A Primary Care-Led NHS
Putting it into Practice

For Churchill Livingstone
Publisher: Peter Richardson
Copy editor: Carolyn Holleyman
Indexer: Nina Boyd
Project Controller: Anita Sekhri

A Primary Care-Led NHS
Putting it into Practice

Edited by

Geoff Meads MA (Oxon) Msc
Director of Performance Management, South and West NHS Region

With Foreword by
Alasdair Liddell
Director of Planning, NHS Executive

CHURCHILL LIVINGSTONE
NEW YORK EDINBURGH LONDON MADRID MELBOURNE
SAN FRANCISCO AND TOKYO 1996

CHURCHILL LIVINGSTONE
Medical Division of Pearson Professional Limited

Distributed in the United States of America by Churchill
Livingstone Inc., 650 Avenue of the Americas, New York, N.Y.
10011, and by associated companies, branches and
representatives throughout the world.

First Published 1996

ISBN 0443 05570X

British Library Cataloguing in Publication Data
A catalogue record for this book is available from the British
Library.

Library of Congress Cataloging in Publication Data
A catalog record for this book is available from the library of
Congress.

Medical Knowledge is constantly changing. As new
information becomes available, changes in treatment,
procedures, equipment and the use of drugs become necessary.
The editors/authors/contributors and the publishers have, as
far as it is possible, taken sure that the information given in
this text is accurate and up to date. However, readers are
strongly advised to confirm that the information, especially
with regard to drug usage, complies with the latest legislation
and standards of practice.

The
publisher's
policy is to use
**paper manufactured
from sustainable forests**

Printed in Great Britain by Bell and Bain, Glasgow

Contents

Contributors

Adrian Dawson MB ChB FFPHM
Acting Director of Public Health, Dorset Health Authority

David Dungworth
Locality Manager, Gloucestershire Health Authority

Rosalind Eve BA (Hons)
FACTS Project Director, Sheffield Centre for Health and Related Research

Caroline Glendinning BA (Hons) M Phil
Senior Research Fellow, Centre for Primary Care Research, University of Manchester

Anita Grabarz MA
Assistant Director, New River Health Authority, New Southgate

Peter Greagsby
Director of Strategy and Development, Rotherham Health Authority

June Huntington PhD
Independent Consultant and Visiting Fellow, Kings Fund, London

Carolyn Larsen MBA ACIS MHSM
Associate Director, South Essex Health Authority

Angela Jeffrey
Associate Director of Primary Care, Southampton and South West Hampshire Health Authority

Edmund Jessop DM (Oxon) FFPHM
Director of Public Health, West Surrey Health Authority, Surrey

John Kirtley BA (Hons) MHSM Dip HSM
Director of Primary Care Portsmouth and S E Hampshire Health
Commission

Camilla Lambert BA MA (Econ)
Director of Primary Care Development,
Isle of Wight Health Authority

Alasdair Liddell
Director of Planning, NHS-Executive

Ed Macalister-Smith MSc MBA BSc
Assistant Director of Primary Care, Wiltshire Health Authority

Gavin McBurnie MB ChB MBA
Director of Public Health, Fife Health Board

Andy McKeon
Head of Primary Care, NHS-Executive

Geoff Meads MA (Oxon) MSc
Director of Performance Management,
South and West NHS Region

Philip Milner
Director of Public Health, Wiltshire Health Authority

Geoff Newbery BA MBA Dip HSM
Director of Primary Care, West Yorkshire Health Authority

Joanna Parker BA (Hons) RGN RM Dip HV E.N.B 176, Diploma in Research
Methods
Nurse Adviser, West Midlands NHS Region

Brian Maynard-Potts MSc
Primary Care Manager, South and West Devon Health Authority

Bob Ricketts MA (Cantab) MIHSM MIPD MBA
Director of Purchaser Performance Management, NHS Region
Anglia and Oxford NHS Region

Alan Torbet
Director, PRCSA, Surrey

Mike Warner BSc Dip HSM
Director of Primary Care Support, Wiltshire Health Authority

Ray Wilcox DMS MHSM AITD
Independent Consultant, Wilcox Penfold Partnership,
Norwich

David Wilkin BSc MSc PhD
Chief Executive, National Primary Care Research and
Development Centre, Manchester

Fedelma Winkler
Visiting Research Fellow, Queen Mary and Westfield College,
University of London

Foreword

Since the launch of the strategy, the *Primary Care-Led NHS* has been rapidly absorbed into NHS 'management-speak' but, more than a year later, I am still asked the question 'What does it mean?'. My first response is to ask ' what do you think it means?' because I do not think it is helpful for those at the centre to provide a 'correct' and precise definition, which in practice would in all probability stifle the innovation and development which we are seeking to stimulate. Indeed, I have been impressed by the way in which people at local level in the NHS have set about defining for themselves what it might mean in their own local context.

So much so, that we are now able to draw out some general messages from this work which (fortunately) match well with the NHS board ideas we had in launching the strategy. So, on this basis, what are the key features of a *Primary Care-Led NHS?*

First, it is about decision-making. The idea is to shift decision-making about health and healthcare as close to patients as possible. In the NHS, it is GPs and their teams who are closest to patients and in the best position to identify their needs, taking account of the 'whole person'. Secondly, it is about the process of delivering and managing care. Then idea here is that the GP should be the **Coordinator,** not just of the primary care team, but of the whole care system. Thirdly, it is about strengthened relationships. What we are saying is that primary care is in fact the basis of the healthcare system, with secondary care in a supporting role. This is hardly a new idea but it means a shift from the perception of primary care as the 'feeder' of secondary care. This requires effective partnerships between primary care professionals and patients, secondary care professionals, health authorities, social services and other agencies.

But it is equally important to emphasise that a Primary Care-Led NHS is not just about GPs – it is about all members of the

Primary Care Team. It is not just about shifting funds from secondary to primary care – it is about the *right* location of care – funding the most appropriate setting for the specific needs of individual patients.

It is against this background the Secretary of State, Stephen Dorrell, recently announced that he wanted a wide-ranging debate about the future of primary care. How do we want primary care to develop, within the context of a *Primary Care-led NHS*, into the next century? This is an important debate for all parts of the service – GPs, Trusts, Health Authorities – who have a real opportunity to help shape that part of out future. This book is a valuable contribution to that debate. It is both thought-provoking and informative, and I certainly commend it.

The vision of a *Primary Care-led NHS* certainly seems to have struck a chord with many parts of the NHS. The challenge is to get beyond the slogan, to make it a reality, and I have seen plenty of evidence of that challenge being tackled with enthusiasm in different parts of the country. This book draws on the enthusiasm and the experience of the past year. I hope it will stimulate many more to set out vigorously to find the answer to what *Primary Care-led NHS* means in the local context and to put that answer into practice.

ALASDAIR LIDDELL

Preface

This is a book without waffle. Its purpose and design are straightforward. Taken as a whole it provides an essentially pragmatic guide to those responsible for managing the delivery of a Primary Care-Led NHS, at practice, provider and authority levels, Taken in sequence the individual chapters are a step-by-step progression through every aspect if contemporary primary care management, from the meaning of the policy to the monitoring of its implementation. Each has been prepared by contributors whose distinctive quality is that they can write not about what they plan to do but what they have already done. During the past 5 years when the radical shift towards primary care has often relied on the missionary zeal of one-off entrepreneurs, rhetoric has sometimes plagued the NHS. What follows is designed to get away from this trend. It is firmly in the tradition of turning abstract theory into practical reality.

This is also a book in which many of the chapters are without references. June Huntington's opening vision is the main exception as she seeks to root the Primary Care-Led NHS in its history. But, arguably, there are very few references for managers in the next phase of the post-1990 reforms. Even when placed in an international context there are few models to emulate. Indeed countries as far apart geographically and culturally as Spain and New Zealand, Sweden and those of the emerging CIS are looking to the UK for leadership. There is currently a healthy trade in NHS consultants abroad as such countries as those mentioned above seek first to establish systems of gatekeeping general practice and then to build into these the combination of clinical referral powers, financial controls, and service development functions that now so distinguishes the British approach. The focus for UK managers has to be themselves. The lessons today are essentially local. A Primary Care-Led NHS has to be re-created in every district.

This is not a book, however, without new ideas. Its concentration on good practices does mean that those readers wanting to know, for example, if and when to apply research or new IT developments will be readily satisfied. There are, for example, specific checklists and timetables for compiling surgery registers, establishing localities and transferring specialties. Every contributor has deliberately covered the same territory. What is the transferable good practice and learning? What are the opportunities and obstacles? What can the Primary Care-Led NHS mean to me and to my role and my responsibilities? The answers reflect the growing diversity of the NHS which is now years apart in its different local stages of development. For some of those at the leading edge, inevitably, the answers have actually meant their contributions offer at least a glimpse of the next stages of NHS policy development. For those in this position this is actually an essential part of their practical purpose and adds to the utility of the book. Brian Maynard-Potts, for example, as Project Manager for the Dawlish Total Purchasing Pilot, indicates how realistically the concept of managed care can become operational in the UK while, equally lucidly, Ed Jessop from Guildford points to the potential impact of more evidence based medicine on what have become over simplistic assumptions about the efficacy of secondary to primary care transfers. The need for realism is equally apparent in the mature historic perspectives offered by Ray Wilcox and David Dungworth based on their long association with primary care.

Whilst the 1996 Health Authorities can be increasingly expected to commission health care through localised agreements, primary care in UK is essentially still regulated centrally and will remain so for the foreseeable future. Dentists, doctors, community pharmacists and opticians all work to the terms of nationally negotiated contracts. The importance of these only grows as the local internal market mechanisms extend their scope. These contracts and the values they embody are the cement which holds the NHS together still as a national institution. Andy McKeon is currently head in one of the Department of Health's teams in the annual negotiating round with the different national professional representatives on these contracts. His is the job of both liberating and, sometimes, constraining the types of local developments described in this book through an ever changing framework of national regulations, statutes and guidance. It is fitting, therefore, that he should have the last word in this guide to future good practice.

To Andy and to all other contributors go my thanks, not least for delivering a product that is so well timed. Publication coincides directly with the legislation for new Health Authorities and extended fundholding coming into force. Achieving this coincidence has meant working fast and hard; writing, I hope, in the white heat of inspiration!

And lastly a note of appreciation is due from all the contributors to Alasdair Liddell, NHSE Director of Planning, not only for his foreword, but for placing primary care at the top of the NHS Medium Term Priorities, and for keeping it there. A Primary Care-Led NHS seems the sensible and self-evident direction of travel now; 5 years ago it was a pipe dream. Alasdair and the NHS have travelled down thus route well together.

These introductory remarks must close with some personal appreciations: to Jane Harding and Tony Laurance especially, in the South and West Regional Office for their forbearance and support; to June Huntington and Ian Carruthers for their inspiration; to Peter Richardson for his readiness to back creativity and innovation, and to Tricia and our children. The latter have now had to tolerate my obsession with a message that has meant continuous escapes to the study over the past year, often at the least convenient times. The product has been a family of publications, with this the third and final progeny in 9 months. Its dedication fittingly, therefore, is to Rebecca, our third and last child.

Reference:

1. National Health Service Executive 1995 EL(95) 68 Priorities and Planning Guidance for the NHS: 1996/97, NHSE, Leeds

Geoff Meads
Winchester, 31 October 1995

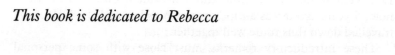

This book is dedicated to Rebecca

List of Abbreviations

ACE	Angiotensin Converting Enzyme
CHC	Community Health Council
CMDS	Contract(s) Minimum Data Set
CMIS	Central Management Information System
DCGP	District Committee of General Practice
DHA	District Health Authority
DoH	Department of Health
ECG	Electro-Cardiograph
FHS	Family Health Services
FHSA	Family Health Services Authority
FPC	Family Practitioner Committee
GMS	General Medical Services
GMSC	General Medical Services Council
GP	General Practitioner
HCHS	Hospital and Community Health Services
HoN	Health of the Nation
IM&T	Information Management and Technology
IT	Information Technology
LMC	Local Medical Committee
MAAG	Medical Audit Advisory Group
MIQUEST	Morbidity Information Query Syntax
MPC	Medical Practices Committee
MQSA	Monitoring Quality in Service Agreements
MS	Multiple Sclerosis

NHS	National Health Service
NHSE	National Health Service Executive
NHSiS	National Health Service Executive in Scotland
NMET	Non Medical Education and Training
NPCRDC	National Primary Care Research and Development Centre
NVQ	National Vocational Qualification
PCLP	Primary Care Led Purchasing
PGMDE	Postgraduate Medical and Dental Education
PHCT	Primary Health Care Team
PPG	Priorities and Planning Guidance
RCGP	Royal College of General Practitioners
REDG	Regional Education Development Group
RHA	Regional Health Authority
SNMAC	Standing Nursing and Midwifery Advisory Committee
SSD	Social Services Department
UK	United Kingdom
UKCC	United Kingdom Central Council for Nursing, Midwifery and Health Visiting
VFM	Value for Money
WFP	Working for patients
WHO	World Health Organisation
WTE	Whole Time Equivalent

1. A *Care*-Led NHS?

June Huntington

CAN AN ORGANISATION CARE?

In trying to understand the term *Primary Care-Led NHS*, we risk focusing on the *primary* rather than the *care*. If one of the reasons for promoting a Primary Care-Led NHS is to bring care closer to patients and to make it more responsive to their needs, we must ask whether the practice as well as the practitioner can care? I was first given a positive answer to this question when as a researcher I went into General Practice for the first time. While waiting to interview a health visitor, I got talking to an elderly patient. She obviously felt 'at home' within the practice, and with no prompting from me said that when any of her neighbours had problems she always told them 'Go to the Caversham, they'll help you'.

Eight years later, I had a similar experience in a practice in Sydney.[1] While interviewing one elderly woman in her own home, I learned a lot about the place of *The Ashby Medical Centre* in her life. Like her counterpart in London, she told me that if any friends or neighbours came to her with problems, she told them 'Go to the clinic, they'll help you'.

Interestingly, these two women were attached to their own GPs and would by choice see them if they needed to see a doctor. What they conveyed though was a real sense of relationship with the practice as an organisation. Reflecting on these two examples, conditions which predisposed these patients to sense that 'the organisation cared' become apparent:

- They were elderly women, who probably used the practice frequently, perhaps well beyond its average consultation rate. Consequently, they would be known by name and personal circumstances to staff. Elderly people suffer progressive loss of relatives and friends who 'recognise' them in both their biographical and social contexts.

- As part of the stable population of the community, these two women probably saw the practice and its staff, and certainly their own GPs, as embodiments of their own biography, deepening their sense of being known by the organisation as well as by their own GP;
- Significantly, as this was unusual in the 1970s, these two practices as organisations and as buildings had a name: *The Caversham Centre* and the *Ashby Medical Centre*. Buildings embody corporate identity, as well as generating attachment, as the current fight over London's historic teaching hospitals demonstrates;
- It is also possible that the positive relationship these two women experienced with their individual GPs enabled them to extend that positive perception to what they perceived as his organisation.

I was reminded of these two examples when I read Julian Pratt's book *Practitioners and Practices: a Conflict of Values?*[2] His subtitle questions whether these values are irreconcilable or whether, like Marx's thesis and antithesis, they can produce a new synthesis.

Practices are growing in size.[3] Over the past 20 years, the proportion of practices with one or two partners has declined, while that of practices with over five partners has increased. The national average practice now has four partners. In the early 1970s, practice nurses and practice managers were found in only the most 'advanced' practices; in the 1990s they are found in the majority, and many primary care teams include physiotherapists, counsellors, psychologists, and others. 'The Practice' has become a larger, more complex, and more costly organisation the management of which has become a burden for many GPs, especially those who wish to go on working as if they were solo practitioners.

To my question whether the practice can care, most GPs who cleave to the practitioner model would probably say 'no', but recent research in Wessex suggests that there are now some GPs who would answer 'yes', and a growing number who would say: 'We're not sure, but we've got to test it — in the interest of ourselves, our staff, and our patients, given the current environment'.[4] In other words, developing an *organisation* that can care is in part a strategy for practitioner survival.

Most practices that have achieved a state of 'organisation as relief' rather than 'organisation as burden' have done so through applying certain basic principles of organisation and management that apply to any organisation, be this in the public, private, or voluntary sector. Most of them do not apply the principles of the business world aggressively, but they do think about their organisation as a corporate whole; about their staff as individuals and groups who can be motivated or demotivated depending on the quality of their management; and about their patients as 'customers' in the sense of asking their opinions on the current pattern of service and involving them in planning future services.

MANAGING HUMAN SERVICE ORGANISATIONS

Many GPs and practice managers, like their NHS manager colleagues, have pursued an interest in management through reading the standard management literature which derives from the business schools; particularly in the USA. While finding some of this valuable, many are aware of its limitations in helping them manage organisations that are significantly different from those on which this literature is based. Most are unaware that there is a literature which addresses the particular management challenges of their own organisations which have at their core the diagnosis, treatment, and continuing care of individuals who are ill, or believe themselves to be ill.

This is the literature on human service organisations, much of it developed in schools of social work administration in the USA,[5] but also at the Tavistock Clinic and Institute in the United Kingdom.[6,7] Human service organisations are those where the task is to bring about personal change in the user, the agent of which is the worker and/or the organisation itself. The means through which change occurs is the personal encounter between the user (client, patient) and the professional (doctor, nurse, social worker) offering the service. It is 'the work' they do together which creates its healing potential. The linked assumption is that if the primary task of the organisation is to be achieved the worker must be enabled to use his or her 'self' therapeutically. It is the job of management to make that possible, to create the enabling environment.

The ethical and technical assumptions underlying the theory of human service organisations must be contrasted sharply with that of 'Customer Care' as an aspect of marketing in some commercial service sector organisations:

In March 1995 First Direct Bank ran a full page advertisement in the quality press featuring a young cat, eyes closed, on a human lap as a human hand stroked it. You could almost hear the purr. In bold type beside the photograph, was printed: *'As a First Direct Customer, you're always treated with courtesy.'* In bold type underneath the photograph, was printed: *'The more you stroke your cat, the more affectionate it becomes ... cats are not affectionate by instinct, and need constant handling to break down their suspicion. Stroking works well; it soothes your cat by imitating the grooming action of a mother cat licking her kittens. Note: cats who are not stroked when young will be very resistant to stroking when they become adults.'*

The photograph and the statement were a flagrant attempt to con-jure the image of caring, softness, nurturance. Down the right side of the page was printed a mix of credo and information under headings such as 'A Customer Focus'; '24 hours a day'; 'Free Banking'; 'Bill Payment Service'; including the information that First Direct is a bank 'that's lean' because it does not have to staff all these high street branches.

Such 'Customer Care' is often achieved at the cost of manipulat-ing not only customers but staff who directly provide the service. In *The Managed Heart*, a study of flight attendants in which the author described much of their work as 'emotional labour'[8], the fol-lowing example was cited. During a long flight across the USA, a businessman summoned a flight attendant. When she arrived at his seat, he said: 'you're not smiling'. She invited him to smile at her first. When he did so, she said, 'Right, try holding it like that for the next 5 hours'.

This is an extreme example of a service-provider's response to a customer who believed in his right to service with a smile, and there are many questions we would need to ask in order to judge its appropriateness or inappropriateness. Regardless of the manner adopted by the customer, we would want to know how effectively management understood the demands of the front line and whether this understanding was reflected in its staff management practices. While many organisations now realise that in the com-petitive world out there keeping customers is as important as get-ting them in the first place, they do not always go on to recognise the increasing complexity of the front line relationship, in which staff will not make customers feel cared for if they themselves do not feel cared for by management.

Health care organisations are an extreme form of human service organisation. To them, users bring the most intense and painful emotions, particularly that of anxiety. In order to address the patient's problem, the clinician/worker has to be psychically as well as physically 'there for' the patient. This puts the worker 'at risk'

— of becoming overwhelmed or engulfed by the patient's own anxiety, pain, or despair; yet his capacity to get in touch with these in himself as well as the patient is part of the healing process.

One of the best descriptions of this 'risk' or 'threat' to the psychic integrity of the worker comes from a different profession, that of acting. Ben Kingsley, when interviewed about his role in the film *Schindler's List*, said:

'*Schindler's List* nearly wiped me out. I was pretty burnt out after that. I really had to consciously work hard on allowing the boundaries not to completely dissolve between myself and the character. We all know that if those boundaries get loose and wobbly, and out of the actor's control ... there is a list of my colleagues who have had nervous breakdowns. It is a very serious business. And anyone who laughs at those who take risks and injure themselves psychologically or physically, ought really to examine what we do for a living. It's bloody hard, actually. It has its danger zones, and we have to learn to negotiate them'.[9]

Actors know the directors and companies who enable them to 'manage the boundaries' and those who do not, and often speak of directors who have 'set them free' or enabled them to push their boundaries safely, with manageable risk to themselves. In these circumstances, the director and the company function as a 'container' for the anxiety generated by the risk.

One of the best introductions to this approach to managing human service organisations is Mattinson and Sinclair's *Mate and Stalemate*,[10] a study of marital therapy conducted in the contrasting organisational settings of a Social Services Department and the Tavistock Institute of Marital Studies. There is no better model of a 'bottom up' approach to management. The model begins with an analysis of the nature of the clients' disturbance and demands, from which is produced an analysis of what the worker needs to do and to be in order to address the clients' needs. From this in turn is produced an analysis of what the organisation needs to do and to be in order to help its workers work effectively.

The issue is one of boundaries, and whether the organisation functions in such a way as to ensure that the boundaries between doctor and patient, social worker and client, are managed constructively or destructively. This is why general practices cannot be construed solely as businesses nor indeed as public sector organisations. Neither model of management takes account of the fact that at the heart of these organisations are diagnostic and therapeutic encounters which put huge psychic demands on clinicians. In its eagerness to persuade GPs and their practices to promote health, governments sometimes seem to forget that those GPs are *clinicians* and that the word *clinical* means 'of or pertaining to the bedside'.

A major assumption underlying the management of human service organisations is that only clinicians who themselves feel cared for can care for patients in the way just described. This is not difficult to understand when we look at the definition of *care* in the Shorter Oxford English Dictionary:

> *Care (noun)*: Oversight with a view to protection, preservation, or guidance.
> *Care (verb, as in 'to care for')*: to feel concern or interest;
> to have regard or liking for;
> to give serious mental attention to.

We tend to assume that caring is about feeling, but it is also about thinking. Caring responses to a person result from empathy which has both affective and cognitive components. Empathy with the user is as vital in the design and maintenance of an organisation and its operational systems as in the interpersonal encounter of doctor and patient.

THE CARING ORGANISATION

How then can a practice convey 'care'? The following features of the practice will reveal the degree to which empathy with its patients or users has influenced its design and continues to influence its management:

- Physical facilities (space, light, warmth, comfort);
- Waiting times (whose time is valued?);
- Opening/closing times (whose convenience is valued?);
- Privacy (for talking; undressing/dressing);
- Indications of performance and quality adopted;
- 'Routines' — in whose interest?;
- Procedures adopted to handle deviation from the normal;
- Presence of checklists, protocols (underlying aims, motivation for);
- Availability of information on the service and its providers (in user-friendly form).

All of the above will convey deep organisational assumptions about the user's entitlement to be cared for. The user's sense of whether the organisation cares will also be sharply coloured by its social climate: by whether the 'temperature' of interaction is warm or cold, by the relative weight given to differences of status and the embodiment of these in degrees of formality or informality.

Most of these features are shared by other service organisations which take pride in their 'Customer Care'. In order to feel cared for by a health care organisation, however, its users need to feel *entitled to be patients*, and not simply users or customers. At times in their contact with the organisation users will feel anxious, fearful, distressed, confused. At such times, they will feel cared for only if those on the front line are able to:

- Listen to them actively;
- Touch them sensitively;
- 'Be there' for them as well as 'doing for' them;
- Be there psychologically as well as physically;
- Make connections between different kinds of loss, trauma, and transition — as a basis for empathy;
- Take in and connect with the patient's experience yet not be incorporated or engulfed by it;
- Accept and work with patient's needs for dependence, independence, and interdependence;
- Help the patient to understand and manage the physiological, psychological, and social aspects of her condition and to repair so far as possible any breakdown in the integrity of their interrelationship.

New Health Authorities with their new core task of support to a Primary Care-Led NHS need always to be aware that those on the front line, all members of the primary care team, will be able to do this only if:

- They feel *entitled* to work in this way;
- They feel *supported* in working in this way;
- 'Management' understands the psychological burden of their work;
- The organisation is managed so as to help them 'contain' their own and their patients' anxiety and dependency;
- There is agreement on the organisation's primary task and on the (sometimes varied) means of achieving it;
- There is a strong corporate culture and identity which celebrates diversity — of skills, talents, interests;
- There are high levels of mutual respect and affection among staff;
- Staff share and care for patients and each other;
- 'Staff' means all staff — clinical, managerial, clerical — all of

whom see clearly their own contribution to the primary task;
- 'Systems' promote personal recognition and care of patients as individuals.

To manage any human service organisation successfully, managers must recognise staff's motivation for choosing to work in them. Most people who work in public service organisations do so because they perceive their own values to be embodied in the organisation and its primary task. Many are also fuelled by idealisation (of patients, professions, areas of work, or specific organisations), by projection of their own dependency needs, and by fantasies of repairing past hurts in their own lives.

While these fuel the motivation to work, they also put staff — and sometimes their colleagues and patients — at risk. The managerial challenge at both Health Authority and practice levels, is now that of helping those on the front line to manage the boundaries between fantasy and reality, and to ensure that the organisation functions so as to enable its members to contain the powerful emotions evoked by their work. The managerial task is particularly challenging in primary care organisations where relationships between clinicians and patients are often long-lived and may be marked by deep affection as well as ambivalence.

IMPLICATIONS FOR THE NEW HEALTH AUTHORITIES

The new Health Authorities have been charged with the promotion and development of a Primary Care-Led NHS. They will be supported by those GPs who have been personally, professionally, and organisationally stimulated by the policy changes of the past few years. In many districts of the country, these GPs are as yet a minority, and if NHS managers allow their perceptions of local general practice to be too influenced by these GPs, they will prejudice their own chances of success.

Many GPs remain seriously alienated. This is often breeding a destructive cynicism that is damaging to their own organisations as well as to the broader NHS. Because EL(94)79[11] and its accompanying brochure[12] linked the idea of a Primary Care-Led NHS to GPs' role in purchasing, there is a risk that the new Health Authorities will neglect to develop the provider role of GPs and their practices, particularly as only one form of GP-led purchasing has been centrally sponsored.

At the heart of much GP alienation is the sense that the core of the GP role — that of the diagnosis, treatment, and continuing care of those who are ill or believe themselves to be ill — has been progressively devalued by the policy changes of the 1990s, and that government's promotion and development of 'the practice' is driven by managerial and public health agendas of which many GPs remain suspicious.[2]

In delivering a Primary Care Led-NHS, managers of the new Health Authorities will need to understand that this suspicion is not manifested solely by GP reactionaries. In its consultation document on *The Nature of General Medical Practice* published in May 1995,[13] the Royal College of General Practitioners used terms such as 'the depersonalised wall of the population perspective'. The document also gave no attention to the practice or to partnership as the organisational context of the clinical practice it described. It was as if the present and future nature of general medical practice were a professional, but not an organisational or managerial issue. It amounts to ostrich-like escapism to ignore the new models emerging of managed primary care organisations in the UK.[14]

If a Primary Care-Led NHS is to become reality rather than rhetoric, Health Authority managers will need to help GPs and their organisations reframe their provider role in ways which promote the capacity of the practice and the people within it to care. A strategic shift from secondary to primary care will not occur unless the practice, as a provider organisation, is able to contain the anxieties of its clinicians and its patients. Practices will be more able to do this as and when NHS managers demonstrate an understanding of the nature of the practice as a human service organisation as well as a business in contract with a public sector NHS.

REFERENCES

1. Huntington J 1981 Social work and general medical practice: collaboration or conflict. George Allen and Unwin, London.
2. Pratt J 1995 Practitioners and practices: a conflict of values? Radcliffe Medical Press, Oxford.
3. Fry J 1993 General Practice: the facts. Radcliffe Medical Press, Oxford.
4. Huntington J 1995 Managing the Practice: whose business? Radcliffe Medical Press, Oxford.
5. Perlmutter F D 1984 Human services at risk. D C Heath and Co., Lexington, Mass.
6. Menzies Lyth I 1988 Containing anxiety in institutions: selected essays. Free Association Books, London.
7. Obholzer A, Roberts VZ (eds) (1994) The unconscious at work. Routledge, London.

8. Hochschild A 1983 The managed heart. University of California Press, Berkeley.
9. Stock J 1995 Heavyweight champion. The Independent on Sunday, 23 April: 27.
10. Mattinson J, Sinclair I 1981 Mate and stalemate: working with marital problems in a social services department. Blackwell, Oxford.
11. National Health Service Executive 1994 Developing NHS purchasing and GP fundholding — EL(94)79. NHSE, Leeds.
12. National Health Service Executive 1994 Developing NHS purchasing and GP fundholding: towards a Primary Care-Led NHS. NHSE, Leeds.
13. Royal College of General Practitioners 1995 The Nature of General Medical Practice — draft for consultation. RCGP, London.
14. Meads G (ed) 1995 Future options for General Practice. Radcliffe Medical Press, Oxford.

2. Communicating the message: what does it mean?

Geoff Meads

DEFINITIONS

Even the most ardent supporter of the recent NHS reforms does not classify as communications successes the policy documents on which these have been based. *Working for Patients* left a legacy of suspicion and doubt about the future of the NHS itself; marginal continuing health care cases have sometimes plucked disaster from the clutches of *Caring for People*'s original public relations triumph, while the jury is still out on *Health of the Nation*. As for *Promoting Better Health* and *Primary Health Care*, discussion papers that helped spawn the new 1990 GP contract, ordinary people are still simply confused.[1] Demand suggests they like the very same new screening and health promotion services which, 6 years on, many General Practices continue to complain about as a futile imposition. The need to restore public confidence through a renewed sense of ownership in the NHS is crystal clear.

The move to a Primary Care-Led NHS in the aftermath of April 1996 provides this opportunity. Indeed putting into practice the vision already provided by June Huntington on the preceding pages, with all the sound management lessons set out in the following chapters, depends first and foremost on effective communications strategies. For the modern NHS it is essential that these begin with its own staff, too many of whom have too often been either bypassed or even, on occasion, alienated by official explanations of reforms that have concentrated on the mechanisms of change, rather than their underlying values or intended outcomes. 'Improved patient care' has often seemed simply an object of lip service in much the same way as attaching the initials 'GP' to what have been perceived by many as dogma driven innovations, has been too ready a source of easy legitimacy. The post-April 1996

NHS wants to be at ease with itself once more, to regain the sense of normative integration upon which all complex public service organisations still rely for their overall effectiveness.[2]

So what does it mean: The Primary Care-Led NHS? Different things to different people in different places is the too easy answer, given in particular, the highly variable nature of individual general practices. And, of course, it is important locally that each and everybody finds their own answer for the message to be truly internalised. But there is nevertheless a national common denominator. Across the UK a Primary Care-Led NHS now, in essence, is about where priorities for health care are agreed, and who takes part in this process. It signifies the convergence in the primary care setting of NHS clinical referral powers and financial controls (especially over acute and continuing care), with service, but not strategic, planning responsibilities. It means a different locus for NHS decision making.

DEBATE

For much of an establishment rooted in institutional edifices, both physical and psychological, this is turning the NHS on its head. For others, including the influx of those now drawn into NHS funded employment from other sectors through the business and career opportunities afforded by the recent reforms, it is aligning the modern NHS with their personal experience. For the vast majority of UK citizens, a Primary Care-Led NHS is one based upon their General Practice, where the bulk of their health care contacts are already made. Moreover, while general practice as a partnership organisation is now having to diversify to respond to the twin pressures of providing and purchasing responsibilities,[3] as a principle it is a constant. Indeed the tradition of comprehensive, continuous personal care is now stretching out from the individual to the whole practice based Primary Care Team. For most people 'Primary Care-Led' means turning the NHS the right way around at last.

While, however, it is fundamentally attractive to equate the new policies of devolution with individual personal experiences, it would be naive to assert that the latter are the exclusive source of a Primary Care-Led NHS. Financial, clinical and political expediency also all point this way. Hence the scepticism from those who argue, wrongly, that a Primary Care-Led NHS is simply a cover up for more fundholding, a back door route to further unresourced secondary care transfers or even managed competition in disguise. Such doubts are perfectly understandable. The individual catch-phrases of the NHS have sometimes seemed perversely flexible in their meaning. 'Primary Care-Led Purchasing', for example, start-ed its life back in 1992–93 in the former Wessex region as a steer to new health commissions and the antithesis of funding. By 1995 it had become the official term for describing the full range of exten-sions to the GPFH scheme! Such changes as these point to an imperative. A Primary Care-Led NHS is a policy which absolutely requires discussion and debate at every level if policy is to be turned into practice. It needs thinking time and space. In perfor-mance management terms it requires new health authorities to operate far more through development than monitoring mecha-nisms. Descriptive commentaries, far more than statistical data, are the accounting currency of a Primary Care-Led NHS.

Development based on effective communications does not just happen. It requires planning, management and milestones. And this is especially true for an increasingly decentralised health care system in which power is more diffuse and the interactions between a growing number of stakeholders often unpredictable. Mapping power in the modern NHS has relatively little to do with understanding formal organisational diagrams and hierarchic management structures.

DIMENSIONS

For managers in new health authorities and general practice alike, usable frameworks are essential. Accordingly, to be successfully communicated a Primary Care-Led NHS needs to be first unpacked. It has at least four dimensions. These can be set out as shown in Table 2.1.

Table 2.1 offers therefore a simple checklist of synonyms, with their component features for a Primary Care-Led NHS. For each heading there is a civilised argument to take place, a target to be set, a timescale to be agreed. As a working tool it is a framework, for example, that can be used to track such key development indi-cators for a Primary Care-Led NHS as the investment levels in interprofessional education, the availability of extended primary care teams in Medical Practice Areas, and their contribution to Care Programmes. These are the new trademarks of the NHS; being able to recognise them in the future depends on the commu-nications now set in train.

Table 2.1   The four dimensions of a Primary Care-Led NHS

A Primary Care-Led NHS is:	
A Locally-led because it: • complies with Euro-principle of subsidiarity; • aligns with associated developments in locally governed schools, housing associations, social services, care management, etc; • supports the shift away from central bureaucracy; • builds on the idea of Community as a collective of self-help and voluntary initiatives.	**B Relationship-led because it:** • is founded on general practice tradition of continuous comprehensive care; • is derived from frontline, direct personal contacts about the whole of a person's well being; • creates new accountability processes less reliant on structure and tactics; • reacts against past paternalism of consultant to patient relationship in parent–child or expert–casualty mode.
C Citizen-led because it: • moves patients from mere registration rights to the status of public subscribers; • meets the requirements of the Patients' Charter and allied 'Rightist' developments; • responds to modern telecommunications and the resultant much wider range and availability of information to the general public; • builds on the principle of individual needs assessment.	**D Consumer-led because it:** • offers choice of services and service outlets; • promotes more business-like health care enterprises in the NHS; • links financial viability on income and cost directly to need/demand; • promotes a modern economy of small service businesses in the independent sector.

COMMUNICATIONS

These communications rely for their effectiveness on both the spirit in which they are undertaken and the standards they set. This combination in turn depends upon leadership. Herein lies a major challenge: for managers of new health authorities of course, but also more particularly for non-elective Chairs and Members and GPs themselves. The latter are used to working outside the

St Albans and Hemel Hempstead NHS Trust

LIBRARY AND INFORMATION SERVICE
Hemel Hempstead Hospital
Hillfield Road
Hemel Hempstead HP2 4AD

Internal extensions2185/2662
Direct lines (01442) 287185 / 287662
Fax (01442) 287992

With compliments

system: for many this is what their independent contractor status has been designed to protect. For NHS members the transition to purchasing has often been painful enough, often requiring those on Health Authority boards to put aside their natural affiliations with local providers. Moving now to a process in which decision making is shared, variation is the norm and differential partnerships with small businesses are essential, becomes a major learning exercise.

In such an environment post-April 1996, top-down local strategies are out of the question. The strategic process now becomes all important. Table 2.2 sets out the product of one such process.[4] Useful though the headings and aims in this widely adopted framework are, however, their value is really only as strong as the partnerships developed in their formulation. Behind the objectives, in this case, lay a 2-year programme of workshops, presentations and pilot schemes which forged a genuine tripartite strategic alliance between the general practice, the executive and non-executive leadership of a region. As a result the framework has been widely used at all levels, from that of guiding local surgery investments to that of influencing national policy developments in both England and Scotland.

Table 2.2 The product of the Strategic Process

Wessex Strategic Framework

The five main objectives are:

1. Practice-based primary care to be the preferred setting of services, wherever this is appropriate and effective for patients, and an efficient use of resources.
2. Extended practice-based primary care team services to be responsible for meeting the health needs of the majority of the population.
3. Practice-based contracts for primary care services to be the local responsibility of integrated Health Authorities.
4. Primary care led purchasing to be the guiding principle to apply in meeting and responding to a population's needs.
5. Participation of the public to be a right throughout the planning, delivery and assessment of primary care.

February 1994

CONCLUSION

The lessons to be drawn from communicating a Primary Care-Led NHS effectively are straightforward. It is, therefore, perfectly and pragmatically possible to succeed and to get the new message across. Patience and professionalism are the bywords and conviction is the key. With these three qualities sound NHS management can again demonstrate its resilience and deliver an NHS which is held in as high a level of public esteem in the year 2000 as at its inception just over 50 years ago. Then it was right for the NHS to be hospital led. Now is the time for primary care.

REFERENCES

1. Department of Health, Primary Health Care. An Agenda for Discussion (1986), Promoting Better Health (1987), Working for Patients (1989), Caring for People: Community Care in the next Decade and Beyond (1990) and The Health of the Nation: A Strategy for Health in England (1992). HMSO, London
2. Etzioni A 1971 A comparative analysis of complex organisations. Free Press, New York
3. Meads G (Ed) 1995 Future options for General Practice. Radcliffe Medical Press, Oxford
4. Meads G 1993 RHAs and primary care: the new alliance. Primary Care Management 3: 2–4

3. Applying research

David Wilkin and Caroline Glendinning

INTRODUCTION

Since the appointment of Professor Michael Peckham as the first Director of Research and Development for the whole NHS in 1991, we have seen the beginning of some fundamental changes in the relationship between academic research and the development and delivery of health services. In the NHS there is a growing commitment to the provision of knowledge-based health care and, therefore, to ensuring that the provision of care is founded on the best available research evidence. Within the academic community, there is an increasing recognition of the importance of involving the users of research at all stages, from formulating the research questions through to disseminating the findings. The 1995 international conference sponsored by the NHS Research and Development Programme ('*The Scientific Basis of Health Services*') brought together managers, professionals and scientists from many disciplines to emphasise the importance of partnership between the academic and health service communities in supporting the delivery of effective, efficient and appropriate health care. Research and development needs to underpin the future development of the NHS, being both responsive to the needs of the service and proactive in helping to shape the direction of change.

The development of a Primary Care-Led NHS presents immense opportunities and challenges for research and development, if we are to translate political and managerial rhetoric into a reality which will result in improved health service provision. However, rather like another key contemporary social policy — community care — the concept of a 'Primary Care Led NHS' is capable of many different interpretations. These various interpretations are, in turn, likely to lead to a wide range of diverse implementation strategies at local levels. Policy makers, purchasers, providers, clinicians and other professionals are increasingly facing uncharted territory in developing services. They will need to know what has been tried elsewhere, whether it works and with what costs and benefits. Moreover, they will need this information quickly and in forms which are easy to understand and to relate to their own practice, if mistakes are not to be repeated and wheels reinvented.

In this chapter we set out some of the ways in which research and development can contribute to the building of a primary care-led service. First, we describe the range of different contributions which research and development can make; we then illustrate these through two important areas of work which we are undertaking in Manchester at the newly established National Primary Care Research and Development Centre. We are concerned primarily with health services, rather than clinical research, but many of the issues raised are equally relevant to clinical research.

THE CONTRIBUTION OF RESEARCH AND DEVELOPMENT

In the past, NHS staff and researchers have had somewhat narrow and rather unhelpful views of the relationships between research and the development and delivery of services. For their part, academic researchers have tended to emphasise the pursuit of knowledge, perhaps involving complex research methods, and have tended to give less consideration to the practical application of that knowledge to the current problems faced by the NHS. On the other hand, policy makers, managers and professionals have tended to see academic research as too remote, not reflecting their immediate concerns and taking too long to produce answers which even then are equivocal or heavily qualified. Research has also often had a broader or longer-term focus than the immediate problems faced on a day to day basis by service providers.

However, research and development have major roles to play in helping to shape a primary care-led service. These twin activities must underpin and support the process of change, from the formulation of policy to the delivery of individual patient care. This must involve abandoning old stereotypes and instead forging new alliances between the research and practitioner communities, at all stages in the development of services. In particular, it means that research activity must be linked closely to the development and delivery of primary health services; helping to promote and shape innovative developments on the basis of existing knowledge; evaluating the impact and effectiveness of services on a post hoc basis; and working closely with both purchasers, providers and users to ensure that research evidence is disseminated widely and effectively to those to whom it is most relevant. While much research will undoubtedly continue to need specialist skills and expertise (in just the same way as clinical practice will continue to do), it is in the area of service development where immense opportunities and challenges lie for researchers and NHS staff to forge new partnerships, to the ultimate benefit of the NHS as a whole.

Policy analysis and development

While the broad brush strokes of the policy commitment to a primary care-led service are present, the details necessary for a clearer picture of what such a service might look like are lacking. Detailed policies and implementation strategies need to be developed at all levels, from the NHS Executive to individual General Practices. This is not to imply a blueprint which will determine the precise shape of service provision in all areas, regardless of local circumstances. However, there is a need for greater clarity in both national policy frameworks and in local implementation strategies which set out how this might best be achieved. Research and development have important roles to play in examining the range of options in the light of current knowledge. What evidence is there to support or reject different options? What are the likely implications of one policy change on other aspects of the service? The knowledge derived from research can contribute to the formulation of new policies and to the development of implementation strategies.

Basic research

In the absence of knowledge about many of the factors which shape people's health experiences and use of health care services, the behaviour of clinicians and the outcomes of different treatments, there is a continuing need for basic research, which may not necessarily have immediately obvious applications. For example, we need to know much more about why people choose to seek health care from a range of potential sources; how doctors, nurses and other clinicians make decisions about appropriate treatments; and how best to measure the outcomes of treatments. Some of this sort of research may seem far removed from the immediate concerns of the purchasers and providers of primary health care. However, without answers to these more fundamental questions our attempts to develop a primary care-led service will be at best a 'stab in the dark' and, at worst, may result in poorer health care.

Systematic reviews of research evidence

The development of techniques for systematically reviewing the results of randomised controlled trials through the Cochrane Collaboration, and for systematic reviews of other research on the costs and effectiveness of health care by the Centre for Reviews and Dissemination at the University of York, provides a valuable resource for the NHS. These initiatives, which rely on extensive — often international — networks of researchers, attempt to draw together the results of many studies and to summarise their implications for professional practice. Although much of the work to date has focused on specialist care, there is enormous scope for conducting systematic reviews of major issues in primary care which can help determine the most effective and efficient treatments and ways of delivering services.

Evaluation

If we are to learn from our experiences of innovation and change in primary health care, it is essential that we invest in systematic evaluations of the cost-effectiveness of different treatments and of different ways of funding, organising and delivering services. Without such evaluations it will be impossible to make informed choices between possible alternatives. It is not surprising, for example, that debate about the impact and future of GP fundholding remains largely at the level of political and ideological controversy, in the light of the decision by Kenneth Clarke (then Secretary of State for Health) that fundholding should not be introduced on a pilot, experimental basis and only extended after careful evaluation. However, evaluations must involve a close working relationship between purchasers, providers and researchers if they are to be relevant to the needs of the service. For example, researchers will need to be involved well before the introduction of a new service or treatment so that baseline information essential to proper evaluation can be collected. It should also be acknowledged that good evaluation may be time consuming and expensive if it is to provide definitive answers. However, it is essential if we are to learn from earlier mistakes.

Dissemination

It is in this area that academic research has commonly failed the NHS; all too often the results of research have languished in reports and academic journals, making little or no impact on the actual provision of health care. Researchers, health commissions and primary care professionals will need to work much more closely than has previously been the case if the potential benefits of research based knowledge are to be fully realised. We also need more research into which forms of dissemination in primary care are effective in reaching and changing the behaviour of professionals and managers.

Education and training

Last, but by no means least, it is important to recognise the importance of education and training in research. Hospital-based medicine has long emphasised the importance of research (usually clinical) and has provided opportunities for research training, particularly for doctors. However, primary health care has lagged far behind. It will be essential to increase the research capacity of primary health service professionals and ensure, at the very least, that those not directly involved in research have the necessary skills to enable them to interpret and use the results of research.

THE NATIONAL PRIMARY CARE RESEARCH AND DEVELOPMENT CENTRE (NPCRDC)

In January 1995 the Department of Health established this new Centre at the University of Manchester, with collaborating teams in the Centre for Health Economics at the University of York and the Public Health Research and Resource Centre at the University of Salford. The fact that this is the first such centre to be established under the NHS Research and Development Programme reflects the importance which the Department has attached to research and development in primary care.

The new Centre has a 10-year contract to deliver high quality research, disseminate research findings and promote knowledge-based service development in primary health care. It will work closely with the NHS at all levels and with the many other research and development groups contributing to the development of primary health services. The 10-year perspective which the Centre's funding makes possible provides an opportunity for research and development to make a significant contribution to the shape of primary health care in the next century. From the extensive portfolio of NPCRDC we have selected two areas of work which illustrate the potential contribution of research and development to building a primary care led service: the development of a programme of work around 24-hour responsive care; and an evaluation of primary care resource centres.

24 HOUR RESPONSIVE PRIMARY HEALTH CARE

Steadily rising demands for night and weekend visits by GPs and the increasing, allegedly inappropriate, use of hospital Accident and Emergency Departments have become sources of considerable friction between patients, professionals, managers and politicians over recent years. Moreover, current service provision at night and weekends is fragmented between many different professions and agencies; even within the health service, GPs, community nurses, ambulance services, pharmacists, dentists and hospital Accident and Emergency Departments are all involved. A range of different solutions to these problems have been sought, including walk-in Primary Care Emergency Centres, nurse-run minor injuries units, GP staffing of Accident and Emergency Departments and, most recently, a negotiated financial settlement between GPs and the NHS. Nevertheless it seems likely that the present system, with its division of responsibilities between different service providers, will continue to come under pressure as demands and expectations continue to rise.

There is therefore an urgent need to understand the underlying reasons for this increased demand; to assess the appropriateness of current methods of providing emergency and out-of-hours health care; and to evaluate experimental and innovative models of dealing with this difficult problem. NPCRDC is addressing these issues in three ways.

Research into demand

There is clear research evidence of a steady and consistent rise in demand for out-of-hours visits by GPs over the past three decades.

However we know precious little about why demand is rising or whether there might be more appropriate ways of meeting the underlying needs which are giving rise to the increased demand. NPCRDC is therefore designing research which will address these questions. It is unlikely to have any immediate impact on the provision of care, but is nevertheless essential if we are to develop more effective strategies for meeting demand in the medium term and identify effective longer term solutions to the problem.

Evaluation of Primary Care Emergency Centres

While it is essential to mount research which will inform the longer term development of appropriate services, innovations in service delivery will not await the results of such research. In the meantime, research is also needed to inform and support these service developments. NPCRDC has therefore undertaken an evaluation of the costs and effectiveness of walk-in Primary Care Emergency Centres which, it is hoped, will relieve some of the pressure on night visits by general practitioners. This work begins with a descriptive study of some of the Emergency Centres already in operation, and goes on to work closely with those involved in the Centres to devise an appropriate evaluation. It is essential in this sort of work that the evaluation is designed in close collaboration with both the providers and the users of the Emergency Centres and that the results of research are disseminated rapidly so as to inform others planning similar initiatives.

Models of 24 hour primary care for the 21st century

Research and development have important roles to play in the development of new service models which will best meet the needs of patients in the future. The current provision of primary care services at night and weekends is fragmented between many different professions and agencies. One of the features of a Primary Care-Led NHS should be the improved integration of the various different services. NPCRDC is therefore also working with the range of different providers of out-of-hours services, to try and develop integrated models of 24 hour responsive primary care. We then aim to work with commissioners, providers and users to pilot innovative approaches, evaluate them and disseminate good practice.

EVALUATION OF PRIMARY CARE RESOURCE CENTRES

A second example of the kind of research and development work likely to be increasingly important in moving towards a Primary Care-Led NHS is our evaluation of Primary Care Resource Centres. These new Centres are the outcome of an initiative by the North West Regional Health Authority to channel capital funding to areas of high health need in order that primary care services can be expanded and improved. Agreement has already been given to the funding of some 20 Centres throughout the north west; plans for further Centres are in the pipeline up to and beyond April 1996.

Primary Care Resource Centres have no standard definition, their precise configuration of services depending on local needs and the objectives of the various 'stakeholders' involved in their development. However, most Centres contain a range of conventional general medical, community health and health promotion services; diagnostic and treatment services previously provided in secondary settings, such as physiotherapy or outpatient clinics; innovative services such as nurse-run minor injuries clinics; social work and other welfare services; and facilities for use by local groups. Primary Care Resource Centres should also have the active involvement of local GPs, whether or not a practice is actually located in the Centre (see Glendinning et al. 1995).[1]

The evaluation of Primary Care Resource Centres presents a number of major challenges. First, the Regional Health Authority's 'vision' of Primary Care Resource Centres, its requirements for the development of local funding bids and the criteria on which such bids are approved have evolved gradually. In addition, within the overall framework set by the Regional Health Authority, each Primary Care Resource Centre has a different set of objectives, depending on the needs and priorities of the particular locality. Also influencing the development of Primary Care Resource Centres are extraneous, idiosyncratic local factors, such as the reprovisioning of local hospital services. Each Primary Care Resource Centre is therefore different, with its own distinctive features which reflect the needs and priorities of the locality and the particular 'stakeholders' involved. Secondly, the evaluation was only commissioned after funding had already been agreed for a number of Centres. Therefore opportunities to establish 'baseline' data were already restricted. Thirdly, the evaluation has to take into account the processes by which Centres have been developed as these are likely to have a major impact on key outcomes, such as a Centre's acceptability to and use by a range of professionals and local people. Fourthly, demonstrating the cost-effectiveness of Primary Care Resource Centres may be difficult, as increasing the accessibility of services in deprived areas may well increase their use. Broader and longer-term measures of overall health gain may therefore be more appropriate, but will take longer to obtain and may be harder to attribute specifically to the impact of a new Primary Care Resource Centre. Fifthly, identifying and measuring the 'added value' obtained by co-locating a range of services under the same roof is particularly problematic. Finally, Primary Care Resource Centres are intended to be flexible and responsive to changing local needs. Within this context of regular change, baselines are difficult to establish, as is the point at which outcomes should ideally be measured.

In short, this particular piece of work involves the evaluation of an evolving initiative which is being implemented locally in a variety of different ways. This presents major challenges to conventional research methodology. In addition, there has been a constant demand for information about the Primary Care Resource Centre initiative, both from those within the region who are preparing their own bids for capital funding and outside, from others keen to learn from the north west's experience. The project therefore also involves a considerable amount of development work, as well as more traditional research. A well-attended seminar was held early on in the project to share the early findings with purchasers, providers and professionals; and the research team is regularly asked to advise groups developing proposals for similar initiatives both within and outside the north west region.

CONCLUSIONS

The NHS Research and Development programme has already had a major impact on the culture of health services research, by encouraging the extension of academic research to embrace policy and service development activities and by locking both of these firmly into the current and future concerns of commissioners, managers and professional providers. This process needs to be consolidated and extended, to ensure that research and development can — and docs — play a central role in the implementation of a Primary Care-Led NHS. This means that at all stages in the development of new services and treatments, commissioners, providers and practitioners must build in opportunities for systematic review, appraisal and evaluation. Conversely, researchers must work closely with NHS staff in formulating research questions and in disseminating and implementing the results of research. It is only through this closer integration of research and service development, at all levels, that knowledge and evidence will be acquired about which particular primary care services, in what configurations and with what types of relationships to the wider health and welfare service systems, provide the best examples of a Primary Care-Led NHS.

REFERENCE

1. Glendinning C, Bailey J, Jones J, Morley V. (1995) Primary care resource centres in England: an initial survey. National Primary Care Research and Development Centre, University of Manchester, Manchester

4. Maximising information

Geoff Newbery

INTRODUCTION

This chapter is about the opportunities and the pitfalls arising out of the information bonus in prospect when, in April 1996, the managements of DHAs and FHSAs will formally come together. As we have learnt in West Yorkshire, the collision of these giants potentially creates a new range of opportunities for information flows which can support the decision-making processes of new authorities and, in particular, give a sharper focus to information developments in primary care. The chapter will therefore cover:

- What are the data and what are their sources?
- What are the problems with using the data?
- What are the potential information network developments?
- How to make practical sense of it all.
- Summary.
- Conclusions.

The chapter also comes with two disclaimers; it is unashamedly written from a primary care viewpoint and by someone who regards computers with the deepest suspicion.

WHAT ARE THE DATA AND WHAT ARE THEIR SOURCES?

It would take an entire chapter to list all the data now available to DHAs and FHSAs jointly, and at the end of such a list the reader might be none the wiser. However, it is worth reviewing three major sources of data which form the basis of discussion here, and the proposals for their more effective future deployment.

(i) Family Health Services Registration System

This is the core system that has existed for the General Practice side of FHS administration ever since FPCs were progressively computerised from the 1970s. Basically, each system holds the registration details (e.g. name, address, age, sex) of every patient who is registered with a GP in the authority's area. Much of the information on the system is used to fuel the payment process for General Practitioners as, for instance, GPs are paid in part on the basis of the number of patients they have on their lists.

(ii) Contract/Hospital Activity Systems

All Health Authorities have a core system to support their commissioning and contracting of principally acute-based clinical activity. These systems hold the monthly 'Contract Minimum Data Set' information provided by Trusts. Apart from contract monitoring, therefore, this represents information on the *supply* of acute service. Over a number of years, this builds up a picture of *notional demand*, but is clearly some way short of a true 'health needs' picture of the resident population.

(iii) General Practitioner Systems

The emphasis is on plural because there are a number of different GP systems and they are also each used differently. At the very lowest level, some GP computers are little more than glorified word processors being used for such routine activities as repeat prescribing. The main systems, however, will hold the GP's register of patients and can additionally retain a wide variety of clinical detail relating to patients. The obvious link here is between GP systems and the FHS system which I will return to later.

The common theme running through this and other systems is that they all hold potentially relevant data — *or is it information?* — that can help the NHS in its decision making. The point about the distinction between data and information is important and needs to be understood early. Although there are many definitions of the word 'information' they generally fall into the following two categories:

1. information is data *in a context*, and
2. information is data *plus meaning*.

Straightforward data, in the form of, for example, a list of figures showing the number of people on waiting lists for various specialties, is by itself meaningless. It only becomes useful when some context is given to it such as a comparison with Patient's Charter waiting times or a comparison with a similar set of figures from a previous time period. The context here is the management of the waiting list and it is at this point that if data informs the management of the waiting list then it indeed becomes **information**.

WHAT ARE THE PROBLEMS WITH USING THE DATA?

There are a variety of problems with present NHS information systems and unless these problems are recognised and addressed together the combining of DHA and FHSA information resources will achieve nothing in terms of maximising the benefit from the potential outcomes available. There is no particular priority to a list of these outcomes so they are presented in alphabetical order as follows:

- Access
- Accuracy
- Completeness
- Confidentiality
- Consistency
- Fragmentation
- Timeliness
- Too much data
- Utility

Access

This title might, to the uninitiated, suggest that computer systems are your veritable, flexible friend but, in fact, access to the data contained, especially in GP systems, is not nearly as simple as it seems. A major example (which will also feature in other contexts) is that of the well-meaning attempts to obtain morbidity information from GPs.

There is a perception which is still being tested, that GP computer systems contain a wealth of morbidity information which, if made available to the new Health Authorities, would significantly improve the quality of decision making. However, early attempts to involve significant numbers of hard-worked GPs and their practice staff in churning out yet more data for authorities for no obvious immediate return to the practices has often meant that the responses contained references to Norman Tebbitt and bikes! This is not so surprising if you appreciate that General Practices have so far existed by supplying significant amounts of data to FHSAs in order to receive payment for the services they provide to you and me.

This problem has been partly resolved by such devices as computerised payments, and also by developing user-friendly software through the MIQUEST* project which has helped overcome some of the problems surrounding obtaining comparable data from different systems.

However, it cannot be automatically assumed that because there is potentially usable data lying around in various systems, that the new Health Authorities will have access to it.

Accuracy

Just because it is data it does not mean that it is accurate. The small but significant example of this was illustrated in a study undertaken in Calderdale FHSA which was again built around the assumption that there was useful morbidity data held in GP systems. The study concentrated on diabetes and GP information systems were trawled to identify all diabetic patients. Other sources of information on diabetic patients, (the register of patients in a Chiropody Department is a simple example), were then checked to provide a cross-check with the GP information and lo and behold, the cross-check revealed that there were other patients with diabetes who were not so identified on the GP systems.

Completeness

The prime example of this comes from successive central costing guidance for contracting: an ever-increasing volume for the local NHS to apply on how to achieve both consistency and accuracy in costing systems, so that purchasers can be sure that when comparing costings they are comparing like to like. One identified short-

---

*MIQUEST. Stands for Morbidity Information Query Syntax. A piece of software designed to sit on different GP systems (to date, only works on Emis and Meditel) and to extract morbidity data in a common format. It is potentially of more value to Authorities which want aggregated population data; individual practices may be better off with system-specific enquiry software. As ever, it is still dependent on the quality of data it extracts and so does not detect and correct coding errors!

fall is with community systems. The 1995 central scrutiny into bureaucracy in General Practice estimated that there can be up to a 60% variance between community nurse activity as recorded separately by practices and community trusts. Meanwhile, the development of community systems nationally is running well behind that of acute service systems.

Confidentiality

Anyone looking at information from GP systems or about GPs and their patients will sooner or later run up against confidentiality. GPs are understandably concerned about information on their patients being passed from pillar to post and are equally sensitive about information in regards to practice organisation being passed around. In Calderdale one GP objected to the fact that a small number of LMC officers and senior managers have been able to compare real data on a small group of practices in order to evaluate methods of distributing GMS Funds — even though the practice managers themselves had agreed in a working group that this information could be exchanged.

Medical Audit Advisory Groups have assembled potentially significant information on clinical activity in general practice. In West Yorkshire, as elsewhere, this has always been held at confidential arms length from the FHSAs regardless of how useful it might have proved. As MAAGs start to move into issues of practice organisation, this will potentially test the boundaries of confidentiality to breaking point.

Consistency

The major inconsistency between GP and FHSA-based practice list data is now being eroded by the progressive introduction of GP *Links*, although it will still be a few years before all the remaining non-computerised practices are brought into line. The scale of this exercise is dwarfed, however, by the inconsistencies of the potentially more valuable medical data held on GP systems. The medical information that goes on to the system depends on the GP's diagnosis of a patient's condition and naturally that diagnosis could vary from GP to GP. Even the Read coding system which attempts to give a coding framework for recording medical information is subject to that variability of interpretation. Many GPs have also improved their recording of medical information over the years so that information collected 2 or 3 years ago may be far more variable than recent information. All this makes it very difficult to rely absolutely on medical information held on GP systems as GPs will often be the first to admit. To achieve consistency it is often necessary to discard retrospective information and start prospective studies on an agreed basis.

Fragmentation

Not only do we have different computer and information systems in different parts of the NHS; even within one sector of the NHS, namely General Practice, there are a number of different systems. This is a result of the uncontrolled entry of computer suppliers into the GP market in England, a situation that is only gradually being redressed by the central accreditation of specific systems with reimbursement ultimately expected to be tied to this accreditation by Health Authorities. However, even this process is still leaving several systems in the market each with their own pros and cons and with no apparent hope of moving to a unitary General Practice system in the foreseeable future.

Timeliness

Managers can now choose between Real Time Systems which deliver up to the minute information and Retrospective Systems which deliver information which is 'x' period of time (days, weeks etc.) old. However, Real Time is very expensive and the benefits of such a heavy investment need to be well justified.

Too much data

There is a veritable mountain of data in and around the NHS and the mountain seems to grow daily as new demands for new information appear but old information is not necessarily laid peacefully to rest. Somewhere within the mountain are the odd nuggets that managers are seeking; the temptation however is to take the easy route and simply ask for whatever information is available in the hope that this will lead to the nugget. The danger is that this leads to the reaction described by a colleague of mine as 'fancy that'; an NHS manager looks at information placed in front of him, says 'fancy that' and does nothing else. It is a reaction that has broken the will if not the heart of many an information manager down the years.

Utility

One of the requirements of an effective management information system is that data can be effectively extracted so that they can be used. A problem with some of the existing systems is that they were not designed for this management purpose but, like the FHS registration system, to merely administer a process (in this case the GP contract) and not to be manipulated for other management purposes. At worst, the appropriate analogy is that of the comedian Victor Borge's waterproof watch; once he got a drop of water into it he couldn't get it out again.

This section may seem an unduly pessimistic way of reviewing the opportunities that arise in information terms from the 1996 merger of DHAs and FHSAs, but it is important to appreciate the foundations on which hopes and aspirations are now to be built.

SUMMARY

Accordingly, drawing on the experience of bringing together an FHSA, and a DHA in West Yorkshire diagram in Figure 4.1 gives a simplified graphic illustration of just some of the problems listed above.

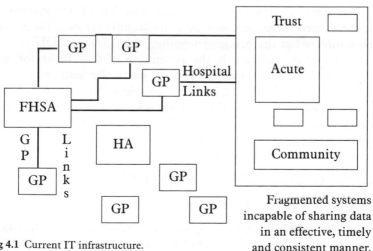

Fig 4.1 Current IT infrastructure.

Fragmented systems incapable of sharing data in an effective, timely and consistent manner.

WHAT ARE THE POTENTIAL INFORMATION NETWORK DEVELOPMENTS?

What could it look like? The diagram in Figure 4.2 gives an illustration of all the potential links that can now be established across the 105 Health Authorities of the NHS from 1996.

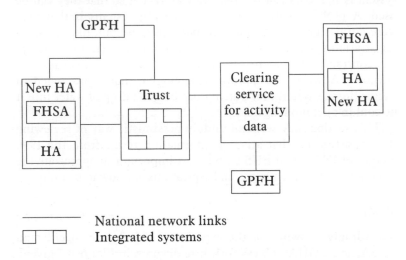

National network links
Integrated systems

Fig 4.2 Implementation of the national IM&T strategy supplemented by local linking activities with LAs, voluntary organisations, etc.

Arguably, it did not need DHA and FHSA integration to achieve these links, because they are technically possible in any structure. What the bringing together of FHSAs and DHAs does now, however, facilitate is the generation of data flows for new managerial purposes which will be of particular assistance to the new authorities both in their strategic role and their roles of supporting and monitoring the development of a Primary Care-Led NHS. In short, maximising information effectively is central to the performance of their functions.

HOW TO MAKE PRACTICAL SENSE OF IT ALL

(i) Decide what you want to do

The first trick in finding a way through the information maze is to be very clear about the managerial decision that you want the information to support. In the case of the example given below, the fundamental management decision was that we needed to have a clear picture of all the resources that are being committed to the care of the resident population on a practice by practice basis. At a time when the Authority, like many others is expecting nil growth in resources it is very important to have an understanding of where the resources are being committed as a first step towards deciding how, if at all, to redistribute those resources on any geographical basis. This is not a locality system; as any locality boundaries would be arbitrary. Instead, the exercise is based on practice boundaries as a pragmatic decision of accepting that practices each have a defined catchment area (even if they do overlap in urban settings,) and these relate to a defined segments of the population.

There have been partial forms of practice profiling around for some time, principally in FHSAs. These profiles typically related such information as practice earnings, practice staffing and list size in whatever combination was required, and, more recently, information on other practice activity such as cervical cytology or health promotion banding has also been variously employed. One of the main uses to which such information has been put has been attempts to define nationally ways of distributing GMS resources.

In terms of secondary care, partial profiles have emerged through fundholding practices as the information systems have rapidly developed to serve the fundholding agenda and so give examples of far more sensitive practice-based purchasing information.

However, these profiles have been partial; the view in West Yorkshire is that by putting together every piece of information about both the money that is going into each practice and, as far as is measurable, the activity that is being generated by the practice (both in terms of normal primary care activity and referrals to secondary care), it should be possible to build up a much better picture of what sort of overall deal the patients in any particular practice are getting. Set this against district health needs information and it should also be possible to identify the use of resources against the needs of the population, and this should be a further powerful piece of information for cash-strapped authorities in making decisions about the transfer of resources.

Even without this addition, the picture of resource commitment will be of fundamental importance in giving the new authorities a picture of where resources are going and a basis for asking 'why'.

(ii) Decide how to do it

Crucially, with the merger of separate organisations into a single body, it should be possible to build such an information base into a unified network that serves the whole organisation and so allow such an information base to be available to all the senior managers and directors dealing with both primary and secondary care issues. If this achieves nothing else it will at least give a unifying set of information about resources and activities in an entirely new format to all managers many of whom will have only dealt with parts of the equation in a previous life.

A final crucial benefit is that it helps give a sense of identity to the phrase 'Primary Care-Led NHS'. This identity, which many have sought since the phrase first came into use, comes from the fact that all the information is based around individual General Practices and helps to iron out the primary/secondary care split by identifying a single unit (namely the General Practice) as the consumer of all the resources devoted to the healthcare of its patients.

(iii) Other examples

Drugs cost control is a rather grand example of the opportunities for maximising information as DHAs and FHSAs come together in pursuit of VFM but there are other simpler examples that could equally be considered. Central Planning and Priorities Guidance repeatedly requires authorities to consider containing the total cost of prescribing. The costs of primary care prescribing have been well identified for several years, but the costs of secondary care prescribing are wrapped up in contracting costs. The information must, however, be there and if the control of prescribing costs is to be properly tackled by new Health Authorities then it is arguable that an information system around the total commitment to prescribing would be of significant use.

A different sort of benefit comes from bringing together the data that FHSAs hold and the information skills that more often seem to have resided in DHAs in both their information departments and in research departments. It is these skills and manipulation of data that have released an inventiveness that was not always available to FHSAs and though less spectacular than some other projects should not be under-estimated.

A final more detailed example of the advantages of bringing together the information and data systems has been the availability of information in one authority that has helped identify problem areas for another authority. In West Yorkshire, we had the opportunity to use RHA funding to develop primary care in one, and one only, deprived location. From all the various sources of data available, it was the powerful arguments presented by the Standard Mortality Ratios held by the Department of Public Health in the DHA which clearly identified the location that was most in need of this type of FHS project support.

SUMMARY

To summarise; the bringing together of FHSAs and DHAs into a single organisation does create powerful opportunities for creating new information flows which should, if properly used, create decision making opportunities that were simply not available while the organisations themselves were kept separate. The crucial point, however, is that this potential for problem solving can only be realised once the problem itself is properly identified and this vital pre-requisite at this stage is overlooked at your peril.

CONCLUSIONS

So how does all this relate to a Primary Care-Led NHS? I hope I have indicated that the bringing together of disparate data previously owned by separate authorities creates the opportunity for the role of primary care both in its historic provider role and as the off-quoted gateway to secondary care to be quantified for the first time in a way that will allow decision makers to compare, contrast and ask leading questions about the way resources are used, mis-used or exploited. The comprehensive and integrated approach that we have developed for the new Calderdale and Kirklees Health Authority aims to achieve that, but I would hesitate to recommend that it should be universally adopted at this stage throughout the NHS as we are still in the testing stages. However, I hope that it does serve to illustrate just what can be achieved provided that all the health warnings in the earlier part of the chapter are properly observed.

The challenge, therefore, is first to make sure that data and information systems are developed in such a way that they can be put to more effective use; until this is done it will always be possible to query the accuracy of the results that such studies produce and therefore cast doubt on their value. Once these basic building blocks have been put in place the next challenge is for managers to be very clear about the purposes to which they wish to put information. This is often still put together at significant expense and information needs to help both develop this managerial discipline and then its full expression.

For a Primary Care-Led NHS, the challenge is to find ways of exploiting the potential information flows to consolidate the position of General Practice as the pivotal organisation for the delivery of care to the population. This will only happen when we make the cultural shift from having information available to being **'informed people'**.

ACKNOWLEDGEMENT

I would like to acknowledge the very considerable assistance provided by Annette Holbrook, Director of Information for the Calderdale and Kirklees Authority, in preparing this Chapter.

5. Supporting secondary care transfers

Adrian Dawson

INTRODUCTION

The movement of health services away from hospital and into the primary care setting is not new. The systematic movement of people with learning disability and mental illness into the community had already paved the way for the NHS and Community Care Act 1990 and the substantial effort now going into community care care planning and care management.[1] Technology is now making possible the development of home and community based therapies. Equipment which was once the preserve of hospital clinicians is now portable enough and cheap enough to place in General Practices; and telecommunication is ushering in the telemedicine age enabling patients in home and community settings to be 'seen' by consultants who are geographically at long distances from the patients.

THE DORSET HEALTH COMMISSION APPROACH

The following is offered as a case study. It is drawn from my experience over the past 3 years as an executive board member of the UK's first Health Commission: the forerunner of the April 1996 new Health Authorities.

In October 1992, Dorset Health Commission officer task groups met to discuss a series of issues, one of which was to consider the shifting balance of services from secondary to primary care. The resulting paper laid out the reasons for moving services, the implication of such moves, the opportunities and the action plan. The group then considered that the reasons for moving services were:

- General practitioners have a more holistic approach and are less likely to view patients in terms of a single condition or specialty;

- This shift would capitalise on the wide-ranging skills of general practitioners;
- Aftercare was more likely to be relevant and to take into account the home and family circumstances of the patient;
- Care would be more convenient for patients and likely to have a smaller emotional impact than attending and receiving treatment in a hospital;
- Patients would be able to exercise choice;
- The communication between practitioner, professional and patient would be better and clearer;
- There would be better accountability as patients and relatives were more likely to know and have more personal contact with the practitioner and professional and the closer and more intimate contact would result in better outcomes for patients;

However, fundamental practical implications had to be taken into account. These included:

- The safety of procedures, treatments and required skills, cost, criteria for procedures to be carried out, who should carry them out;
- Clear guidelines were required;
- The roles of the team — including the general practitioner and consultant — needed to be clarified;
- The extension of the team and cascading of skills were necessary;

Supplementary factors to take into account were identified as:

- The size of practice which was seen as determining the pace of transfer;
- The role of facilities (such as community hospitals) was bound to be placed under scrutiny;
- Career development was likely to be an issue;
- The majority of general practices would require major organisational development;

At that time in 1992 the opportunities were seen as: a shift of most outpatient work, the development and shift of services such as physiotherapy, audiology, orthodontics; the opportunities for shared care that would arise with optometrists; minor surgery schemes would develop and there would be opportunities for hospital-at-home schemes.

The task group considered the following as the first actions required to realise these opportunities:

- Undertake a literature search on shifting secondary to primary care;
- Obtain patients' views on such shifts.
- Draw up a list of specialties which could move to primary care.
- Ensure managed development programmes for practices.
- Ensure dissemination of best practice, such as the agreed production of service specifications and the development of quality and audit measures.

To a large extent, the report produced by the task group became the blueprint: the work that grew out of it is described in this paper.

HISTORY OF LOCALISED AGREEMENTS AND RANGE OF SERVICES COVERED

The Dorset Health Commission Strategy 1992–1998[2] set out a number of strategic aims, the first of which stated that 'Primary care should be the principal focus for health and health care'. The primary care section of the document emphasised the potential for the transfer of services to primary care as one of its foremost objectives. Following publication and consultation on the strategy, a sum of £1 million was invested in primary care to purchase services over and above General Medical Services. In other words, the Commission started to develop extended primary care services.

The Commission was keen to ensure a process of accountability by individual practice and an investment programme following a planning cycle. To draw these strands together each practice was asked to produce a health plan according to an agreed format, the plan would be analysed, a view taken on the need for resourcing the plan and a service agreement drawn up with each individual practice. The idea for a health plan evolved from a desire within the Family Health Services Authority that greater value for money on training for primary care staff could be achieved by asking practices to produce a training plan which identified practices' development needs. Discussions about a training plan led on to discussions about a health plan and what would a health plan look like. A framework for a Practice Health Plan was drawn up in the Commission and tested with individual practitioners. The plan included guidance on the practice population, patients' health needs, current service delivery patterns and thoughts on changes, the practices' level of commitment to quality and using resources efficiently and the patients' use of the practice. The framework was then sent out to practices for comment. Finally a number of practices were approached to see if they were interested in writing plans linked to additional resources.

Discussions also took place on whether practices would report information on their practice consultation rates and specific diseases and would also agree to a number of national and local priorities: the management of prescribing, involvement in clinical audit, the production of a practice charter and involvement in the GP Links scheme. At this point, sensitive discussions took place with some practices about moving the plan to a contract. Acceptability varied by practices and eventually the Local Medical Committee became involved in negotiating parts of the service agreement for extended primary care. During this period, as practices expressed their interest in writing plans, visits were made to the practices to discuss the plans. Arrangements were made in the Commission for officers to read and analyse the plans and for the plans and their resource consequences to be agreed by the Chief Officer group. Subsequent visits were made to the practices to begin negotiations on contracts and the agreements. Over this period of time negotiations had also taken place to provide management consultant support to practices to help them develop their plans.

The range of services covered is now extensive and growing. By April 1996, contracts cover audiology, chiropody, counselling, physiotherapy, dermatology, rheumatology, mental health, ophthalmology; investigative techniques such as primary care based ultrasound, echocardiography and urodynamic screening; service issues such as the management of back pain, cardiac rehabilitation, hyperbaric oxygen therapy; and service provision such as shared care schemes and hospital-at-home schemes. The Commission has learned a great deal from these developments. The response from General Practices was overwhelming and has fully tested the managerial capacity of the new Health Commission.

As a result the Health Commission has learnt to focus its efforts on facilitating and managing primary care rather than administering it. The culture of the Commission has had to change to respond to these functions. This has meant that roles and responsibilities of Commission staff have had to be continuously clarified because General Practitioners who were used to dealing with single individuals found themselves telephoning and meeting different people about their plans and contracts. At the same time the process which was unclear at the beginning has become clearer and therefore response times to GPs have improved. The planning process raised issues which have become wider than just individual practices. Examples are: the development of the district nursing service; the need to start benchmarking activities and volumes related to size of practice; the development of primary care capital programmes and the process for handling these. The central focus for shifting services has now become the Practice Health Plan which is now integrated into the business cycle of the new Dorset Health Authority.

IMPACT UPON PRACTITIONERS, PATIENTS AND PROVIDERS

The NHS reforms have meant considerable change for practitioners and providers. Because the focus is on the shift of secondary to primary care services, there has been a need for general practitioners to work collaboratively with the Commission and to focus on long term goals. Needs assessment was required; clinical and managerial functions were developed; and some clinical skills were transferred to primary care staff. GPs have had to come to grips with the derivation and apportionment of costs, have had to learn negotiation and contracting skills and the need to monitor service developments.

Practice managers have had to cope recently with incredible change, having to learn new financial skills, computing skills and information analysis. A number have become extremely knowledgeable about services. Many practice managers now directly link and negotiate with individual hospitals and hospital consultants and some are actually leading their practices. They are having to run additional appointment and booking sessions, establishing outpatient consultant sessions in a practice, producing leaflets and questionnaires for patients. Practices have had to confront the need to discuss skillmix and the cascading of skills among the team. Sometimes they have had to examine totally new ways of providing services within the practice; for example, how a practice copes with follow-up patients coming to the practice instead of going to hospital outpatient clinics. One local practice is using a physiotherapist to triage patients within the practice.

An important dimension of the Primary Care-Led NHS is the practice's ability to innovate as more team members have been added to the practice. In one Dorset practice the physiotherapist and counsellor who originally provided separate practice-based services now work together on the management of chronic pain. It is only a matter of time before practice personnel begin to develop teamworking across different professional groups and create multi-disciplinary teams able to tackle a range of patients' problems which in the secondary care sector would be managed by different specialties.

Consultants have faced a period of adjustment through the development of fundholding and General Practitioners exercising their choice about who should provide services and where they should be provided. Some consultants have embraced the change while others have fought it. Consultants are facing issues relating to loss of control, loss of function and loss of purpose. Discussions have been difficult with regard to the value of their service and some have been reluctant to discuss the value of General Practitioner referrals. Consultants in their turn have questioned the cost-effectiveness of community services, the need for consultant level expertise in practices, the types of cases they are seeing, their lack of availability in the hospital while they are in the community and their ability to provide teaching to their junior staff and carry out research projects. They have also questioned the lack of interest among General Practitioners in their services within a practice, their lack of available equipment and diagnostic facilities and the lack of administrative staff to support them.

Others have found the links with practices stimulating, the attitudes of staff and patients encouraging and welcoming, and support facilities available to them. In many instances although consultants are affected by the changes, middle grade staff on the wards may not be aware of the influences now being exerted upon senior staff, and negotiations between primary care and consultant staff are only now beginning to permeate the wards. At senior manager level in the provider Trusts there has been a responsiveness to the changes and an understanding of the strategic aims and priorities of the Dorset Health Commission to develop services in the community and primary care setting. Nevertheless there is not as yet a strong belief among hospital managers that a Primary Care-Led NHS is the way forward. There have been some interesting tactical situations where provider Trust managers found it useful to build alliances with Health Commission purchasers in order to shift professional attitudes and stances.

Local patient surveys by practices who are providing secondary care services have been overwhelmingly positive. Practices are inviting patients to give their views on the type of service provided in the practice and the hospital. In a few instances, patients are now asking for changes in the patterns of service on an individual basis, for example, patients are now asking for their appointments to be made at closer geographical locations.

The work on transferring services from secondary to primary care over the past 3 years has provided the following learning points. Commissions are moving into performance management; at the same time they are having to support and facilitate practice development. Information strategies within Health Commissions need to take account of what is happening in primary care computing, information technology and information analysis. Commissions will both be able to hold and share more openly information about practices and their populations. General Practices are having both to compete and collaborate and understand where they stand to gain or lose by adopting the strategies — their world is more uncertain and less stable. At the same time they are becoming more knowledgeable about secondary care services and the work of hospital specialties which in turn is enabling practices to customise services as they transfer to the practice.

Both consultants and General Practitioners are learning more about each other — at a very practical level consultants have learnt that most GPs do not welcome consultant clinics on Monday mornings, while GPs are learning about consultant contracts, consultant interview processes and the way patients move around inside hospitals. General Practitioners and consultants are now directly negotiating sometimes outside the formal contracting processes. They are more aware of the change process and the time it takes to shift attitudes and behaviour rather than services. Planning and implementing change requires discipline and is not linear. The transfer of resources must take place in a focused framework. Holding the process together requires effort and luck. There are significant transaction costs.

These are highlighted by a retrospective analysis of the local community dermatology initiative which indicated 70 different actions over a year. These actions involved consultants, medical directors of Trusts, managers of Trusts, private hospitals, fundholder and non-fundholder General Practitioners, practice managers, a Royal College, a National Association of Hospital Doctors, a national charity, national newspapers and medical newspapers.

COST AND CLINICAL EFFECTIVENESS

Cost

It is the case that costs of service shifts to primary care are easy to measure as these services are often single specialty costed shifts or developments. The complexity occurs when attempts at comparison are made. In Dorset, fundholding has presented the opportunity to consider comparisons as shifts have been made by practices. The benchmark for comparison has been the tariff price quoted by the secondary care provider.

Overheads are apportioned to tariff prices including a return on capital. In primary care overheads are invisible appearing as cost or notional rents and are within the General Medical Services allocation. Tariff prices quoted by fundholders who wish to provide in-house services cannot therefore be compared with secondary care tariffs. Comparisons become even more tenuous when practices wish to build on to premises in order to house these services. Primary care needs an accounting mechanism such as 'costing for contracting' in the secondary care sector in order to facilitate cost comparisons.

Tariff prices should also vary according to volume. Volume in secondary care is high, depending as it does on referral from large catchment populations. Catchment populations in primary care are much lower. In summary, total service costs in primary care often appear lower because the overheads are invisible but in terms of volume tariff prices may actually be higher than secondary care.

In Dorset, a good example exists of the need to consider primary care and secondary care tariff prices carefully. Fundholding practices with local community hospitals are considering total purchasing. They wish to make more use of community hospitals and wish to shift care from the acute sector. In this case there may be step-up costs which translate into return on capital and higher tariff prices for the community hospitals. Cost advantage between the community hospital and acute hospital may diminish for the practices as purchasers, as community hospital tariff prices rise because of new building schemes. A total purchaser can be further disadvantaged if the acute hospital loses significant volume and tariff prices rise as a result of cost restructuring in the acute sector.

Clinical effectiveness

In shifting secondary care transfers and supporting service developments which otherwise would have gone to the secondary care sector, the question of clinical effectiveness has been partially addressed by the Dorset Health Commission and by fundholders. As clinical effectiveness for much of medicine is unknown, emphasis should be on best practice and ensuring evidence for effectiveness is incorporated into primary and secondary care service provision. The examples that follow are of work in progress in Dorset to address these issues.

Two early developments included provision of counselling and physiotherapy in practices. A key consideration was that such services should be appropriate for practices. Criteria for inclusion and exclusion according to clinical presentation were drawn up as part of the service specification. Following the introduction of these services, sampling surveys of casemix were carried out.

Information on physiotherapy indicated that 30% of patients suffered from back pain. Guidelines on the management of back pain have been drawn up by both the Dorset GP Guidelines Group and the Clinical Standards Advisory Group at national level. GPs, rheumatologists, orthopaedic surgeons and therapy services are now discussing in 1995/1996 the guidelines to enable best practice across primary and secondary care. General Practitioners and physiotherapists are now working together to ensure the management of back pain conforms to best practice. Some GPs have access to psychologists and approaches to the management of back pain now include psychological support for patients with chronic back pain.

Information on counselling indicated that the majority of patients attending have some degree of anxiety and/or depression. The counsellors in primary care are supported by psychologists who have drawn up guidelines on best practice. The GP Guidelines Group is examining the management of depression in primary care. These two examples illustrate a process which begins by stating what services should be in primary care (physiotherapy and counselling), what is appropriate (inclusion and exlusion criteria), what is best practice (local guidelines, national guidelines), and translation into practice (meetings between General Practitioners, consultants, therapists).

Two further examples illustrate how this process is now evolving in 1996. The Dorset Health Commission has supported shared care schemes between General Practitioners, optometrists and ophthalmologists. Two schemes — monitoring of diabetic retinopathy, and glaucoma — are worthy of mention. The essence of these schemes is that patients are seen by optometrists, information is sent by optometrists to ophthalmologists who decide, on the basis of the information, which patients require further eye examination. General Practitioners are kept informed of what is happening to their patients. These schemes have been running for 2 years. Optometrists draw up criteria for monitoring and agree these with the ophthalmologists. They agree the standard information sheet to be sent by the optometrist to the ophthalmologist and that evaluation should be carried out. The evaluations have recently been undertaken by the diabetologists and an ophthalmologist. Both evaluations consider that optometrists are as capable as other professionals in providing high quality eye examinations.

The optometrists and ophthalmologists have held feedback sessions on the evaluation, supplementing regular joint educational sessions between these two groups. The Local Optical Committee is now considering educational and training programmes as part of an accreditation process for further shared care schemes. These schemes demonstrated not only agreement of selected appropriate activities, guidelines and standard information format; they extended the process to incorporate an evaluation of quality. Furthermore, the feedback sessions identified the need for education, training and accreditation to support good practice. In these cases, the components for supporting secondary care shifts are almost all in place.

The provision of technology and personnel in primary care also offers opportunities for service development which currently are unsupported by evidence. For example, opportunities exist for colon cancer screening, aortic aneurysm screening and glaucoma screening in primary care. However, as yet these screening opportunities are not linked to national programmes. Should such programmes be introduced, primary care is well placed to provide them.

Appropriate shifts imply that targeting from secondary care is important. For example, many practices are interested in developing sexual health clinics linked to the Health of the Nation objective of reducing teenage pregnancy. Across Dorset, teenage pregnancy rates are higher in some areas than others; it is therefore appropriate to consider investing in practices in those areas.

Some information exists on compliance in primary care compared to secondary care. By providing services in-house at least one practice has been able to reduce its 'Did Not Attend' (DNA) rates by one half. Attendance is particularly important in the areas of mental health problems linked to substance misuse and sexual health for teenagers. As surveys suggest that teenagers are wary of attending sexual health clinics in primary care, pilot studies in primary care supported by the Health Commission have incorporated this element into existing monitoring arrangements.

The key message is that:

In terms of making decisions about shifts of secondary services to primary care a balance has to be struck between the need for analysis and the desire to test the process. Not all shifts will be subject to randomised controlled trials and it seems likely that such shifts will be considered as part of an overall approach to developing services in primary and secondary care in order to ensure value for money.

FUTURE OPPORTUNITIES AND CONTRACTING REQUIREMENTS

Future Opportunities

There will continue to be opportunistic initiatives. However, it is likely that as current initiatives develop in primary care and the culture of 'if it can be done in primary care, it should be done in primary care' grows, better coordination of transfers and shifts will occur. It is the task of new Health Authorities to facilitate through creating infrastructures that enable the processes for discussion and debate, followed by dissemination and implementation of best practice. A recent example is the discussions in Dorset which have covered the specialty of rheumatology and the development of a back pain service. These have centred on the respective roles of primary care and secondary care in service development. Meetings have covered issues such as planning, service specification, guidelines and audit, best practice, training and accreditation.

Progress will occur against a background of skills transfer in primary care which enables roles such as the nurse practitioner to develop, and enhances roles for therapy services. This must occur at pace and a primary driving factor is the absorption of additional workload in the primary care setting, accentuated by low levels of GP recruitment.

After April 1996 opportunities will increasingly exist and emerge for alliances between primary care and local authorities. In Dorset work with disadvantaged children and families demonstrates that there are opportunities for child and adolescent mental health services at primary care level; and for exercise prescription schemes where General Practitioners and primary care services will foster links with leisure and activity services provided by the local authorities. The hospital Trusts are keen to extend their outreach services through specialist nurse links particularly in the field of chronic disease management, such as asthma, epilepsy, diabetes and Parkinson's disease, and may well manage community hospitals.

The infrastructures can be created to enable progress on many initiatives. These infrastructures cover General Practitioner guideline groups, effectiveness forums, primary and secondary care audit groups, locality groups of GPs, education and training groups. It is necessary to strengthen links between them which in turn will lead to a more coordinated movement of services from secondary to primary care.

The movement of secondary services to primary care has thrown up the issue of risk management. This has still to be tackled in a cohesive way and will occur as more of the decision-making begins to take place in primary care. However, it seems likely that new Health Authorities will continue to manage risk and will be expected to prepare a risk management strategy.

Contracting requirements

The Dorset Health Commission now has a range of contracts with the secondary care sector, General Practitioners and voluntary agencies. The extended primary care contracts with GPs are developing as the first round of practice health plans have now progressed to contracts. As certain practices have gained additional services these have also been negotiated through to the contract stage and represent 'add ons' to the extended primary care contract already in place. Discussions are taking place with a view to certain practices becoming locality or preferred providers of services for other practices. If these initiatives proceed then some practices will have a contract with the Health Authority to provide services to other practices. The extent to which this occurs is reliant upon the extent to which practices compete or cooperate in the provision of services.

The content of the contract will increasingly focus on best practice and evidence-based service provision and will be considered from both primary and secondary care points of view.

The new Health Authority will therefore require sophisticated information from primary care as contracts increase in complexity. This depends on the state of primary care information systems and standardisation of information such as disease definition. The Health Commission is now beginning this work by linking a software company to selected practices.

In turn, new Health Authorities are likely to establish individual patient contracts with practices. At present, care plans are driven by the secondary care sector but this is likely to change as General Practitioners integrate their practice teams with primary care teams of community units.

EL(94)79 stated that District Health Authorities would work with general practitioners, local people and other agencies to undertake strategic monitoring and support functions more effectively.[3] In Dorset the shift of services to the primary care sector is taking place within a broad strategic framework. Increasingly, monitoring and evaluation systems are developing and support for General Practitioners is seen as the lynchpin to making this happen.

In the short term, Health Authorities will continue to be the main contractor, with General Practitioners increasingly wanting to influence the content of the contracts. The longer term depends upon the extent to which fundholding or its variants are encouraged: this will determine whether Health Authorities contract through primary care for both primary and secondary care provision. If this scenario becomes reality, the scene will be set for further considerable shifts of services to the primary care setting.

REFERENCES

1. Vetter N 1995 The hospital: from centre of excellence to community support. Chapman and Hall, London.
2. Dorset Health Commission Health Strategy 1992–98.
3. National Health Service Executive 1994 Developing NHS purchasing and GP fundholding. EC(94)79, NHSE, Leeds

6. Extending primary care teams

Angela Jeffrey

A CORPORATE APPROACH TO THE USE OF HCHS/GMS RESOURCES

The need for a strategy

A strategic framework for developing primary care for a 'new' Health Authority in 1996 within the context of a Primary Care Led-NHS is essential, or it will not know where it is going, when it has got there — or indeed if the rest of the commissioning organisation and its associated providers (including contractors) are working towards the same vision.

A modern jazz musician was once asked where he thought modern jazz was heading. His response was that if he knew he would be there now. Do we know where primary care is heading — and if the answer is known, has anybody out there arrived yet? A note of caution too about improvisation, you can only improvise for a defined number of instances before you start to go over old ground and reinvent the wheel!

The new Southampton and South West Hampshire Health Authority does have a strategy for developing primary care.[1] In order to enable primary care to stand firm as a core element of the NHS throughout episodes of constant change it regards the following principles as fundamental:

- General Practice and extended primary healthcare teams should be the cornerstone for Family Health Services;
- Shifting the emphasis of healthcare from hospital to the community is better for patients and should result in health gain;
- There will always be a need for hospital based services;
- Patient choice, clinical/cost effectiveness and value for money will all be important considerations in the deployment of local services and the provision of care.

RESOURCES AND A CORPORATE FINANCIAL APPROACH

Within this strategy for primary care development, specific links are made to the health strategy of the Authority, to which each individual purchasing strategy is also then linked.

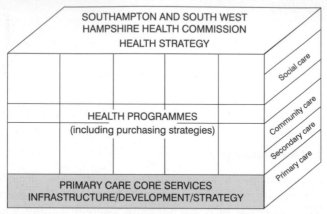

Fig 6.1 Health Strategy of Southampton and South West Hampshire Health Commission.

We have an overall health strategy within which there are a number of health programme areas covering the following — injury, mental health, cancer, circulatory disease, infection and internal disease, pregnancy and the newborn.

Related to each programme area are purchasing strategies. Every purchasing strategy will have a primary care dimension to varying extents. Commissioning authorities are gradually expanding the number of purchasing strategies, but none can afford to wait until the set is complete before investing in General Practice based infrastructure and services. A pragmatic approach is required that is continually realigned as more service/ or condition specific purchasing strategies are developed.

Since mid-1993 the Southampton and South West Hampshire Health Commission has been increasingly developing a corporate approach to the use of HCHS and GMS funding. For the last 3 years the DHA has contributed recurrently to GMS allocations in order to supplement premises development, staffing, training, computing and GP links programmes. Without this investment primary care development would have been minimal.

In addition, non recurrent allocations varying between £350 000–£500 000 have also been invested in pilot projects. Examples of such projects covered are:

- Outreach outpatients in dermatology/ultrasound;
- Practice based dietetics, physiotherapy, counselling;
- Healthy Village Project, (Brockenhurst);
- Provision of condoms in General Practice;
- Organisational quality standards in primary care;
- Practice Charter development.

The overall objective has been to develop a financial framework which, set against relatively low growth prospects for the period of the primary care development strategy (1994–2000), would:

- Aim to remove as much uncertainty as possible relating to the provision of cash limited GMS funds year on year;
- Address issues of equity between practices, and increasingly localities (this relies heavily on good management information systems);
- Recognise the need to provide good quality clinical care through supporting the practice as an organisation;
- Ensure value for money;
- Identify opportunities to redeploy the use of existing funds through a combination of greater efficiency, the relocation of services to more appropriate settings (e.g. from secondary to community to primary care) in conjunction with targeting agreed priority areas (e.g. a Purchasing Strategy for Mental Health Services);
- Relate increasingly to a managed health care system based on assessment of health needs and local targets;
- Cope with moving goal posts, such as potential changes to the nature of the current GP contract.

OUTCOMES OF A CORPORATE APPROACH TO FINANCIAL RESOURCES

The development of primary care has been accelerated due to a corporate approach. Developing primary care requires investment, but it need not always be major, in order to bring about significant changes. For the future, one of the key issues relates to the restrictions imposed by having separate financial allocations, i.e. HCHS, cash limited GMS and non-cash limited GMS. Currently one of the most problematic areas relates to the funding of General Practice premises. The rules still need to be urgently reviewed if extended primary care teams are to have the physical bases they require.

THE PRIMARY CARE TEAM AND ITS MEMBERS

The practice is a partnership of independent contractors. GPs are in contract with the Health Authority. The core primary health care team can be loosely defined as GPs, primary health care nurses, other professional staff and administrative support.

Examples of services which currently complement the work of practice primary health care teams include:

- Audiology
- Chiropody (mobile unit, and practice based)
- Community psychiatric nursing
- Counselling
- Dental practitioners
- Dietetics (practice based pilots)
- District nursing
- Family planning (practice and community based)
- Health visiting
- Mental handicap meeting
- Midwifery
- Occupational therapy
- Ophthalmic optical services
- Pharmaceutical services
- Physiotherapy (direct access)
- Practice nursing
- School nursing
- Social services
- Specialist nursing
- Speech therapy
- Voluntary sector services
- Informal carers
- Self help groups.

Currently, not all these services are provided on an equitable basis to practices and localities.

The role of the primary health care team can be seen as follows:

- Health promotion/ill health prevention — surveillance and targeting of those at risk
- Assessment and presymptomatic screening diagnosis
- Early diagnosis and diagnosis of established disease
- Responding to emergencies
- Management of access to secondary care
- Management of disease and chronic ill health

- Continuing care
- Management of non-differentiated ill health and health related distress
- Supporting rehabilitation at home/in community/post acute hospital care
- Supporting the development of mental health services, services for people with a learning disability, maternity services with a primary care focus
- Terminal care
- Supporting carers/families
- Counselling
- Information and advice dissemination
- Mobilisation of the voluntary sector to support primary/community based services
- Involvement of the community in looking after their own health and determination of priorities for health services 'responsible patients'
- Management of the lay-primary care interface
- Achieving health gain

General Practice also has a major role in mobilising social care and facilitating seamless health and social care. This role is an increasing one, particularly as a result of 'care in the community' policies. This particular aspect of the work of GPs and their extended teams is a major area for development, requiring the full examination of skills, resources and access to services needed. The overlap between the health and social care aspects of General Practice and primary care is recognised as a continuum in the delivery of services and the fulfilment of the roles described above. Seventeen of our local practices are involved in four community care projects, ranging from a district nurse acting as a care manager to employment of a care manager. The collective outcome of these projects will influence the primary and social care interface for the future.

PRIMARY CARE TEAM: THE OPPORTUNITIES AND CHALLENGES FOR THE FUTURE

The challenge from April 1996 is to deliver PHCTs working as true teams, members communicating with each other within a recognised framework.

Many FHSAs will have worked with practices to implement team building events, but how often have these initiatives been 'one off' or temporary? The key to the future will be to ensure adequate investment is made which is tailored to ongoing individual practice development initiatives. It is our intention in Southampton to develop practice specific training and development plans, with each of our practices and their extended teams. Such training plans will be multi-dimensional and multi-disciplinary.

Skill mix within the PHCT is changing. GPs need to take a radical look at how they are delivering medicine and what can be delegated to others. Their effective interface with nurse practitioners, practice and community nurses will be a critical success factor in solving clinical workload issues. Potential medical and nursing manpower shortages may force the issue, as will the need to utilise competent professionals within the team to the level of their training and ability (e.g. CPNs).

Organisational development within practices needs to be considered in conjunction with the concept of directorship with the PHCT and the potential for the role of 'medical director'. The role of medical director could be a useful vehicle for ensuring leadership within the practice; someone needs to be steering the organisation into the future. Reliance on total consensus management will no longer be appropriate.

Local factors need to be taken into account. Changes in the structure and service provision of General Practitioner provision in areas with different socio-economic characteristics[2] demonstrates the need for more substantial support to urban and inner city practices.

A useful summary definition of the key management and organisational skills needed for PHCTs has emerged from a joint initiative between this Health Authority, a fundholding General Practice and Norwich Union Healthcare.[3]

The role of Community Trusts

PHCTs will continue to develop in a flexible manner, depending on the needs of the practice population and locality. A constructive partnership approach with Community Trusts must be developed where appropriate to ensure the most effective use of community resources relating to such attached staff as community nurses, chiropodists, dietitians, physiotherapists, counsellors, etc. Practices and Trusts will need to be proactive in determining for themselves their own areas of effective collaboration. There may be several or there may be few. Locally a three-way partnership has developed with the Southampton Community Health Services Trust in relation to premises development, and a collaborative training initiative in the inner city of Southampton. As a result the Community Trust is exploring different organisational models of community nursing with local practices.

Table 6.1 Summary of key management and organisational skills needed for PHCTs

• Organisation development	— Particularly team building, leadership and corporateness (within both the partnership and the practice as a whole).
• Rules and role definition within the practice	— In order to facilitate sound and responsive management
• Business and strategic management skills	— Particularly in the area of decision analysis, option appraisal and decision making
• Innovation	— Requiring further consideration environmental analysis tools (e.g. BCG and Porter)
• Risk management	— Particularly corporate risk and total fundholding risk
• Alliance building and private networking	— To maximise benefits from the private sector and other parts of the public sector

The role of Acute Trusts

The growing demand for additional 'direct access' services and the acknowledged need to engage those in primary care in the decisions about the development of local services also impact on the functioning of the PHCT both in its development and ongoing training needs. This is another area for collaboration between Trusts and primary care.

Implications for education and training within primary care teams

Primary care teams within the new Primary Care-Led NHS need to be able to respond quickly and flexibly to local health needs and patient demand. There is a need to deliver evidence based, cost effective medicine and to promote health strategies in line with the Health of the Nation strategy and other local health targets.

Continuing professional training has, to date, been controlled by the professional bodies with little input from past health commissions and the growing body of fundholders. However, training and education which relies exclusively on professional input may inhibit service changes, prevent commissioning authorities from developing their General Practitioners locally and fail to relate to local priorities. Postgraduate Education Allowance (PGEA) arrangements are often arbitrary and frivolous and training reimbursements, through FHSAs, random and unplanned. Purchasers need training geared to future service direction, together with educational programmes that demonstrate a commitment to evidence based medicine, link primary and secondary health care and promote local priorities. Such programmes need tailoring to individual practice needs; they should cover all aspects of practice activity and be ongoing.

From April 1996 the NHSE will set two levies, one for Postgraduate Medical and Dental Education (PGMDE) and one for Non-Medical Education and Training (NMET). The former will cover General Practitioners and dentists, the latter physiotherapists, midwives, nurses, and other non-medical staff in the PHCT. Those whose training is outside the remit will continue to be administered at national level. The NMET levy is administered locally via consortia. The PGMDE levy will be administered by Regional Education Development Groups (REDGs) at regional level.

New Authorities need to ensure that in order to achieve a truly Primary Care-Led NHS members of PHCTs are appropriately trained. The development of postgraduate programmes covering clinical expertise, professional and practice management issues, which are ongoing and no longer ad hoc will be managed by REDGs and implemented through Regional Advisors in General Practice.

The new Authorities will need to ensure PHCT training and practice development is funded through GMS on a recurrent basis, properly planned and programmed. This should cover, for example:

- Management in Primary Care (e.g. at Certificate and Diploma levels);
- NVQ courses for administration staff;
- Quality Standards awards — Investors in People Standard;
- Practice Nurse professional development (e.g. at Diploma and Degree level);
- Collaborative training, e.g. with the Community Trusts;
- Joint Social Service/Health Service Training.

The 1990 Contract provided GPs with the opportunity for continuing their professional education in the form of the Postgraduate Education Allowance. With NMET and PGMDE new Health Authorities need to work closely with Postgraduate Advisers and GP Tutors to ensure that coherent GP training and continuing professional education programmes link as appropriate with the training of the PHCT. Such training needs to be multi-disciplinary and involve others such as Community Trusts in joint approaches.

With the forthcoming changes to the funding of postgraduate education and training, it is essential that commissioning authorities have an overview of all aspects of the education and training requirements of the PHCT. Fundholders will have both a purchaser and provider role in this respect.

THE ROLE OF THE PRIMARY CARE DEVELOPMENT AND RESOURCE CENTRE

Southampton and South West Hampshire Health Authority is now developing a Primary Care Development and Resources Centre at the Commission offices/headquarters in Southampton. The accommodation and facilities to support this initiative are available within the headquarters building and it became operational in November 1995. The scheme has been developed as a result of the firm recognition that General Practice-based primary care and the associated primary health care teams should be the cornerstone in the provision of locally based, easily accessible Family Health Services.

The Primary Care Development and Resource Centre for General Practices within the Commission's boundaries will focus on the development of the practice as an organisation to:

- Provide support to practices which will enable them to develop a range of high-quality, consumer responsive services geared to local needs;
- Develop capability in:

— training
— financial support and advice
— effective use of staff/manpower
— practice development planning
— business planning
— practice health plans
— audit (both organisational and clinical).

The objective is to achieve a coordinated approach within which this can be achieved building on what is specified in the Primary Care Development Strategy and existing work already underway in the areas specified above. In particular the focus is on the development of General Practice as an organisation to:

- Purchase and influence the purchasing of a range of health services through primary care led purchasing and General Practice fundholding.
  (The purchasing of health care will include aspects of secondary, community and primary care and their relationships to social care.)

The attention to practice development within a dedicated facility will enable current resources to be shared more widely and facilitate the development of the following:

- The sharing of experiences relating to operational issues within and between General Practices;
- The development of a strategic focus for the practice and primary health care team;
- The prevention of insularity within some practices, through the forgoing of links with other practices, particularly within localities;
- An increased contextual understanding of NHS changes, both local and national;
- An understanding of the inter-relationships between the managerial/organisational and clinical issues in the delivery of health care (managed care).

The funding of the Centre will be achieved through joint initiatives with other bodies including both the NHS and the private sector. It is a clear signal of a Health Authority demonstrating its new core function of support to extended primary care providers and it exploits the new capacity of 1996 Health Authorities to mobilise and integrate resources in ways that were really achieved prior to 1996 and the advent of a Primary Care Led-NHS.

REFERENCES

1. Southampton and South West Hampshire Health Commission (1994) A strategy for developing primary care 1994–2000
2. Leese B. Bosanquet N. 1995 Change in general practice and its effects on service provision in areas with different socioeconomic characteristics. British Medical Journal 311: 546–550
3. Southampton and SW Hampshire Health Commission and Norwich Union Healthcare 1995, Into the future — The lessons learned from a partnership of public and private sector healthcare organisations. Report of the 4P Project (unpublished)

7. Coordinating practice

Rosalind Eve

Three questions spring out at me when thinking about a Primary Care Led-NHS. The first is how can we help General Practitioners and their staff to participate in the multitude of complex decisions that need to be made? The second is how can we ensure they acquire the skills to accommodate the accelerating pace of change brought about by, for example, technological advance, demographic changes and patient expectations? The third is how can we ensure that they are accountable for their decisions? There are no simple answers. General Practice is diverse and operates in a highly complex environment.

THE PRE-REFORM LEGACY

The problem

Traditionally, General Practices have been isolated — geographically, organisationally, financially and culturally — from each other and from the rest of the health service. This isolation is exacerbated by the rigorous training doctors have, to take clinical decisions on their own, guided by a powerful set of ethics concerning confidentiality. It mitigates against the good communication and flow of ideas necessary for well-informed decision-making and is particularly unresponsive to traditional line management command structures.

Worse still, like many professionals, GPs and their staff have never been satisfactorily accountable for the decisions they make. Prior to the 1960s, GPs were accountable to nobody but their own conscience. In the 1970s the professional organisations developed mechanisms to increase GPs' accountability to their peers (for example, the introduction of vocational training). The recent NHS reforms endeavoured to introduce financial accountability to the government and the nineties have seen a tentative exploration of accountability to patients. GPs now find themselves potentially accountable in all four directions simultaneously. Since these constituencies sometimes have conflicting criteria, accountability cannot be a simple process of separating the competent from the incompetent, a judgement of good and bad.

To complicate matters further, there are few straightforward clinical outcome measures that can be usefully applied to a consultation. What is or is not 'effective' is a highly subjective opinion.

How can GPs give evidence of effective performance such that their professional discretion (and therefore a key factor in their ability to respond quickly and appropriately to problems on the ground,) is left intact? An appropriate response — one that will satisfy both themselves and the various constituencies to whom they are accountable — is only possible if they develop an understanding of the context in which they work. They need to be able to place themselves within the range of practice variation and to know how their actions may impact on other sectors of the Health Service.

In short, new Health Authorities need in 1996 to facilitate a dynamic relationship between GPs and those to whom they are accountable so that everyone is on an upward learning curve. The success of this approach hinges on overcoming their isolation — breaking down the barriers between General Practices and the rest of the world, so that external scrutiny becomes an opportunity for learning rather than a threat and does not demand that they neglect their core activities. Practices need to become 'knowledge-based' organisations able to generate, transfer and share knowledge.[1] It is a two-way process. GP understanding of the broader context demands a complementary understanding of general practice by others involved in the dialogue.

Everyone inhabits their own 'different assumptive worlds'[1]. People from different organisations can look at exactly the same information, draw quite different and sometimes contradictory conclusions and be 'right' within their own terms of reference. Furthermore, much knowledge, in any organisation, is tacit, subconscious, unspoken and unwritten. General Practice is no exception. For GPs and their staff to participate in meaningful dialogue with others, they need to gain an understanding of how 'we' and 'they' see the world. This includes some insight into the tacit knowledge of other organisations.

Advantages

There are advantages in the way that General Practice is currently organised. Almost by historic accident, they have some of the organisational characteristics necessary for effective change management. They are small units. Decisions are not hampered by layers of command. Solutions to problems can be found quickly — and self management allows jobs to be continually redefined. General Practice is well on the way to being the sort of flat, web-like organisation that management literature suggests adapts rapidly and appropriately to change, produces most innovation and can be most responsive to client needs. New Health Authorities involved in supporting General Practice and facilitating its development can build on these characteristics.

SOME ANSWERS

The work that we have been doing in Sheffield has been exploring how knowledge-based General Practice can be achieved, drawing on a multitude of approaches. Our starting point has been to help to address common problems identified by members of practice teams. Although much of our work has been funded by the District Health Authority, its management and direction has been determined by the practices to whom we are accountable and we have not had to wrestle with the contradictory roles of both developing practices, which demands trust and openness, and policing them, which inevitably generates secrecy.

Shadowing and networking

Shadowing has often been promoted as a tool for career development for managers and administrators in the Health Service. We have adapted its use so that it assists the learning of tacit knowledge, particularly amongst clinicians. GPs and hospital consultants or senior health service managers 'shadow' each other as peers. They follow a written protocol to avoid false expectations or misunderstandings and to help participants make the most of the opportunity.

Similarly, small multi-disciplinary groups from one practice shadow their counterparts in another practice for one morning, so they can compare a particular aspect of care. A visit is prepared for in advance by agreeing its purpose and exchanging organisational profiles. On the day, time is allocated for the visitors to watch, to ask questions of their counterparts and to compare notes with each other. Afterwards the visitors compile a brief report giving constructive feedback to their hosts which provides the basis for discussion back at their own practice. The host and visiting practices then reverse roles.

These learning exercises give people the opportunity to step back from their daily routines, place their clinical activity in a wider context and look afresh at their way of working. They carry Post Graduate Education Allowance accreditation which reinforces the message that GP time away from their core function (that of consulting with patients) is valued and not to be taken for granted.

Skill sharing and learning may demand little more than simple informal networking. Putting people in touch with each other so they can learn from each others' experience underpins more formal approaches and assists the breaking-down of barriers. Practice staff may want to compare anything from appointment systems and disease management clinics to building design. Such networking can be easily arranged for the convenience of those involved by someone who commands both trust and respect and has an intimate working knowledge of the practices involved — someone whose role is unequivocally to respond to the needs of the practice, as the practice sees them.

Translation

Every organisation has its own culture, language and world-view, reflecting differences in structure, function and professional values. If General Practices are to participate in complex multi-agency decision-making these differences need to be explicit, negotiated and explicated to avoid misunderstandings and mistrust. Communication and dialogue with General Practice is more likely to meet with success if it does not jar on normal practice culture.

The local Health Commission's communications have often been lengthy — for example, in report form, whereas GPs are more accustomed to reading and writing shorter texts — patients' notes and test results. Ideas and proposals need to be put into a form that can be readily assimilated by their audience. The first written communication of, say, a proposal, is more likely to elicit a response if it is in a form that can be easily read on the hoof, in between consultations or visits. More detailed communication needs to be available once their interest has been 'hooked'.

Similarly, Health Authority staff are accustomed to long meetings — lasting perhaps one to two hours, whereas GPs are steeped in short consultations — lasting 5–15 minutes. At these meetings, Health Authority staff are likely to make infrequent, big, definite and unreversable decisions that are wide ranging and impact on a greater number of people. GPs, on the other hand, make many small decisions, usually relating to the individual in front of them, frequently couched in terms of uncertainty — 'let's do this and review in a couple of weeks' — and rarely require any advance preparation (agendas, background reading etc). When these two worlds meet it is easy to see how they may have conflicting implicit expectations of both the process and outcome.

Careful preparation before meetings to make sure that time is well spent away from core practice activities is very obviously useful. GPs and their staff need to learn the art of preparation and the onus is on those who already have these skills to help them to learn. (Since a Primary Care-Led NHS does not demand that managers develop the skill of making quick reversible decisions on the basis of little evidence, this learning is not a two-way process.) Chasing people up, being their memory and providing routine prompts need to be built into the system, and not seen as an additional nuisance.

First contact meetings are practice friendly if they are brief — aiming to establish the credentials of someone who values their time and is willing to listen. Too many meetings cannot be sustained without impinging on patient time.

Data sharing and information feedback

Critical review of clinical practice is stimulated by routine feedback of comparative data.[2] Many practices compare and review changes in their own activity over time but few can routinely compare their activity with others. Reducing isolation by providing them with comparisons of standardised, routinely collected work load, morbidity and financial data puts variations into context, and promotes organisational learning. When significant numbers of practices in one area are involved it also allows the larger picture of what GPs and their staff actually do, together with the associated costs, to emerge. Shifting patterns of care and costs in primary care can be identified that may be invisible to any single practice.

Successful collation of practice held data depends crucially on it meeting expressed needs of practices rather than a means to monitor quality. In Sheffield, collection, collation and control of the data rests firmly within General Practice. This has meant that practices find it much easier to hand over sensitive information. Ultimately, anonymised but otherwise unavailable data is released to the Health Authority, making the range of variation explicit; over time, changes in patterns of work will be identified. Practices are willing to compare and discuss differences (without fear of being judged and possibly penalised) — highlighting areas that might benefit from closer scrutiny and stimulating tangible organisational learning.

Each new set of comparative data is discussed at meetings of GPs, practice managers, receptionists and practice nurses. This gives them the opportunity to ask questions of one another and make sense of what it all means. One practice realised they had an exceptionally high nurse visiting rate, so they invested in a centrifuge to enable doctors to take blood on home visits and successfully improved services to patients whilst reducing nurse visits.

Another realised it had unusually high insurance costs to cover partners who fall sick and subsequently changed its policy. Yet a third realised its need to have computerised accounts and have invested in training to provide more accurate budget forecasts.

It is new information. The skills have yet to be developed to reliably offer definitive interpretation. It is likely that there are many different but valid interpretations of the data, depending on criteria and viewpoint. What is true for the clinician considering the health of an individual may not be true for those considering the health of whole populations. Our strategy for interpretation is in its infancy and highly pragmatic. However, it is a tentative stab at describing to the outside world, in numerical terms, what actually happens in General Practice.

'Up to now General Practice has been a black box shielding both activity and costs from the sight of even the participants. Opening the black box should enable both Health Authorities and practitioners plan services better and enable the appropriate transfer of resources from secondary to primary care.'[3]

Coalition building

Some problems in General Practice may only be overcome if complementary change occurs simultaneously in other organisations. Difficulties may well not be related to cussedness or lack of professionalism on the part of the GP. Often there are real practical problems that are not within the gift of those working in general practice to overcome. With the best will in the world, moving anticoagulation monitoring en masse from hospital to General Practice for example, demands changes in city-wide contracting and hospital services that even consortia of GPs, acting on their own, cannot achieve for a whole city.

In Sheffield we have found there is a clear role here for 'change agents', familiar with local networks, to mediate between organisations and develop coalitions of interest around clearly defined specific issues. This is best achieved by engaging the interest of key influential enthusiasts in each organisation. It may require no formal, collective meetings at all; instead individuals can be met one at a time.

The discussion will then have fewer hidden agendas to second guess and negotiate. It can be sensitive to cultural and organisational differences giving the key players the opportunity to express their reservations in confidence. The change agent then has the opportunity to anticipate and overcome problems and construct win–win solutions without generating a lot of extra work for those whose core task may well not be to bring about that particular change in general practice and who are already beleaguered by over-taxing schedules.

Training

Difficulties in developing knowledge-based General Practice may simply reflect formal training needs. The most obvious of these needs revolve around management, computing and information and clinical training (to accommodate treatments or investigations once performed in hospitals by specialists). Enthusiasm and commitment to learning will be more likely to be forthcoming if the need for training is identified by those who will directly benefit from it and the course is developed in consultation with them. This demands an environment where admission of ignorance does not involve public loss of face or retribution.

Management

General Practice has undergone spectacular organisational growth over the past 40 years — from single-handed GPs to large partnerships with teams of supporting staff — induced and supported by financial reward but little accompanying organisational or managerial direction. Skills such as negotiation, liaison, delegation and organisational development need to be learned so that they emanate from within General Practice and are not seen as aliens from without. Again, this can only be achieved if the need for the learning is felt by the practice staff and doctors themselves. It needs to be seen to respond to the difficulties they are currently facing and giving voice to.

Difficulties within partnerships are common and can generate a lot of grief for everyone involved. There are no instant answers. However, responding to the difficulties with support can also be an opportunity to promote organisational learning that will be welcomed if offered by someone who the partners and practice staff trust — and who has the appropriate organisational development skills.

Computer skills

In our experience computer skills are frequently overestimated. Simple requests to identify patients maintained on a particular drug often present difficulties. Skills for routine computer use are often more than adequate, but anything demanding a slightly out of the ordinary report may well present problems that practice staff wouldn't necessarily anticipate. Developing the confidence to experiment and explore the computer's capabilities is key to enabling practices to generate, transfer and share knowledge.

Ascertaining general practice views and concerns

A Primary Care-Led NHS will be established once the values of primary care dominate. If GPs (be they fundholders or non-fund holders) and patients are to influence improvements to the quality of services given by provider units or the Health Authority planning process many new, routine and sustainable mechanisms need to be established.

One such system, established since 1991, is the Monitoring Quality in Service Agreements project (MQSA). Its purpose is to monitor the quality of care given to patients by the local Trusts from GP and patient perspectives. A total of 57 Sheffield practices participate, serving 60% of Sheffield's population. Funded by the Health Authority, it is firmly rooted in general practice, responding to issues identified by GPs and their staff.

GPs are systematically and regularly canvassed to identify their main areas of concern. Having identified the services to be monitored, assessed what is methodologically feasible and consulted widely with Health Authority managers and public health physicians, evaluations are carried out.

GPs are asked to complete one questionnaire (one side of A4) for every patient admitted or referred to a given service over, say, a 2 week period (depending on the sample size required). Topics have included the quality of communication from hospital, the level of investigation and the ease of access to an acute bed. Because of the large numbers of participating practices, any one GP is unlikely to have to devote any more than one hour per month to the project. The response rate is often as high as 95% and always higher than 80%. The results, which give GP opinion an unprecedented cohesion, are published and circulated widely.

We have also carried out an extensive survey of women's views of the quality of maternity care they received from hospitals, General Practice and the Community Trust. Our hypothesis is that, by using GPs and their staff, patients will respond more readily and at a deeper level than is usual with most survey instruments of patient experience. This was born out by the maternity care survey which, despite being 30 pages long, achieved a 72% response rate covering many areas of urban deprivation.

MQSA complements its evaluations with routine semi-structured interviews to identify, in-depth, the issues that currently concern GPs and their staff. The results of these interviews give collective voice to GP experience.

CONCLUSION

The work described in this chapter is just the beginning of what promises to be an extraordinary journey for all involved. For practices to become knowledge-based organisations able to generate, transfer and share knowledge many complementary techniques and support structures will be needed to build and strengthen the webs and networks that already exist to promote dialogue and learning. To create these locally is a major challenge for new Health Authorities in 1996 and General Practice may frustrate those who endeavour to manage using the techniques that worked well in large bureaucracies. However, for the very same reason it frustrates, it offers a multitude of opportunities for fast moving innovation that responds directly to patients' needs as they stream through the door.

ACKNOWLEDGEMENTS

I would like to thank all who have worked with and for the Towards Coordinated Practice project, the Monitoring Quality in Service Agreements project, the Practice Data Comparison project and the Framework for Appropriate Care Throughout Sheffield project, without whose commitment, ideas and enthusiasm none of this work would have been possible. I owe special thanks to Dr Paul Hodgkin whose inspirational ideas have permeated and underpinned much of the issues discussed in this chapter.

REFERENCES

1. Dawson S 1995 A research basis for health services management. Paper given at the Scientific Basis of Health Services Management conference. London, Oct 1995
2. Keller RB, Soule DN, Wennberg JE, Hanley DF 1990 Dealing with geographic variations in the use of hospitals. Journal of Bone Joint Surgery 72 (9) 1286–1293
3. Eve R, Hodgkin P, Jenkins P, McGorrigan J 1995 Activity and costs: collecting data on the hidden aspects of general practice. Paper given at the Primary Health Care Specialist Group (The British Computer Society) conference. Cambridge, Sept 1995

8. Combining with Public Health

Peter Greagsby and Philip Milner

INTRODUCTION

Rotherham Health Authorities, at strategic discussions in 1995 around a set of local initiatives drawn together in a paper titled 'Preparing for a Primary Care-Led NHS', accepted as policy a number of key issues which will direct the work of the organisation in understanding structural, operational and organisational culture issues to take it beyond April 1996.

First, the Authorities accepted as a mission statement that their overall vision moving towards a Primary Care-Led NHS is:

'Enabling people to enjoy good health by providing, in partnership with other agencies, equitable high quality primary, community and social care services, sited in appropriate settings, at the heart of local communities, appropriately accessing hospital services.'

Secondly, they re-affirmed their commitment to a number of guiding principles to which Rotherham had worked over the past few years which, although they needed refocusing in the context of a Primary Care-Led NHS, they still held good. These are:

- Every person should have access to a comprehensive, locally based, personal primary health care service, and be able to exercise reasonable choice. The service should be sensitive to local need;
- Services that can be, should be provided within primary health care, adopting the simplest appropriate technology whilst ensuring high quality of care;
- The delivery of health care in Rotherham should be primary health care-led where appropriate. Access to secondary health care should normally be by referral from primary health care;
- A comprehensive primary health care service is best provided by a multi-disciplinary primary health care team working from

well-sited, properly equipped and adequately designed premises, serving a defined population registered with a practice or practices. Properly functioning primary health care teams are of paramount importance for the future development of services;
- Primary health care services should address the needs of their local people. Information obtained from primary health care teams should form the basis of the assessment of health needs, together with information derived from local public health advice and other sources, local authorities and the consumers of the service.

In Rotherham, we are clear that the most appropriate place for purchasing health care lies at the point closest to the patient where understanding of need is individually and collectively focused, based on day-to-day contact with a clear understanding of the particular environment. That point of focus is the General Practice and the wider primary health care team. They will be at centre stage in purchasing all health and (alongside the local authority) social care services.

Placing primary health care at centre stage of purchasing focuses even more clearly the need to accept General Practice as the building block for health needs assessment and population level information, to harness its purchasing to ensure clinical and cost effectiveness. It is essential that the skills of the organisation work alongside General Practices in developing their new role to ensure they are 'fit' to do so.

THE ROLE OF PUBLIC HEALTH AND HEALTH PROMOTION

The role of Public Health is the key player in ensuring this happens. Public Health working closely with General Practices in both their purchasing and providing role is an essential if General Practices are to purchase health care services clinically and cost effectively for the benefit of their patients. In Rotherham we feel that Public Health should provide the following range of advice and services to General Practice.

HEALTH CARE NEEDS ASSESSMENT

The concept of health care needs assessment as elaborated by the NHS Executive[1] needs marketing to General Practitioners. In essence this consists of describing the scale of a particular health problem in General Practice, understanding what works in addressing the problem, and then monitoring that improvements are actually occurring. Given that much of General Practice is currently demand-led, moving to a needs-led service is a major challenge. In the short, medium, and perhaps even long term, the workload in primary health care teams will increase. Politicians, NHS managers and policy-makers, and financial reward systems need to recognise this. The approach will only succeed if health problems are chosen that are a major concern for the practice, preferably one at a time initially. An example of this in Rotherham is coronary heart disease. Public health physicians can help the primary health care team identify all patients with coronary heart disease and try to ensure they have all their health needs met. This will mean referring many people with chest pain for direct-access exercise ECG testing to detect those most at risk of severe coronary artery disease. It will also mean increasing drug expenditure on lipid-lowering, ß-blocking, and ACE inhibitor drugs on a massive scale. But the health gain will be an immediate and prolonged reduction in the number of deaths from coronary heart disease. Interestingly the greatest health gain will come from the prescription of an unglamorous drug which costs next-to-nothing: asprin.

EPIDEMIOLOGY, STATISTICS, AND SOCIAL SCIENCES

Public Health physicians can promote this process through their knowledge and skills in epidemiology, statistics, and social sciences. Epidemiology is the study of diseases and their causes. Having epidemiologists associated with primary health care teams can only improve the organisation and outcomes of health services. For example, raising awareness in primary health care teams about the risk factors for coronary heart disease will ensure all opportunities are taken to influence people to stop smoking, take more exercise, keep a normal weight, drink sensibly, and take their medicines. Understanding which routine statistics are available for primary health care teams will lead to better clinical practice through using them in clinical audit and outcomes monitoring. Understanding what is known about changing people's behaviour and clinical practice in the social sciences will allow PHCTs to structure their activities so as to maximise the likelihood of securing health gain. Perhaps the most important development would be for all primary health care staff to possess critical appraisal skills. These have evolved out of the joint practice and study of epidemiology, statistics, and social sciences over the last 20 years. With this new mind-set practitioners would more readily reject clinical practice of proven ineffectiveness and conversely adopt those of proven clinical effectiveness and cost-effectiveness.

CLINICAL INFORMATION SYSTEMS

The health needs of larger populations could be best described if they were built up from constituent sub-populations such as those covered by primary health care teams. This information would be invaluable for allocating resources appropriately, formulating local health strategies, and monitoring progress towards local health objectives.

Opening up the flow of information from secondary and tertiary health care use to PHCTs will help shape clinical practice and even the organisation of primary care services. For example, in Rotherham it seems that practices with the highest death rate from coronary heart disease have the lowest rates of cardiac surgery. We are currently enlarging the dataset for this analysis. If the finding is confirmed, we will have to work with the disadvantaged practices to ensure that patients who need cardiac surgery are being identified and having their needs met.

PRACTICE ORGANISATION

Public health physicians understand diseases and the ways in which health and other sciences are delivered. With practice-based health needs assessments they are then ideally placed to advise on how best to organise tackling health problems, be they dementia, diabetes, or renal failure.

EVIDENCE-BASED CLINICAL PRACTICE

Only about 15% of clinical practice is based on good quality research evidence.[2] The challenges for the NHS are to ensure that primary research is undertaken as soon as possible to provide the missing evidence and to facilitate and promote the dissemination of the current research evidence. Public health physicians should be able to help with this dissemination to primary health care teams. There needs to be improvements in information networks as well. We know that just providing information to health professionals does not change clinical practice. We therefore need to develop action plans for improving clinical practice which are developed and owned by stakeholders such as the Continuing Medical Education Advisor, the Local Medical Committee, the Postgraduate Dean, and the Research and Development Director. Currently we know that there is not much we can do to change clinical practice for the better. There are about six types of activities which work in various settings and which have been derived from research evidence.[3] Academic detailing as practised by pharmaceutical representatives works, as do computerised or manual reminder systems at the point of patient contact, changing organisational and financial rewards and sanctions, influencing patients directly, and well-constructed clinical guidelines. The net benefits of doing these types of activities together is greater than the sum of doing them separately.

ANNUAL REPORTS

General Practice Annual Reports are being replaced by business plans. These contain health needs assessment, action plans, and resource needs. Public health physicians have helped produce District Annual Reports on the health of the local populations since 1990. They can therefore use this experience in aiding General Practitioners develop their business plans.

TOTAL PURCHASING PROJECT

An interesting example of linking public health time directly into General Practice is within the context of Rotherham's national Total Purchasing pilot project. Benefits from this to date have been:

- Jointly agreed priorities for Health Needs Assessment exercises;
- Appropriate/relevant advice and support;
- Assistance with Health Needs Assessment exercise;
- Increased understanding of each other's roles.

An early decision was taken within the project to develop an information system to support purchasing which could be realistically extended within available resources to other practices. This meant the practice had to work with the Authorities Central

Management Information System (CMIS). The cost of this for each practice is around £10 000. Linking in this way has allowed the practice to key into a whole range of information to support their purchasing decision-making process. Examples of this information and how it is being used includes:

- Health Needs Assessment;
- Identification of priority areas to be tackled in the next contracting round;
- Comparison of practice activity with the District as a whole e.g. re-admission rates, average lengths of stay, death rates, etc.

From April 1996, these developments will need to be set in the context of a local 'Primary Care-Led Purchasing Information Management and Technology Strategy' to underpin the development of a Primary Care-Led NHS.

HEALTH PROMOTION

In 1992, recognising the importance of integrating the health promotion activities of Health Authorities and GPs, individual senior health promotion officers were directly linked to a number of General Practices to cover all Rotherham practices. Their aim was to liaise and coordinate health promotion in the primary care setting with particular emphasis on General Practice and other primary health care professionals.

The process over the years has involved the utilisation of existing networks and resources and the identification of other opportunities for developing health promotion in primary care. The health promotion support network for all Rotherham GPs and their teams provides opportunities for primary health care terms to liaise and discuss health promotion issues with a health promotion specialist. Specific examples of the results of this work include:

- Establishment of a young people's sexual health contraception clinic;
- Development of an ethnic cervical cytology project with several practices;
- Training programmes for primary care staff;
- Development of Occupational Health project to provide GPs and other primary health care professionals with a service for patients who suffer from an occupational health related illness or condition;
- Health education leaflets in pharmacies;

- Introduction of a training programme for pharmacists in health promotion;
- Sessions in conjunction with the Post Graduate Medical Education Tutor on Health of the Nation key areas for GPs, practice nurses and other primary health care professionals. Particularly well-received were sessions on alcohol, cervical cancer, accident prevention, heart health, mental health and sexual health.

The relationships between health promotion specialists and GPs' PHCTs continues to mature and grow in understanding.

This section has described the actual and potential role for Public Health and Health Promotion specialists working alongside general practitioners and their teams. General Practice recognises that the wider health and effectiveness dimension in their purchasing and providing is often not a priority and by and large welcome help in developing that understanding.

INFORMATION AND INFORMATION TECHNOLOGY

General Practice, working alongside Public Health in health needs assessment and clinical and cost effective purchasing, needs to be underpinned by the development of high quality and effective information systems in General Practice. The practice database needs to be the building block to bring together practice and population level information and intelligence together. That population level information and intelligence needs to recognise the wider health issue by integrating information on deprivation and social care to produce a comprehensive package of health and social care needs assessment. Uniquely, a Primary Care-Led NHS will lead to primary health care purchasing and providing services which recognise this wider 'need' dimension.

In Rotherham various initiatives are guiding us in this direction. Three examples are:

- Population information systems
- Healthy alliances
- Deprivation mapping.

EDUCATION, AUDIT AND RESEARCH

Also underpinning the development of GPs as purchasers and providers is the need to integrate education, audit and research into the primary health care team.

Any attempts to improve clinical practice in primary care will always come back to basics. Education, research and audit are fundamental. Undergraduate medical education is almost entirely built around hospital medicine. This is wrong. The medical schools know it is wrong and are trying to base much more training in primary health care. But there has not been much progress. Similarly generalist medical training should cover General Practice. Currently it does not unless doctors are aiming to be General Practitioners. Continuing medical education should always cover developments occurring in General Practice if these will impinge on the medical specialty in question. Public Health physicians have worked with GPs, hospital consultants, pharmaceutical adviser, medical adviser, and the CME adviser to integrate the development of clinical guidelines with postgraduate medical education. We have handled guidelines for the investigation, management, and rehabilitation of patients with strokes and guidelines for anticoagulation, childhood asthma, and lipid-lowering drugs in this way.

Research brings three major benefits to primary health care. The first is that it keeps alive and nurtures a questioning spirit. Given that we do not know the effectiveness of much clinical practice, a discerning doctor who challenges orthodoxies for the benefit of patients is an essential component of a PHCT. The second is that through undertaking research doctors can develop critical appraisal skills. This will then allow them to judge better the mass of claims and counter-claims on clinical matters made by pharmaceutical representatives, medical magazines, academic journals, hospital specialists, colleagues and others. The third is that there is great need for research to be undertaken in General Practice. Hospital practitioners have proportionately undertaken more research and also better quality research than have workers in primary health care.

In Rotherham we have led the way with the development of ear-care training for practice nurses. This innovation has been evaluated by the Sheffield Centre for Health and Related Research (SCHARR) in a before-and-after comparative study with patient-assessed health outcomes in Rotherham General Practices, the intervention group, and Barnsley practices — the control group. We have also worked with GPs in identifying younger people with dementia to create a register. This register has been developed from a Care Programme in the local Community Trust and is being used to ensure that these disadvantaged people and their carers receive the social, health, and other services they desperately need.

Clinical audit in primary health care is inextricably linked to education and research. Practitioners should set standards based on clinical knowledge, which is itself derived from good quality research. Undertaking clinical audit well demands many of the skills needed for undertaking research. In fact good quality clinical audits often are original research. For example, in Rotherham we have undertaken through the Clinical Audit Advisory Group a multi-practice audit of referrals for glue ear. This has embedded within those practices the most up-to-date knowledge for this condition plus an awareness of new knowledge as it is uncovered.

THE HOW

This chapter has to this point considered the 'what' that can be provided by Public Health, Health Promotion and the other parts of the skilled resources within Health Authorities which should be available to General Practice to ensure that primary care is 'fit' to meet the challenges and opportunities of a Primary Care-Led NHS. The 'how' requires a continuing change of organisational culture, systems and operation. This means moving away from the old style of generally centralist activities, whether undertaken by staff in Public Health, Strategic Planning, Information, Contracting, Finance, Quality Assurance, Personnel or Training. The management culture of new Authorities needs to be one that recognises its role as supporting and facilitating primary health care in its purchasing/providing. The organisation of an Authority needs to link resources into practices and operationally in-house skills need to be used to support General Practice explicitly and flexibly in a 'partnership contract' mode.

If we are now to successfully develop a Primary Care-Led NHS the skills of the organisation must be linked into individual or clusters of practices. They must support and develop practices under the umbrella of a locally-agreed Primary Care-Led NHS strategy and in the context of individual practice development plans. The focused development of General Practice as purchasers and providers and their role in partnership with new Health Authorities in health strategy are essential in the inexorable movement towards a Primary Care-Led NHS.

This new way must ensure meaningful health needs assessment at practice level with clinically and cost effective purchasing and providing. It is essential that Public Health support to practices, along with Health Promotion and Information and Information

Technology, is explicit in the management structure, culture and operation of the new Authorities after April 1996.

REFERENCES

1. Stevens A, Raftery J 1992 Health care needs assessment: Volumes 1 and 2. NHSE, London
2. Smith R(1991 Where is the wisdom. British Medical Journal 303: 798–799
3. Expert Advisory Group 1996 Methods to promote the implementation of research findings in the NHS — priorities for evaluation. Report to the Central Research and Development Committee. Department of Health, Leeds

9. Managing chronic diseases

Edmund Jessop

The first clause of the Act of Parliament which set up the National Health Service laid upon the Secretary of State a duty to 'secure improvement in the physical and mental health of the population'. How will a Primary Care-Led NHS help to secure improvement in the physical and mental health of people with chronic disease? What will it do for people who have diabetes, or paraplegia, or schizophrenia?

BENEFITS

Primary care is local care, and the key benefit to patients with chronic disease of a Primary Care-Led NHS is the development of services which are more local and more accessible. This is particularly important for patients with diseases which need lifelong treatment and hence lifelong follow-up; a number of models of good practice are available, including treatment clinics at surgeries and local health centres, and a variety of locally available in-patient facilities.

The most important single benefit may be avoiding the long trek to an inaccessible hospital for an appointment which achieves little. Ten years ago Marsh noted that 'of 260 follow up outpatient consultations analysed by GPs in the Northern Region, a large proportion appeared to be complete waste of time'.[1] Control over follow-up appointments will be an important feature of a Primary Care-led NHS, and the benefit is already seen in Surrey in a number of fundholder contracts which clearly specify 'for opinion only'. For chronic disease shared care schemes are a good way to reduce the need for frequent out-patient attendance; many such models have developed for the care of people with diabetes mellitus. Such schemes may involve primary care services other than those provided in general medical practice; in the Spelthorne part of Surrey a protocol is being developed to make use of optometrists in screening for diabetic eye disease.

Therapy services such as physiotherapy, dietetics and chiropody have historically been organised for the convenience of the hospital rather than the patient, and one of the clearest benefits of fund-holding has been the development of practice based therapy services. The development of health centres as 'polyclinics' has been mooted for some time; as therapy services develop this is becoming an almost unnoticed reality. Following a survey in West Surrey, some practices are making space for valuable non-medical services such as Citizens Advice Bureau counsellors; poverty, housing and health are inextricably linked so that ensuring full uptake of social security benefits and sorting out housing problems can be regarded, if not as a health service, then at least as a service to health This is particularly important for patients whose earning capacity is reduced by chronic disease.

It has proved less easy to incorporate personal social services into health centres. Locally some success has been achieved with Neighbourhood Resource Centres directed at particular client groups such as the elderly or those with mental health problems, but the medical element of primary care tends to be the missing element in such ventures. Consultant outreach clinics have also proved problematical. Although on the face of it offering the same advantages as practice based therapy services, consultants are more specialised than therapists, and often use during the out-patient attendance hospital facilities and equipment which are not transportable. Furthermore very few practices have enough patients with appropriate conditions to fill a consultant clinic session. Evaluations of schemes such as practice-based ophthalmology clinics show little evidence of two other potential benefits — reduction in out-patient attendances, and improvement in knowledge among practice staff.

Community hospitals come in many shapes and sizes, but flourish in market towns 15 miles or more from the nearest general hospital. They typically provide a range of outpatient clinics and community services, but also in-patient beds which allow local GPs to admit patients with acute illness. Such hospitals are universally loved by their local populations and disliked with equal fervour by Health Authority finance departments. A curious but understandable feature of such facilities, given their popularity with GPs and patients, is that they are never found in towns and cities large enough to justify a general hospital. Tomlinson's review of health services in London envisaged somewhat similar facilities providing a service to local communities. Giving GPs admitting rights to hospital beds is potentially of considerable benefit to patients with chronic disease which relapses and remits. Securing admission to a general hospital is often time-consuming for the GP and inconvenient for the patient; in principle at least, in a Primary Care-Led NHS, the ease of admission to a community hospital as a step-up from care at home should help the patient to recover quicker. For a variety of reasons, staff turnover in community hospitals tends to be low, and over the years staff get to know patients with chronic disease much better than is possible in the tempo of an acute general hospital. Wheelchair users are particularly scathing about the inhumanity of district general hospitals.

General practices in Yaxley, Lyme Regis and elsewhere have been instrumental in developing a number of 'Hospital at Home' schemes with the aim of avoiding the need for admission to an acute hospital. Although not specifically developed for people with chronic diseases, such schemes have much to offer people whose problems involve all too many hospital admissions. Many are directed at allowing early discharge after operations such as hip replacement. Others, such as the scheme in the Waverley district in Surrey, aim to avert hospital admission; these schemes are particularly useful in avoiding the need for hospital admission when patients with diseases such as chronic bronchitis develop acute flare-ups. A formal evaluation of the Peterborough scheme commented that much of the work in that scheme was the care of people with terminal illness.

PITFALLS

There are two main pitfalls for a Primary Care-Led NHS: lack of coherent strategy; and lowering of technical quality.

The NHS has never been particularly good at strategic planning, but it is clear that devolution of budgets for regional specialties to district, let alone fundholder, level has threatened some specialised services. Where the service has a well defined, well organised constituency, such as people with haemophilia, pressure from patients' organisations has resulted in damage limitation by central guidance from the NHS Executive. Other services, less robust, more uncertain of their role, have fared worse. Regional units for adolescent psychiatry have found it particularly difficult to argue the case for stable funding, and although none have ceased to exist, financial uncertainty has blighted attempts to upgrade facilities and recruit staff. As leadership in the NHS is dispersed to thousands of primary care practices, developing coherent plans for even quite straightforward services such as vascular surgery is becoming increasingly difficult. Even greater difficulties lie ahead in joint planning with social service and other local authority departments because of the conflict between organisations which are geographically defined and general practices which are not. The development of multi-funds may in time overcome some of these problems, but such developments take time and a tricky interregnum is likely.

The rapid spread of counselling in primary care illustrates both the strength and the potential weaknesses of a primary care led NHS. On the one hand it has been known for many years that mild anxiety and depression accounted for a high proportion of GP consultations, but there had been no mechanism to respond to this knowledge. Fundholders were very quick to respond to this need once given the administrative and financial machinery for doing so, and this responsiveness to need is laudable. On the other hand there have been considerable doubts about both the quality of counselling and its cost effectiveness. Hospitals — with certain spectacular exceptions — require their professional staff to have recognised qualifications, but most of the counsellors employed in primary care do not have such qualifications. This is understandable given the lack of training courses, but does highlight a potential weakness. On the question of cost-effectiveness, there is very little scientific evidence that non-specific counselling does any good, yet the NHS, or at least its Medical Directorate, are pressing Health Authority purchasers to base spending decisions on evidence of clinical effectiveness. This leads to a view that a Primary Care-Led NHS may be less rigorous scientifically, and hence waste more money on ineffective therapies. The obvious counter-argument to this point of view is that so few decisions now are based on scientific evidence that things could hardly get worse, but the introduction and evaluation of new therapies will almost certainly need to be based in secondary (or tertiary) care centres.

The introduction of beta-interferon therapy for multiple sclerosis in 1996 provides a case study for this. The treatment is new and very expensive; benefits will not be dramatic and eligibility criteria are quite technical; most GPs will have only one or two patients who might be eligible. The argument for neurologists to control prescribing and evaluate the results is overwhelming. There is a clear threat of clinical leadership remaining in the hospitals, with only managerial and budgetary leadership passing to primary care.

Allied to this move of leadership has been the move of clinical work from the secondary care to primary care. The initial impetus for this was largely financial — an assumption that primary care must be cheaper. Some aspects of the shift — in particular the development of minor surgery in primary care — have also raised concerns about quality. Simple suturing is within the competence of almost any doctor (though the quality of sterile supplies in many surgeries has been woefully inadequate until recently), but more ambitious developments such as endoscopy and vasectomy may be unwise.

Another pitfall for the Primary Care-Led NHS is that it may stand in the way of an even better notion — a Patient-Led NHS. Patients with chronic disease often prefer to be seen by secondary care specialists, and it is important to realise that this applies not only to the consultants, but also to their support staff — specialist nurses and therapists. Patients' accounts of their illness all too often include the phrase 'my GP seemed to know little or nothing about my disease'. Even for common diseases such as asthma, practice staff may not appreciate technicalities such as the range of inhaler devices available, their pros and cons and so on. This lack of detailed knowledge is hardly surprising and not blameworthy, but the implication of such reports is that a Primary Care-Led NHS still needs its specialists. Although the division of labour between general practitioner and consultant has largely been settled, and in some cases made explicit through shared care protocols, considerable thought is still needed to work out how specialist nurses and other therapists can best be used, whether directly — treating and advising patients — or indirectly, passing on their skills to practice nurses. As a Primary Care-Led NHS develops, it will be important to ensure that patients continue to benefit from specialists with wide experience and up-to-date knowledge of specific diseases.

One of the interesting features of the current drive to a Primary Care-Led NHS is the unspoken assumption that primary care-led means GP-led. This is of course understandable; GPs own and run their practices, and it is also the doctors who control the fundholding budgets. Thus as the power of medical staff in the hospitals dwindles, the medical profession is establishing its dominance elsewhere. This is in marked contrast to the unsubstituted loss of power by nurses and therapists, who have few established posts in purchasing organisations. What this means for patients with chronic disease is not clear, but it is often nurses and therapists who are most aware of the day-to-day problems of people with chronic disability.

ROLE OF THE DIRECTOR OF PUBLIC HEALTH

The basic function of Public Health Directorates in the new 1996 Authorities is to analyse the health of a resident population, and then do whatever is possible to improve the population's health: analysis followed by action, typically in the form of a health strategy or policy. Monitoring the health of the population will become particularly important as leadership in the NHS becomes dispersed to primary care, but the task of developing local consensus on health policy will also be crucial.

Analysis of health starts with compilation of routinely available data, such as mortality and hospital admission rates. Both of these sources of information have limitations, which are unfortunately particularly marked for chronic disease. Death certificates under-state the burden of disease from conditions such as arthritis which disable but rarely kill; while for conditions such as Parkinson's disease or dementia the doctor who certifies death may have genuine difficulty in deciding whether the cause of death was the chronic condition or an acute event such as pneumonia. These difficulties are well known and can be mitigated by techniques such as multiple cause coding, but they undoubtedly complicate the task of monitoring the health of the population.

Similar difficulties afflict hospital admission data, which are better suited to the analysis of acute episodes of care such as surgical procedures. Looking at data on in-patient admission provides only a partial view of health services for patients with severe mental illness, for example, who may live in staff hostels and group homes, attend day hospitals and work placements and be looked after by community teams.

Despite these difficulties, population based analyses will remain important and give clues to the standard of local health services. For some diseases, such as diabetes mellitus, the population mortality rate, crude though it is, may indicate problems with the local service. Audits of stroke deaths have been used to assess, at population level, the control of hypertension. Hospital data on operations such as hip and lens replacements and coronary artery bypass grafts all give, albeit indirect, information on how people with chronic diseases such as osteoarthritis, cataracts and ischaemic heart disease are accessing specialist care. At present we usually look at district rates for such procedures, with occasional attempts to analyse by local authority or electoral ward; we must now develop routine analyses, and the statistical machinery for interpreting them, by GP practice.

There is of course a considerable amount of data held by GPs, and much is made of the value of this data. The reality is that at present the data held by GPs cannot be accessed for monitoring the health of populations. Some of the difficulties are technical — incompatible computer systems so that any merging of data from different practices to build up a picture of a locality has to be done by hand; lack of Read codes for basic items such as previous smoking habit. Other difficulties are human — lack of agreement about the definition of hypertension, for example. Even an apparently simple task like counting the number of people who are disabled as a result of a stroke is almost impossible to do accurately from GP records. There are some exceptions, and in particularly a number of research projects give hope for the future. The early years of death certification were characterised by bitter controversy, and the same is likely to be true of primary care data. No data source is perfect, and all need experience and good judgement to be used well.

Analysis should lead to action, and for public health physicians this often means developing and implementing policies and strategies. Although the power of Health Authorities will wane as leadership in primary care waxes, the role of public health departments in influencing policy may not change much. Consider for example development of a strategy for back pain services. At present this starts with a review of the research literature and national guidance. Some visits to well organised services of high repute may be worthwhile, and discussion with local consultants and GPs about current services and areas needing improvement will be necessary. Proposals for development of services can then be drafted and discussed. Any proposal which is to be implemented successfully must command the support of GPs. There are usually doubters to persuade and ruffled feathers to smooth. All of this activity will still be necessary in a Primary Care-Led NHS and Public Health consultants will continue to have the time and experience to do it well.

The next step — translating the proposals into funding for a service through a purchasing contract — may well be different in an NHS with extensive fundholding and total fundholding.

It is this loss of direct control, together with the prospect of another wave of district mergers, which is causing understandable alarm in Health Authorities. The loss of direct control will affect contracting and commissioning staff more than public health staff. Public Health physicians to some extent already have experience in implementing health policy through advocacy and persuasion rather than direct control, for example in immunisation and screening programmes. Re-establishing the pertussis immunisation programme, and introducing the *Haemophilus influenza* programme in areas where immunisation was carried out almost entirely by GPs depended on professional dialogue and persuasion, not managerial control. Admittedly the task was simpler than developing a local chronic disease service because it hinged almost entirely on technical issues such as true contraindications to the vaccine, but the parallel is instructive.

CONCLUSION

A Primary Care-Led NHS has much to offer patients with chronic disease, in particular the convenience of local services. The main pitfall to avoid is the loss of access to specialised knowledge and specialised facilities. For Public Health physicians, the basic task of monitoring the health of populations and working with local professionals remains.

REFERENCE

1. Marsh GN 1982 Are follow-up consultations at medical outpatient departments futile? British Medical Journal 284: 1176–1177

10. Facilitating health promotion

Joanna Parker

INTRODUCTION

In 1892 Florence Nightingale said,

'I look forward to the day when there will be no nurses of the sick, only nurses of the well.'

Over the century since these words were spoken nurses have recognised the importance of teaching their patients about health as well as illness. The concept of positive health has developed considerably, even if nurses have not yet reached the point described by Nightingale! Indeed the need for all health professionals to promote health is recognised; particularly those working in primary health care.

HEALTH PROMOTION

There is often a lot of confusion about what health promotion is. Canada has been using the term since the Lalonde Report of 1974, which has been acclaimed internationally as a turning point in thinking about health policy and as a landmark in the emergence of a 'new Public Health movement'. The essential feature of the 'new' Public Health is an approach which brings together environmental change, personal preventive measures and appropriate therapeutic interventions. This Public Health approach reflects an acceptance of a broad view of the determinants of health, encompassing socio-economic and environmental, as well as biological factors. Many initiatives followed the Lalonde Report starting with the WHO Alma Ata Declaration of 1978 which committed all member countries to the principles of Health for All by the Year 2000.

In 1984, the WHO encapsulated the 'new' Public Health by

summarising health promotion as the process which enables people to take more control over their health. This process combines both a lifestyle approach, focusing on individual behaviour change, and a structural approach in considering their social and economic circumstances.

In England the White Paper 'Promoting Better Health' published in 1987 identified the importance of primary health care in health promotion work. It pointed to:

' ... the next big challenge for the NHS and one especially for primary care, is to shift the emphasis from an illness service to a health service offering help to prevent disease and disability.'

The document placed greater emphasis on health promotion and disease prevention whilst offering patients a wider choice of services and information. Family doctors and the 'primary health care team', it suggested, could contribute to promoting good health by giving advice on life-style and by screening for early signs of disease.

In 1992 the White Paper 'The Health of The Nation' placed the issue of prevention firmly on the political agenda with the 1990 GP contract enshrining health promotion in the duties of every General Practitioner.

The 1990 contract included the introduction of payments for and/or contractual obligations to provide 'health checks' for new patients, three-yearly 'health checks' for registered patients, annual assessments for those aged over 75, payments for achieving 'target' immunisation and cervical screening rates, child health surveillance and health promotion clinics including well-person, diabetes, heart disease, anti-smoking, alcohol control, diet and stress management. These terms were considerably revised in 1993 and the new health promotion structure in General Practice combines opportunistic work with a banding system for the reimbursement of health promotion work, while continuing to stress the importance of a multi-disciplinary delivery of services. In place of the open-ended commitment to health promotion clinics the new banding is linked to HoN objectives to reduce smoking, coronary heart disease and strokes. The key significance of Health of the Nation is that for the first time there is a coherent strategy for securing real improvements in health. There are national targets set in five key areas: Coronary Heart Disease and Stroke; Cancers; Mental Illness; HIV/AIDS and Sexual Health; and Accidents, which can be seen as a way of ensuring that priorities are set and meaningful action is undertaken.

PRIMARY HEALTH CARE: THE CHANGING ENVIRONMENT

Primary health care and a Primary Care-Led NHS mean more than just community services provided by NHS Trusts or family health services provided by General Practitioners, dentists, opticians and pharmacists; although GP fundholding can be understood as a key method of achieving a Primary Care-Led NHS. Primary health care describes a particular approach to health care which is based on the key principles set out in the WHO Alma Ata Declaration:

- Accessibility: health care which is provided as close as possible to where people live and work;
- Acceptability: health care which is appropriate and provided in ways which people find acceptable;
- Equity: all people have an equal right to health and health care;
- Self-determination: people have the right and responsibility to make their own health choices;
- Community involvement: people have the right and responsibility to participate individually and collectively in the planning and implementation of health care;
- Focus on health: primary health care concentrates on health promotion as well as the care of people who are sick, frail or disabled;
- Multi-sectoral approach: housing, food policies, environmental policies and social services have a part to play. In this context a Primary Care-Led NHS can be viewed in 1996 as the shifting of decision making into primary care within a new Health Authority's framework of public health priorities, ensuring the patient, their family and community are the focus.

Primary health care in the 1990s and beyond faces a rapidly changing environment. For example, there is now a revolution in health care technology with non-intrusive surgical techniques; shorter hospital stays and a shift from institutional care; changes in the pattern of disease and ill-health; an ageing population and changes in public expectations; with new forms of organisation emerging with an emphasis on sub-contracting, decentralisation of control and a demand for a more flexible and multi-skilled workforce.

Accordingly, nurses working in primary and community health care are practising their skills in a changing world of competitive market forces. To date little focused work has been undertaken on the variety of models and settings in which these skills might be best practised although 'total fundholding' projects, 'multi-fund' models and 'primary care resource centres' are now being evaluated. Such reviews now become essential prerequisites for new Health Authorities in their support and monitoring functions. There is no shortage of source material for them to call on.

KEY DOCUMENTS

There is a range of qualified nursing staff working in community and primary health care settings bringing a rich diversity of skills, knowledge and expertise which are flexible and expandable. '*A Vision for the Future*'[1] sets out the contribution that the nursing professions can make to the health of the population and the quality of health care provided by the NHS. In the context of key policies such as Health of the Nation this strategic framework identifies five broad objectives for the nursing professions to address: quality outcomes and audit; accountability for practice; clinical and professional leadership; commissioning and purchasing; and educational and personal development.

'*New World, New Opportunities*'[2] sets out the agenda for nursing in the community and primary health care. The report states that the best way to meet health needs of individuals and communities is to focus primary health care services as far as possible on the practice population. This facilitates teamwork, improves communication between professionals and allows a full picture of local needs to be developed.

'*Making It Happen*'[3] the report of the Standing Nursing and Midwifery Advisory Committee (SNMAC) on the contribution of nurses, midwives and health visitors to Public Health, sees nurses, midwives and health visitors as key workers in improving health. They have a major part to play in Public Health for the following reasons:

- The scale of their contacts with the population provides unparalleled opportunities for promoting health;
- They meet a wide cross-section of society;
- They work in a variety of settings: homes, schools, workplaces;
- They have privileged access to information about personal health which can inform the assessment of population health needs;
- They can communicate health information to a very large number of people;

- They are valued by society;
- They are part of a diverse range of professional and voluntary networks.

The report also points to the range of flexible skills nurses can bring to the commissioning process. These include skills in articulating health problems, sustaining alliances and evaluating services. *'Ensuring the Effective Involvement of Professionals in Health Authority Work'*[4] also sets out the benefits of involving professionals in the context of a Primary Care-Led NHS and identifies areas where nurses are essential to ensuring good standards.

In 1994 in support of the *Health of the Nation*, the DoH published *'Targeting Practice: The Contribution of Nurses, Midwives and Health Visitors'*.[5] This document highlights the range of activities being undertaken by nursing, midwifery and health visiting professionals in helping to achieve the *Health of the Nation's* stated objectives and targets by contributing to changes in behaviour of individuals, changes in practice and the delivery of care and changes in the environment.

The activities described are intended to provide examples of 'good practice' and act as a practical guide for implementation, as a 'teaching tool' and as a source of ideas on the range, extent, scope and settings in which interventions take place.

FHSAs AND NURSE FACILITATORS

The NHS and Community Care Act 1990 metamorphosed Family Practitioner Committees into Family Health Service Authorities with new roles and new responsibilities. These are now being placed at the heart of the new 1996 Authorities which need to plan and manage broad integrated primary health care programmes which ensure community involvement in identifying health issues, problems and needs, and ensure that the information needs of patients are met. Developing the concept of primary health care teams across and at every level of these programmes is an essential part of their role.

To achieve effective team development some FHSAs appointed facilitators with a wide range of tasks. The concept of a Nurse Facilitator derives from the work, in the 1980s, of the Oxford Heart Attack and Stroke Project, which pioneered a technique in helping GPs to screen their patients for risk factors in coronary heart disease. The method has been copied elsewhere and facilitators now have many functions depending upon their skills and remit. There is a National Facilitator Development Project and an Association of Practice Facilitators, which view their role as catalysts of change with health promotion, training, team building and developing collaborative work as their major activities. Now facilitators perform a key role in helping general practice exploit information available from practice registers and they have played, and continue to play, a leadership role in developing health promotion.

NURSES IN THE PRIMARY HEALTH CARE TEAM

General practice is the foundation of the system of health care in Britain. It deals with nine-tenths of health care episodes, at least 98% of the population are registered with a GP, and, on average, consult a doctor four times a year. Primary health care teams therefore have unique access to the population.

The need for teamwork has, in the past, been emphasised in various policy documents and publications. The definition of the PHCT has been problematic, not least in the sense of 'teamwork', as primary care is not an homogenous entity, it is an interconnected network of different professionals. The 'team' could be described as a core of people such as the General Practitioners, directly employed and attached nursing staff and practice management and administrative staff who make different contributions towards common goals. It is suggested that PHCTs are becoming more comprehensive, to include counsellors and therapists, but often in reality the term 'team' still describes a situation in which individuals and professions work in isolation with infrequent communication and no real collaboration.

Practice nurses are employed directly by the GP and nine out of ten practices now employ one or more practice nurses. Surveys of the work of practice nurses have shown that they perform a wide range of technical procedures with an expanding role into the preventive area. In reality there is often difficulty in identifying the role of the practice nurse, given the variation of work undertaken by them. Practice nurses may be considered the focal point for screening, health education and health promotion by the General Practitioner as they are often the first point of contact between the practice and the patient; however it cannot be assumed that the health promotion knowledge base that practice nurses have is adequate. There is a broad consensus that practice nursing currently lacks a defined knowledge base and adequate education and training.

The nurse practitioner (a vague term not yet officially recognised by the United Kingdom Central Council for Nursing, Midwifery and Health Visiting), is often seen to increase the availability of primary health care. Originating from the United States the role of nurse practitioner was first introduced to the UK by Barbara Stilwell in the 1980s. The role of nurse practitioner has been hailed as that of the new innovative nurse able to extend the boundaries of nursing. In defining the role Stilwell highlights the autonomous nature of the nurses practice as crucial. She argues that autonomous practice enables the nurse to function in an environment which facilitates self-referral by patients and the development of long term strategies for health. The result of a recent evaluation of 20 pilot nurse practitioner projects concluded that only the nurse practitioners in single handed GP surgeries resulted in measurable cost savings. However, and perhaps more importantly, the study also found considerable evidence that nurse practitioners could provide a safe, effective and complementary service to GPS, and one valued, and in many instances preferred, by users.

With the publication of the document 'The Scope of Professional Practice' by the UKCC in 1992, one of the documents which provides a regulatory framework in which professional boundaries and professional practice are developed, the potential for nurses to expand their role was given a new impetus. The document allows nurses to encompass new activities within their role, based on their own determination of the pre-requisite level of competence.

Many of the elements relating to the nurse practitioner can be identified within other nursing disciplines such as health visiting and district nursing. Health visiting is essentially a health promotion role. It has a unique history in the UK evolving in a particular way, often to meet the needs of society unmet at the time by medical services, especially general practice. Health visiting, however, has increasingly moved away from its origins to a more medical, individualistic model of community child health care. 'Making It Happen' states that health visiting is 100% public health and explores how the focus on health promotion in health visitors work with families with children could be extended across much of primary health care to the benefit of other groups in the community.

The report provides illustrations of the various roles and kinds of work undertaken by health visitors in specialist public health posts. It describes the public health nurse working with the PHCT to coordinate profiling, needs assessment and health promotion activities, the model of a post devoted to community liaison and development work across practice populations within a team of GP attached health visitors and the homeless families health visitor providing a 'safety net' service for families and individuals outside the GP practice register. Other studies also demonstrate the health visitors ability to work with groups. There are examples that demonstrate the potential of groupwork to secure improved access to the pre-requisites for health in respect of disadvantaged sections of society; to instigate a community campaign for a family centre and the involvement of members of the community in its planning; and to enable homeless families to identify unmet needs, to establish a secure and stimulating environment for their children and to play a part in developing support networks.

Other disciplines of community nursing are also developing their contribution to public health. District nurses are undertaking clinical audit to enable them to assess the effectiveness of nursing and therapeutic interventions in relation to their practice population needs. For example, in the treatment of leg ulcers, and the use of pressure relieving equipment and continence aids. School nurses are engaged in screening, surveillance and profiling of school populations with the potential to engage in reducing the risk taking behaviour with adolescents. Midwives are working with mothers-to-be in areas such as pre-conception health, nutrition and diet, smoking, breast feeding, sexual health, child safety and accidents.

There are examples of specialist nurses working in the community such as community psychiatric nurses who have been recruited to provide a service to the local police to assess people who have been arrested and who may be suffering from a mental disorder. Nurses working with people with a learning disability are stimulating client participation in strategic and operational decisions about services and facilitating access to primary health care services by developing health screening protocols to detect and manage a range of conditions which have been under-diagnosed within this client group.

TAKING THE NURSING CONTRIBUTION FORWARD

If the words of Nightingale are to be realised then clearly the emergence of the 'new' public health movement and a Primary Care-Led NHS present considerable opportunities for nurses to make a wider contribution. In order to do so nurses should be able to define the criteria by which they label their health promotion activities 'good practice'. The *'Targeting Practice'* document describes criteria which managers can take as indicators of 'good practice' in this area:

- Nurses should play a key role with clear responsibilities and authority;
- Practice is based on the best research evidence available;
- Practice has clear objectives, targets and standards;
- Practice is clearly defined and well implemented;
- Practice is delivered in an environment conducive to the achievement of objectives;
- Practice demonstrates appropriate alliances; and
- There is evidence of cost benefit/option appraisal and formal evaluation.

There are many possibilities for facilitating health promotion in primary care; however, to ensure that 'good practice' in health promotion is a reality then a number of issues need to be addressed. These are not only issues for health promotion but the delivery of all care in general practice.

Traditionally nursing has been examined from the perspective of individual groups which can lead to 'professional tribalism'; nurses now need to embrace their role as part of a multi-disciplinary team. The different disciplines come together within the PHCT but this is often led by a GP, or under contract to or directly employed by a general practice. The power in the decision making process lies with the medical establishment, GPs need to relinquish this power monopoly and allow nurses to practice to their full potential where they can demonstrate improved outcomes and health gain. In developing PHCTs which are skill-mixed with GPs, a shift of power is inevitable, with the possibility of nurse partners in General Practice. The focus must shift from the individual practitioner to the practice. The development of practice-based primary care contracts from new Health Authorities can encourage new forms of partnership and lead to practice based decision making. This issue of skill-mix and integration of community nursing needs careful management. Skill-mix based on a practice profile is essential to ensure that nurses adapt their practice to meet local need as well as national policy imperatives. What is not being advocated necessarily is new roles for nurses, but new combinations of expertise, tailored to meet specific local needs. To enable this to happen education, training and personal development needs to be addressed as a matter of urgency. Nurses, together with their colleagues need to explore ways of meeting their learning needs in a collaborative way.

Nurses also need to be involved in the commissioning, purchasing and contracting process. The 'top down' approach to health needs assessment by DHA Directors of Public Health was limited as census and epidemiological statistics are inevitably dated and broad brush. Health needs assessment is a part of everyday work for health visitors. The individual, family, practice and community health profiles kept by health visitors constitute a comprehensive database of people's experience of health care and health needs. This information is vital as the changes in health, social and environmental circumstances are kept up to date. This database should now be exploited by purchasers.

Nurses, midwives and health visitors are the largest professional group employed in the NHS and just as their contribution to health promotion cannot be ignored, the changes in primary health care should not be ignored by nurses. As the SNMAC report states involving the nursing professions in Public Health represents a 'window of opportunity' for improving the health and well-being of local communities.[3]

REFERENCES

1. National Health Service Executive 1993 A vision for the future. HMSO, London
2. Department of Health 1993 New world, new opportunities. Nursing in primary health care. HMSO, London
3. Department of Health The Standing Nursing and Midwifery Advisory Committee 1995 Making it happen. Public health — the contribution, role and development of nurses, midwives and health visitors. HMSO, London
4. National Health Service Executive (1995). Ensuring the Effective Involvement of
   Professionals in Health Authority Work. HSG (95) 11
5. Department of Health 1995 Targeting practice. The contribution of nurses, midwives and health visitors. HMSO, London

FOOTNOTE

The author is happy to respond to enquiries for further details of the personal and documentary background to this chapter: telephone 0121 456 1444. For this reason references have been kept to a minimum.

11. Integrating health and social care

Mike Warner and Ed Macalister-Smith

SETTING THE SCENE

Naturally enough, this chapter will describe enthusiastically the early outcomes and the benefits to patients of close working relationships between health and social services. What it will also stress is that in a Primary Care-Led NHS there is particular value in making this happen at the level of the individual General Practice.

SOME COMMON OBJECTIONS: SIX OFTEN-QUOTED ARGUMENTS AGAINST INTEGRATION

Before embarking on the up-side of integrated relationships, it is as well to be clear about the problems of closer working. We have learnt from our experience in Wiltshire that if these problems are not acknowledged and managed appropriately, the attempt to establish closer working relationships can easily go profoundly wrong with a return to the worst kind of 'them and us' relations, and a strong tendency to 'pass the buck'.

Here are six common examples of arguments against integration that we have encountered.

'We don't understand each other'

Organisational culture or 'the way we do things around here' is very different, comparing health services in general, and General Practice in particular, with social services departments. The independent contractor and small business status of General Practice leads to a very particular style and pace of work. The role of the GP as a gate-keeper to other services, and the open-ended nature of the GP's commitment to provide services to a list of around 2000 patients is also quite different from access to services being managed through eligibility criteria, and linked to means testing and charging.

'We don't respect each other'

Of course many GPs and social workers do understand each other's roles and responsibilities very well. But some GPs may think that no social worker can make a decision without holding a meeting and being given several days warning; while equally some social workers may think that GPs are primarily motivated by money, and that they make rapid decisions on behalf of patients without fully involving them, and without taking account of the full circumstances of an individual patient. In a team situation, such differences can hinder integration and can also raise the difficulty of who leads, and whose view of the patient/client has supremacy.

'We can't use our money for your work'

There is a view that, despite Section 64, Section 23 and Section 28a funding arrangements, HCHS and GMS funds are so tightly defined that no significant amounts can be made available for jointly commissioning services. Likewise, it may be felt that social services funds cannot be applied to health issues.

'We like diversity, you like uniformity'

It's those General Practitioners as independent contractors again! They have different sized practices, some with large and others with small lists of patients, and they all seem to work in different ways and to have different interests. How can a Social Services Committee, trying to provide uniform services to its electorate, match locally with organisations which are so diverse?

'We can't charge for services, but you do'

If boundaries between health and social care become less distinct, then any clarity which exists in the public's mind about the difference between health care and social services will be eroded. The public may fail to understand why they are being charged for some services and not for others.

'We only have enough money to pay for our core business'

Some health care and social services agencies, whenever there is a crisis or a lack of funds, redefine the boundaries of the work they perform, and let the other organisation take the blame for any problems which result.

In summary

There are plenty of very real concerns which can explain why a programme aimed at bringing health care and social services closer together may stumble or fail. Not all of these problems need to be tackled head on, but they do need to be recognised. There is a particular need for frontline professionals in health care and social services to acknowledge and understand each other's skills and roles. In particular, they must be willing to let go of some of the traditionally established patterns of power by sharing with colleagues.

SO, WHY INTEGRATE?

The work undertaken in Wiltshire over the last few years has been motivated by a clear vision of how integrated services could be effective for patients, but it has also been responsive to national trends in the development of public services in general. We can now list five practical reasons for integration.

Integration creates user-centred seamless services

When any of us is in need we want care and support — not rigid 'health services' or 'social services' dreamed up by the bureaucracy. Research shows that users want information at the surgery about *all* services. The surgery is not stigmatising, and is accessible to almost everyone.

Integration will create the 'one-stop-shop' for care services

Very often, the first point of contact that a user has with adult social services follows a referral from the primary health care team. In addition, infrastructure costs of providing both health and social care services in many locations are quite considerable.

For these reasons, Wiltshire FHSA and the Wiltshire Social Services Department were keen to exploit the potential benefits of working together. The idea of the 'one-stop-shop' built upon existing good practice in many parts of the county where primary health care and social care teams already worked closely together. We recognised, however, that some groups of users prefer to have their own networks and contacts with social care separate from primary care, so user choice requires other contact points for social services as well as in General Practice settings.

Devolution of resources is happening anyway

Both the devolution of purchasing resources and the development of the internal market are strong forces in health care and social services respectively. Increasing numbers of General Practices are taking on fundholding, and care management budgets are being devolved to a more local level within social services. Thus, the total care purchasing resources for a town or locality are made available locally, and integration is ready to happen under our very noses.

Integrated teams make sensible decisions about care priorities

We expect integrated teams to make sensible decisions about local care priorities, and about using local resources. Our experience suggests that practitioners working together in local teams do not attempt to pass the buck from one agency to another, but work within the constraints of combined budgets.

What is more, integrated teams begin to concentrate on preventive actions, which is real progress.

The 'grey areas' between agencies give scope for creative care service development

If organisations stick very rigidly to the definitions of the terms and conditions under which they are expected to work, it becomes difficult for them to explore new ways of delivering services. This in turn can become an excuse for inaction and defensiveness. Most important however, it can prevent service organisations from viewing problems through the eyes of clients or patients, and make it difficult to provide patterns of care which are tuned to the needs of individual people. Developing and maintaining 'grey areas' of work, near the boundaries of the organisations' responsibilities, gives scope for looking at services in entirely new ways.

STEP BY STEP!

Each new Health Authority and Social Services Department will have their own favoured route towards increased joint working within primary care. The following provides a form of checklist of the main steps needed — but the key must surely be leadership.

Vision

The potential benefits for users of services arising from joint working have been mentioned in the last section. In Wiltshire we wax lyrical about empowering care managers, GPs, indeed the full primary care team, as controllers of resources of an unstigmatised and accessible service.

A vision to which senior managers must be signed up, agreed by Boards or elected Members, provides powerful authority for subsequent action.

Top manager commitment and leadership

Only top managers can swing organisations into action behind such a strategic thrust. Unless the HA Chief Executive and the Director of Social Services really want to move forward together and want to recognise the potential of primary care settings and build mutual confidence, then little more than tinkering will result.

Almost all efforts at integration within primary care will be breaking new ground so the usual tests to apply are to judge what each organisation is investing in collaboration by way of top management effort, prestige and resource. In Wiltshire we make a point of appearing together as top managers at seminars and training days, for example, to explain our vision and to demonstrate our commitment to it — visibility is important.

Helping middle management

Operational managers in social services may need convincing that working closely with primary care teams can deliver better services whilst NHS Community Trusts may feel threatened by stronger primary care teamwork. Top managers need to explain clearly how integration is mainstream work, and to celebrate success.

Who heads the team?

A tricky issue on which successful integration may depend — natural fears about GP dominance, the medical model, loss of accountability to elected members for resource use — these all bubble to the surface. The answer seems to lie in real team maturity when leadership is acknowledged to reside in the appropriate professional contribution.

In Wiltshire, experience of joint commissioning by the primary care team suggests confidence does come with familiarity — but it is still fragile.

Employ managers from 'the other side'

New Health Authorities need staff with experience in social services and vice versa. They are vital as intermediaries with responsibilities for smoothing out confidence sapping obstructions to progress.

Money

Sharing recurring resources demonstrates good faith and invites reciprocation — resorting only to Joint Finance is treading old ground and not moulding how base budgets are allocated. The next section demonstrates how linkworking in Wiltshire has meant reshaping care management towards a practice-based management of resources.

LINKWORKING — WHAT WE LEARNED FROM THE FIRST MAJOR PROJECT

Linkworking was the project that made these general principles real for frontline staff. Nine building blocks in the project were important.

Starting with a project that enjoyed mutual support

The Linkworker Scheme provides practice-based, one-stop-shop access to social services, but linkworkers also act as facilitators and catalysts for change within the primary care teams where they are based.

The scheme started as a pilot project, intending to recruit around ten practices throughout the county (out of a total of 89), which would be prepared to accommodate a 'linkworker'. Because of the facilitating aspect of the work, and the focus of the scheme on adult clients, linkworkers in the pilot scheme came from several professional disciplines including social work, district nursing, health visiting, occupational therapy, plus the voluntary sector.

Committed middle managers

In addition to the support of general management and members, linkworking had the strong support of middle managers in both the FHSA and social services. This is the group that was needed to work through problems on a day-to-day basis. Their positive approach aimed at finding solutions enabled linkworking to become established quickly.

Skilled facilitation on the ground

Another important factor, indeed vital for the implementation of the project, was the availability of a skilled facilitator who understood primary care, and was trusted by primary care teams, but who also had close familiarity with social services. The amount of facilitation time required at each practice site was quite considerable. The approach was to set up a local steering group of key players.

Pump-priming and recurring funds

The pilot phase of the project needed funding. Finance was needed to cover the replacement costs of seconded staff who became linkworkers, and to cover set-up costs in the ten practice sites. Set-up costs include desks and filing cabinets, additional computer terminals linked to the practice system, and a separate telephone line. Telephone bills are paid by the project, rather than by existing teams. Additional clerical support is provided, often in the form of a few additional hours from existing part-time practice staff. Premises are generally provided free by the practice.

External academic evaluation[1]

Additional funds were needed to commission an external evaluation of the scheme. All parties were committed to this. A university evaluation made sure that we were not seeing the scheme through rose-tinted spectacles, and that we were being challenged to obtain the maximum possible benefits from it. The style of the evaluation was also important, being participatory with continual contributions during the evolution of the project. This 'ongoing' approach to evaluation was deliberately chosen instead of a more remote assessment limited to the end of the pilot phase.

Training resources

The linkworking pilot project was very much about changing cultures and learning new ways of working, as well as bringing different frontline professionals into contact with each other. Training resources were required, but in reality the sums involved were modest because an essential role for the linkworkers was that they should be able to act themselves as catalysts and facilitators within their own settings.

Testing of consumer opinion

Naturally we needed to know whether the project worked from the point of view of the patients.

A public opinion survey was carried out as part of a general programme of assessing the views of the public about health services. The public response strongly supported the move towards integrating services.

Dissemination of the project outcomes

Linkworking always benefited from its popularity with General Practitioners who created a demand to have linkworkers in their own practices. The project now covers over 50% of GPs in the county. However, since management of the project has now moved to mainstream adult care teams there has had to be a careful and considered promotion of the scheme to operational managers.

Commitment over time

There were several moments when the linkworking project might have faltered. These included the transition from pilot phase into mainstream business with the realisation that linkworking will only become genuinely mainstream when it replaces existing forms of care management, rather than being seen as an additional resource. In addition, the original development staff have changed and every time senior managers or members change, the new staff need to be brought up to date with the project and must develop their own commitment to it. So far, this process has been consistently successful.

WHAT OTHER JOINT PROJECTS SUPPORT INTEGRATION?

The Linkworking Scheme described above was a pioneering example of integration between health care and social services, and paved the way for further commitment to additional joint work. A range of projects has since developed. At the last count, our Joint Initiatives Group had produced a directory of 27 projects which had either concluded, were in their pilot phase, or had become mainstream.[2] Some of these are translatable to other areas. These are described below.

Joint policy development

It is now exceptional that policy development does not take place in an integrated way. We also have outposted and seconded staff working in each others buildings.

Practice-based joint commissioning of services for the elderly

Practice-based projects in Trowbridge and Malmesbury are being supported by the King's Fund. The projects have three elements, starting with a population needs assessment. Facilitators support joint working arrangements between local health, social services and voluntary organisation teams with input from users and carers. Joint service development will be an outcome. A handbook has been produced as a result of these pilot projects to extend the lessons to other parts of Wiltshire.

Extended home care for the elderly — Bradford on Avon

This scheme aims to give patients and GPs the choice of admission either to the local community hospital, or to the extended care scheme. In the scheme, the coordinator mobilises whatever resources are needed for patients to be cared for in their own home including respite care, terminal care, post-operative care, and assessment.

Assessment and care management — the over-75 annual health check

In compliance with the 1990 GP contract, General Practices have been offering annual health checks to patients aged over 75. Wiltshire FHSA put in considerable effort to get this programme established, and numerous enthusiastic practices around the county now undertake this work. It has always been our view locally that there is more value in the over-75 checks than simply the direct doctor or nurse contact with the patient. The assessment cards which are filed with patients' notes have been designed in such a way that they link directly to social services assessment processes. Thus information gained in over-75 checks can be made available through practice-based linkworkers or other contacts to social services when undertaking social care assessments.

Mental health; children

Building on practice-based work with the elderly, similar pilot projects are being conducted in mental health and in children's work.

Mental health work is based around a facilitator, who can help practices to develop mental health services at primary care team level, and to build relationships with specialist mental health services. There will also be a focus on practice-based joint commissioning of mental health services, with a particular focus on ensuring that the national Care Programme Approach is implemented effectively.

As part of preparation for a joint Children's Services Plan in 1996, two practices in Swindon are working with the local SSD's children's team. A specialist children's linkworker is employed in the practices, doing some case work but also acting in a liaison role between agencies, and with health visitors.

Primary care centres

Inevitably, with the focus on developing services in primary care, it rapidly became clear that 'Red Book' rules regarding the size of GP premises make it difficult to accommodate even basic additional services in General Practice buildings. We have begun the development of primary care centres in a number of locations throughout Wiltshire, as ways of accommodating primary care services beyond GMS services. Amongst these are included practice-attached linkworkers, and also services which are shared between health and social services such as mental health teams, hospital-at-home schemes and children's services. A primary care centre can provide common services shared by several practices on 'neutral territory' to defuse anxiety about the possibility of patients being poached from one doctor's list to another.

Inspection of nursing and residential homes — the role of the community pharmacist

Health Authority and SSD inspection teams are looking at ways of cooperating in inspecting residential and nursing homes. A new element in this process is the national decision to delegate some funding for community pharmacists to provide advice to nursing homes as well as residential homes.

WHAT ARE THE LIKELY NEXT STEPS?

Responding to national initiatives

A number of national initiatives are likely to influence the development of specific programmes of joint or integrated action. Continuing care agreements now need to be made locally, and health authorities will be required to make arrangements to monitor and improve mental health care in the community in partnership with social services. Future Community Care Charters are also likely to define common standards for health and social services for patients. These national initiatives will require local action and local integration if they are to be successful. These sorts of initiatives are likely to be more successful, and less subject to manipulation by one party or another, if there already exists a climate of trust and cooperation between agencies and with users and carers.

Practice-level joint commissioning

The range of pilot projects described earlier will provide a wealth of information about the links between practice-held budgets in fundholding practices, and care manager-held budgets in social services. The projects should also provide experience about possible new service developments, and managerial mechanisms and structures which are needed to facilitate and monitor local commissioning of services.

Gradually, practice-based joint commissioning of services may become the norm, while still working within the very different national and local accountabilities of health and social services.

Challenging and countering the arguments against integration

Some of the problems associated with integration described earlier have been tackled and overcome. Others have not, or they have been deliberately by-passed. This poses a basic question. Is there really a need to tackle the theoretical issue of leadership in primary care teams, when in practice bringing frontline professionals together in a team setting with a common agenda tends to produce practical local solutions with people rarely vying for power?

Checklist for a healthy joint commissioning programme

Joint commissioning of services works at two levels — for the individual user, and at the level of service organisation between agencies. So, to end with a challenge: how do *your* services match up to the checklist in Table 11.1?

Table 11.1 Checklist for a healthy joint commissioning programme

Individual

- Care management through practice based staff
- Shared training and teambuilding
- Social care information outlets in general practices
- Joint commitment of funds on individual care packages

Service organisation

- Shared needs assessment
- Joint development and re-profiling of services
- Complementary charter standards
- Joint production of service priorities
- Involvement of users and carers in developments
- Monitoring systems that work for both agencies

REFERENCES

1. Challis L, Pearson J 1993 Report on the evaluation of Linkworker pilots in Wiltshire. University of Bath School of Social Sciences.
2 Pearson J, Challis L 1995 Wiltshire Joint Initiatives Group. Inventory of Project Profiles. University of Bath School of Social Sciences.

12. Involving patients

Fedelma Winkler

INTRODUCTION

All of us are involved as users of services. But for most of us, most of the time, our relationship with the NHS will be the security of knowing that it is there when we need it. Few of us get involved in activities that are not of immediate concern to us. For those of us who do, involvement has to meet a recognised need. That is the first lesson of putting it into practice. A desire to contribute to the community, to share our expertise, to put right what is wrong, to feel valued, are the motives that must be recognised if we want to involve people. At a societal level, the need to hold those in positions of power accountable is the prime motivation for involvement.

This chapter addresses the reasons for public/patient involvement; it reviews existing involvement. It seeks to distinguish between the more general public involvement and the more specific patient/user involvement. It outlines the integrated systemic approach that is needed for involvement to be meaningful.

WHY INVOLVEMENT?

Everybody is in favour of involvement. To legitimate decisions, to enhance local accountability, to identify local needs, are the principal justifications. For some, it is intrinsically good and needs no other defence. But too often for managers, it is another box to be ticked in the performance monitoring schedule. Clarity about reasons is important because it allows methods to be assessed for effectiveness and value for money. In the Primary Care-Led NHS, responsibility for involvement rests with the new Health Authorities. They will have to be its advocate, help it develop, allocate resources, monitor that it happens and above all lead by example. The next sections review the justifications for public and patient involvement and the problems.

Public involvement

Reasons for public involvement?

Legitimation of policy. The public pay for health care services through taxation. At election time, the perception of how health care is delivered is a factor in how people vote. The government is held responsible. Ministers lay stress on consultation with the public by Health Authorities. Opposition to change is often seen as a lack of public education. Increasing resources are invested in consultation exercises. What the public think is usually known; consultation exercises are designed to enable the public to express their views, in line with central directives. Direct and indirect costs for this kind of exercise in one Health Authority were estimated at £200 000. That did not include the costs to the community.[1]

Uncontested changes enable local legitimacy to be claimed, but in contested changes the outcome is determined by the degree to which the community influences the national politicians.

To provide local accountability. Strategic decisions are devolved to local purchasing agencies. The Secretary of State appoints the Chair of the commissioning authority and the non-executive board members. They and the executive members are responsible for purchasing of services according to local need. The Secretary of State emphasises that decisions are taken in the light of local priorities.

However, non-executive members of Boards may have limited contact with the areas for which they are purchasing services. They are paid by and owe their appointment to the Secretary of State. Accountability is upwards. The Executive Members are likewise accountable upwards for implementing national policy. National policy includes the requirement to listen to local voices. The public as yet do not appear to have accepted that involvement exercises can make good the accountability deficit. Hence, they petition Ministers about the action of local Health Authorities.

There are other ways of making the NHS accountable locally. Some argue that local authorities should be given responsibility for health care. They could then be held accountable at local elections. The Liberal Democrats adopted this as policy in 1995. There are advocates also within Conservative and Labour local authorities, but so far few national politicians advocate this change.[2]

To identify local need. The most frequently given reason for public involvement is to identify need and ensure sensitivity to local communities. Authorities base their strategies on statistical information of assessed need, on usage and outcome data, public priorities and political sensitivities. The methodology for establishing the public will is crude. The difference in public priorities between localities is relatively small. Analyses of local purchasing strategies across the country demonstrates little variation in perceived need. The most significant factor influencing services is the affluence of the community and the links between local and national politicians.

Inherently good. There are those who believe that public involvement is self evidently good. It is a method of empowering communities. In theory, this means decision makers sharing power with the public. There are few examples of this being accomplished. It almost certainly requires longer time scales, continuity of resources and more commitment than is normally possible.

Need for honesty. Each of the above reasons for involvement are valid. Problems arise when the reasons given are false. That leads to public distrust. The proposal to shift responsibility for health to local authorities has not as yet gained mainstream support, but unless effective ways are developed that enable the community to be involved, it may look an attractive solution. Local allocators of the public resources need to recognise the public right to hold them to account and find ways of giving account of their stewardship for the money they are spending on the public's behalf.

Patient involvement

What is patient involvement for?

While the public is expected to be concerned for the common good, the interests of patients/users is more specific. The actual users of services know better how services are meeting their needs. Patient involvement contributes to public accountability through ensuring services reflect users' needs; giving patients a role in monitoring services; and providing external checks and balances to protect users. It also creates partnerships between patients, users, carers and services.

To hold to account. The history of public policy demonstrates that decisions made by managers and professionals often look less enlightened with hindsight. The most obvious is the promotion of tower blocks designed to solve the housing needs of the poor. Medical history is awash with theories that were, in their day, self-evidently beneficial, but later found to have the opposite effect. Managers, less than 10 years ago, justified the closure of small hospitals on the grounds of efficiency and safety. Now small hospitals are the spokes that feed the hub.

The public who challenged these managerial and professional orthodoxies were dismissed as lacking understanding, misguided or politically motivated. We need to make sure that in future decisions are less arrogant. Today's managers believe it is appropriate to care for people in their own homes. Opposition is seen as unenlightened. Managerial promises are not hard currency in the community. Managers who were truly held to account by their users, might find ways of guaranteeing that replacement services were in place before closures took place. Involving the patients and community could ensure changes were tested before implementation.

To ensure that services reflect patients and user's knowledge base. A service is only valuable if it meets users' needs. User knowledge should be the litmus test for professional action. The most effective method is to involve users at each point in the system. Too rarely do plans for services, treatment protocols, or research proposals start from the prospective of the expected beneficiary. Patients are usually enthusiastic and willing to share their expertise to help other users. At an intellectual level there is rarely a dispute about the benefits of involvement; it is simply time consuming to implement.

Monitor services. User involvement is not a substitute for good management. Good managers have systems in place to monitor the adequacy and competence of their services. The ultimate test, however, of the adequacy and sensitivity of a service is patient feedback.

To provide external safeguards for vulnerable people. Organisations are never perfect. Systems need to build in external criticism. This is particularly important when the users are vulnerable. Effective user representatives are a protection against abuse of power. Advocacy schemes are one such way of involving people, so that the most vulnerable are protected.

To create partnerships between patients users and services. Some people believe that the involvement of patients leads to a partnership between deliverers of care and the recipients and a more even distribution of power. This value underpins user group activity. The degree to which this belief is shared by those inside organisations needs testing.

Need for honesty. As with public involvement, the promotion of user/patient involvement will benefit from honesty and clarity of intent. In different situations different functions may and should take priority. For example, the prime function for user involvement in services for people with dementia may be to protect, whereas in mental health services it may be to develop partnerships.

THE PAST WILL INFLUENCE THE FUTURE

The involvement of patients in a Primary Care-Led NHS will be influenced by past activities as well as by new values. To patients, the NHS has always been 'primary care-led' or more precisely General Practitioner led. In planning the future past methods and their degree of success need to be assessed.

Involvement in primary care

The degree of involvement in General Practice is underestimated because it does not conform to the 'public meeting' image of involvement. Many patients are involved, particularly in rural areas, with their local practice. This may be collective action around raising money for equipment or facilities or even supporting medical aid to disaster areas or poorer countries.

Where this form of activity exists the bonds between practice and community are very strong. Practices in some areas have become the secular equivalent of the church, the focus of community activity. At its most highly developed, the practice becomes a community development agency, the ultimate form of involvement.[3]

Nationally, the most recognised form of involvement in General Practice is patient participation groups. These groups succeed when the practice is keen and supportive. They provide feedback to the practice and can proactively support the development of services.

Involvement through General Practice is, however, dependent on the practitioners for focus and leadership. Therefore, they are absent where they are needed most — where the services professionals deliver need to be challenged.

Managers and professional leaders have *not* distinguished themselves as champions of patients registered with poor practices. Attempts by patients to influence the selection of practitioners, to improve access to a practice, to influence the attitude in practices have usually failed. They fail in part because of the autonomous nature of the independent contractor and the inability of management to use the levers at their disposal. These factors have to be recognised when fresh attempts are made to involve patients.

The community health services have had less formalised involvement from the community. What often occurs is *reverse involvement*. District nurses, health visitors, health promotion staff are often involved in community organisations. These channels are undervalued by health organisations, but highly valued by the community groups.

User group involvement

Why should patients get involved?

Collectives of patients, and those who care for them, have sought to influence service delivery over a long time. Women who used maternity services and parents of sick children were early campaigners for changes in organisational and clinical care. Slowly, many of their once heretical views became orthodoxy, even if implementation is still patchy.

Major user groups have experience of being consulted on national policy, but much of their impact has come through their ability to influence public opinion. Their advocacy voice is increasingly being weakened, however, as they themselves become major providers. User involvement in the future may have to be attuned to working with smaller groups, who are direct users. To enable these groups to contribute as partners will require different patterns of working.

Patient as consumer

Patients' Charter

The Patients' Charter is a central directive aimed at improving services by targeting key activities, such as access to surgery. It has raised expectations and put pressure on providers to deliver to Charter standards. It is not a mechanism for involvement, rather a response to the public's expressed concerns about service.

Consumer feedback

We cannot run appropriate and sensitive services unless there is regular feedback from service users. Fashions change in how feedback is obtained. Most methods, whether complex expensive consumer satisfaction surveys, employment of patient representatives or patient-centred hospital schemes, leave the consumer passive. The publication of league tables and outcome measures in contrast enables the patient to choose their carer. This provides the patient with one step on the empowerment ladder. They then have to be able to exercise the choice which is increasingly restricted.

Public involvement in service development

Community Health Councils

Since 1974, the public and patient interests have been formally represented in the NHS by Community Health Councils. Now attracting renewed interest, the characteristic they share with the NHS is their variability and poor accountability for performance. Some are strong lobbyists, a valued advice and support service to individual patients. The good ones have enabled community representatives to learn about, participate in discussions, shape and monitor local services. The contact people have with Community Health Councils influences attitudes to this type of representative involvement.

Community Health Councils remain the one community participation agency set up by statute, independent of the NHS patronage system and part of a national network of lay people involved in health care. Future strategies for involving the public need to learn from them.[4]

Local voices

Alongside CHCs, new Health Authorities are expected to involve people so that services are responsive to local needs and preferences. The 'Local Voices' initiative was launched in 1992. It has received consistent support from Ministers.

Commissioning Chief Executives, in a recent survey, listed community opinion as a high priority when placing contracts, but only a minority had a system for obtaining it. Despite the pressure on Authorities to have strategies, most 'listening to the public activity' is organised on ad hoc basis or during major consultation exercises on closing services. *There is a real danger that community involvement is being equated with legitimation for rationing services.* This creates fissures between communities and the Health Authorities. In future activities, this past has to be recognised.

Locality commissioning

Energy is currently being invested in locality commissioning. It is the latest method advocated for sensitising commissioning to local needs. As commissioning agencies grow bigger to gain purchasing leverage, it is argued that locality commissioning would enable Commissioners to retain local sensitivity. It is an attempt to centralise and localise at the same time. The inherent contradictions in this logic are glossed over. The antecedents of this approach lie in local authorities, who also have had periods in which decentralisation was advocated as a method to increase public participation in local government. Evidence of the aim being achieved is scarce because decentralisation is often followed by recentralisation either because of political change, pressure on resources, or boundary changes. Locality commissioning's primary function has been usually about binding GPs into a relationship with the DHA. That is an important function. If it is also to be a vehicle for public involvement it needs a gear shift.

Involvement in a primary care-based NHS

The activities of Community Health Councils, Local Voices, and Locality Commission have generated expectations and created goodwill, but also cynicism and credibility gaps.

Involvement in primary care has been provider-led. There is no history of involvement being used to hold the General Practice to account for their services. The challenge now is to demonstrate that a 'Primary Care-Led NHS' can and will be different.

NOT JUST ANOTHER BOX, MORE A WAY OF LIFE

The challenge, therefore, is to move from negative to positive equity. The building blocks are commitment to the principle of public accountability, respect for the public, involvement of all staff and sustained development, with continuous evaluation.

Commitment to public accountability

The distinction between patient/user involvement and public/ community involvement needs to be made and strategies developed appropriately. Strategies that start from 'We've been told to' are destined to fail, waste money and generate cynicism. Activities based on a belief that public services should be held accountable, plus a desire to excel, have the potential to build a partnership of trust between patients, community, service deliverers and purchasers. In pursuing this, the NHS has two major assets the public good will towards the NHS and the commitment of its staff to the overall aims of the NHS.

Culture public good will

Public good will means that the public are prepared to be generous with their time and knowledge, if it is respected.

Staff involvement a perquisite of public involvement

Staff are also patients, users and public. If the receptionist does not understand what the organisation is trying to do, or worse actually disapproves it is unlikely that the public will understand or approve. If staff are empowered to provide feedback, decision makers will be challenged on the appropriateness of their proposals. If in turn, there is a system of consumer audit, the basis is formed for the virtuous circle. Involvement in reverse, with the staff recognised for their contribution to community development activities needs to be recognised as an important relationship with the community.

Lead by example: audit by public and users built into system

Credible involvement will only occur when there is commitment from the top of the organisation. If it is an add on to the Chief Executive, it will be an add on to staff. Patient/public involvement has to be an integral part of the entire organisation, present in all its strategies from planning, and service delivery through to education and research. It needs to form part of all monitoring activities.

Commissioning

Build from the bottom

A 'Primary Care-led NHS' needs general practitioners to recognise the value of public accountability. New Health Authorities need to ensure GPs have a structure in place to enable their patients to hold them to account for the services they are providing and purchasing. A review of community nursing chaired by Baroness Cumberledge in 1986,[5] recommended the establishment of community health care associations. This proposal is appropriate to General Practice now. A structure based on practice populations gives involvement relevance. People get involved at a level at which issues have direct relevance to them and their community. Similar models of accountability based on patient involvement at primary care levels can be found in the more democratic of the managed health care systems in the United States.

A new 1996 Health Authority should have targets for the establishment of local patient groups based in practices. The establishment of such groups could be contracted to a community organisation or to the CHC. They can form the democratic base for the umbrella organisation at locality or district level.

Integral to strategies and contracts

All policies and strategies should have public involvement built into development and have provision for auditing by patients. For example, new Health Authorities together purchase training. This should be linked to the problems identified by patients. Training programmes should be expected to have user/patient as tutors on courses. To close the cycle, patient organisations should be included in evaluating the impact of training. Clinical audit and research should be expected in a similar way to include the patient perspective in its work as a condition of funding.

The commissioning authority should expect to see evidence from its providers on the way it involves user representatives and user perspective in its decision making structures. Costs should be built into the contracting process and identified.

Special contracts

Some services such as advocacy or monitoring on behalf of the authority will need to be contracted separately with local organisations.[6]

Assigned responsibility

For an integrated approach to public involvement, responsibility within the organisation has to be assigned to a senior member of the team. The remit needs to include the seeking out of the uninvolved, identification of local organisations willing to contribute and to agree methods for selecting representatives. Budgets have to be designated.

Above all, this role has to include preparing other staff to participate. Staff too need to understand the type of support that lay participants need, particularly when asked to participate on professional committees. Committee chairs and members have to be helped to identify why it is appropriate to include a patient voice and how to facilitate it.

A key lesson to be learnt is that involving people is not about arranging public meetings nor about asking agencies to send a representative. It is about commitment to a long term relationship. It requires education and change within the organisation to ensure the user voice is respected. Community organisations often have the expertise Health Authorities lack. The recognition of complementary expertise is essential to the building of partnerships.

Provider organisations

Existing goodwill

Local hospitals build up goodwill in their communities over long periods of time. Sometimes this is deserved, sometimes not. It usually stems from the professional care members of the community have received and therefore rests with the clinical staff. Yet perversely it is professional staff who find the move to partnership with patients most difficult. It is in Trusts' self interest to have strong community support and to be seen to be listening to the people who use its services. Much behaviour by Trusts, including the exclusion of public from trust meetings, is counter productive. It suggests that there is not a genuine desire for accountability. Trusts anxious to maintain public goodwill will move beyond the annual public meeting and have a clearly established structure for both listening to their users and mechanisms for involving them in care.

Trusts and practices have an additional obligation, which is to recognise that some of their users may not be able to participate or may feel too vulnerable. Trusts responsible for people with mental illness, learning difficulties, the elderly frail or patients whose first language is not English will have established systems for protecting people's rights and amplifying their voices through, for example, patients' councils.

Community supportive

Trusts and practices have the means to go beyond public accountability to partnership in community development. That would include recognising how they contribute to the local economy through purchasing, employment and training policies as well as through the services they provide. Public management loyal only to economic efficiency will be counterproductive in the long run. Public involvement might demand that the good of the community be included within its efficiency criteria.[7]

IN SUMMARY

Those seeking to involve users or the public often fail, because they are not clear about why they want involvement, nor why people might want to be involved.

A key dilemma in the NHS today is that the changes are driven by central directives, while the public are consulted on their local implementation. A Primary Care-Led NHS itself could fall into this trap. It is a policy introduced at national level with no public discussion, yet it may have profound effect on care. It is a policy that aims to increase the responsibility of general practitioners for the provision and purchasing of services, with still weak systems of accountability to public and patients.

Involving patients or public activities need to be an integral part of units that make up the global NHS. Activities designed to involve the public should be subject to the same rigour as other interventions. Part of that rigour should include clarity of aims, openness about intent, well researched methods evaluation and feedback. This is just as true in a Primary Care-Led NHS as in a Hospital-Led NHS.

REFERENCES

1. Edwards J 1995 Public enemy: why asking the people about acute services goes wrong. Health Services Journal, 105: 5469, p. 22–24

2. Cooper L, Coote A, Davies A, Jackson C, Voices Off: (1995) Tackling the democratic deficit in health. Institute for Public Policy Research, London
3. Nehring J, Hill R, Poole L 1993 Work, empowerment and community: opportunities for people with long term mental health problems. Sainsbury Centre for Mental Health, London
4. Hogg C, Winkler F 1989 Community-consumer representation in the NHS. Greater London Association of Community Health Councils, London
5. Department of Health 1986 Neighbourhood nursing. Cumberledge Report, HMSO, London
6. Standish S. 1995 BUG-Ging Mental Health Services Health Services Journal, 100: 5474, p. 25
7. Winkler F, Towell D 1990 Old values in New York. Health Services Journal, 100: 520

13. Delivering quality

Carolyn Larsen

Delivering quality remains high on the agenda for a Primary Care-Led NHS. It is an important part of primary care development. The current national GP contract, however, still does not address the quality dimension and in its absence new Health Authorities now have a clear role in developing quality standards for General Practice in conjunction with the profession and consumers.[1] Quality is the crossover point of their new core monitoring and support functions.

THE ESSEX APPROACH

In 1991 Essex Family Health began to tackle this issue by talking to both professional (LMC and RCGP) and consumer representatives (e.g. CHCs) to seek their views on the sort of quality standards that might be applicable to General Practice. After several draft versions, the FHSA published a policy document entitled 'Quality in General Practice — The Goals for 1995'[2] in July 1992, which was then circulated to every GP in the county.

This approach to developing quality standards for General Practice was recognised in the 1993 Health Service Management Awards, achieving runner-up in the National Purchaser Management category.

THE 'GOALS'

The quality standards developed by Essex Family Health relate to the way General Practice is organised and run. There are 28 'Goals' which are divided into six main categories:

1. Written statement on the aims of the practice
2. Organisation and administration

3. Policies and procedures
4. Staff development and education
5. Premises.
6. Self audit and research.

Further details of these updated 'Goals' are set out in Table 13.1. They are based on a clear understanding that the setting of clinical standards is and should remain the responsibility of the GPs and their primary care teams. This separation of the clinical and organisational dimensions is basic to mutual trust and confidence. The Essex 'Goals' are not intended to be confined solely to the work of the practice and the practice team. The important wider role of the primary health care team is recognised in some of the individual 'Goals' standards; for example, encouraging the involvement of all PHCT members in regular team meetings and in multi-professional audit.

Table 13.1 The 'Goals' for 1995

Written statement of practice aims
● mission statement
● practice objectives (reviewed annually)

Organisation and administration
● regular primary health care team meetings
● patient feedback systems
● patient record summaries
● ages/sex and disease register
● appointment systems

Policies and procedures
● protocols for health promotion/disease management
● repeat prescription policy
● practice formulary
● written procedures for staff (including confidentiality, responding to requests for home visits, health and safety and dealing with complaints)

Staff development and education
● 'core' practice team including qualified practice manager
● up to date job descriptions and employment contracts
● staff appraisal schemes
● staff qualification and training records

Premises
- minimum standards for main and branch surgeries
- minimum standards for village hall surgeries
- essential practice equipment

Self audit and research
- collection of service provision data
- regular review of services in line with practice objectives
- multi professional clinical audit
- self review to identify service improvements and developments.

THE PROCESS

Essex has been committed to the principle that the 'Goals' should underpin how its cash limited resources are allocated. Area managers work closely with individual General Practices to agree practice development plans, which incorporate this link. It is recognised, too, that this is not an overnight process — some practices still have a lot of work to do to achieve the goals. It also needs to be appreciated that it may be necessary to operate through incentives to assist innovative practices which are already achieving all the 'Goals' standards and are keen to further develop the range of services offered to their patients.

All Essex practices are visited by area managers to explain 'Goals' quality standards in detail and to assess practices' current positions. A protocol for each visit was devised with the LMC and a standard checklist used for each practice. Action plans are then agreed with each practice after the visit and annual follow-up meetings are planned to review progress. Systematic evaluation is essential to complete the quality circle.

MONITORING

Using a questionnaire survey, GP responses to the initial visits in 1993 revealed that eight (3%) Essex GP practices achieved all 28 'Goals' standards. However, a significant proportion of General Practices (38%) were also already reaching over 75% of the 'Goals'.

There was a direct correlation between achievement of the 'Goals' and investment in practice staff. The size of the practice was also significant; large group practices with qualified practice managers achieve more 'Goals'. However, actual investment in practice premises does not appear to directly enhance a practice's ability to meet the 'Goals' standards. This is an important message for new Health Authorities. Difficulties in obtaining primary care capital cannot be used to disguise deficiencies on the quality front.

The majority of Essex GP practices have been very cooperative during the monitoring visits. They have regarded the 'Goals' as useful benchmarks by which to measure themselves and as a constructive way of aiding their own practice development. GPs are also keen to learn how they compare in relation to other practices within their locality. Figure 13.1 gives one local example of this feedback with relative levels of performance in tabular form[3].

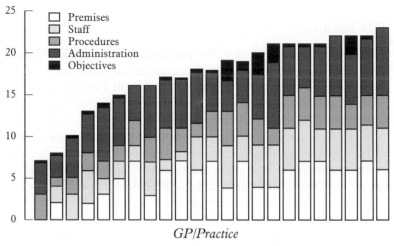

Fig. 13.1 'Goals for 1995'; an example set of the number achieved in Mid-Essex

THE WAY FORWARD

The 1990s have so far seen a radical change in the way General Practice operates; the introduction of the revised national contract in 1990 and the development of GP fundholding especially have promoted these changes. General Practice is now moving away from a reactive demand led approach towards a more managed care model. Proactive teams after April 1996 will have to be the norm to survive. Quality standards should now be a first step in a continuous process of facilitating the development of high quality primary health care. The Essex 'Goals' and their equivalents elsewhere can provide General Practice with the foundations upon which they can develop and extend their provider role to meet the shift of emphasis from secondary to primary care. For new Health

Authorities they are the key to a clear differentiation of roles and thence to collaboration on the post April 1996 agenda.

REFERENCES

1. Butland G 1993 Commissioning for Quality. British Medical Journal 306: 252–252.
2. Essex Family Health Services Authority 1992 Quality in General Practice — the goals for 1995. Essex Family Health Services Authority.
3. Johns C 1994 Developing quality in General Practice. Primary Care Management, 4:9: 6–8.

14. Managing investment

Camilla Lambert

The Example of a GP Premises Register

INTRODUCTION

Developing the infrastructure of GP services was a central role of FHSAs for many years and primary care development continues to be an important part of the support role of new 1996 style Health Authorities.

This chapter concentrates on the experience of one small health commission in working collaboratively with local GPs to agree and manage priorities for investment in premises. It also briefly describes how this experience was extended to joint working on other areas of investment, e.g. staffing and computers.

It is recognised that the issues involved in supporting premises development have if anything become more complex over the time period described here. The debate about the ethics of using fund-holding savings (i.e. public money originally allocated for direct patient care) to build extensions which could financially benefit individual partners rumbles on. The constraints of the Red Book reimbursement scheme devised for a pre-fundholding era and before the impact of the 1990 contract and the increased in-house activity occurring in many practices, has led to increasing frustration. In some areas the new role of Regional Offices has created uncertainty about access to alternative sources of capital. In addition there has been encouragement to develop strategic thinking along the lines of locality provision which brings together a range of primary and secondary care services with the extended primary care team under one roof, variously named polyclinics, primary care resource centres, and family health centres.

However, each area must work within the realities of its own opportunities and constraints. The ability to promote a strategic vision for primary care (and now a Primary Care-Led NHS), while working with the idiosyncrasies of particular practices with their individual histories, personalities and varying degrees of interest in following the national agenda is a crucial management skill, although a somewhat elusive one. It is important to have an overall aim for the future of General Practice as such, but also crucial is a workable set of tools for allocating resources which will achieve that aim in a way which is seen as fair by independent contractors for whom competition is still a key principle.

THE ISLE OF WIGHT CONTEXT

The Isle of Wight is the smallest of the April 1996 Health Authorities, with a population of 126 000 of whom 23% are over 65. There are seven main urban areas where the population is concentrated, set within large rural areas with smaller villages and scattered settlements. There are currently 19 General Practices, with 77 GPs. Only one is a single handed practice, seven have two to three partners, six have four to five partners, and five have six to seven partners.

The average list size per WTE GP is 1769 (ranging from 1108–2173). These GPs employ between them about 70 practice nurses, 19 practice managers, and 96 reception and clerical staff.

The practices work from 19 main surgeries and 11 branch surgeries. Four practices work from two or three premises throughout the week and only four practices use branches for a consultation-only service for limited times during the week. Three practices are based in health centres, two of which are owned by the Community Trust and one by the practice. Fifteen practices are fundholders, which has created additional pressure on space for staff, record keeping and computers. All practices are computerised for GMS, and the aim is to set up GP links in 80% of practices by April 1996.

Work on developing a primary care strategy following the lead set by Wessex RHA, started during early 1993. The strategy emphasises the importance of the Health Authority enabling the development of GPs as both purchasers and providers, but over time the limits on expanding the GP provider role have become evident. Paramount among these are a shortfall of space and the sense that GPs cannot take on much more extra work without a considerable shift of resources from secondary care. The rapid growth of fundholding over the last 2 years has been a major influence on pursuing strategic intentions for primary care. It has created opportunities: many practices have used fundholding to bring additional services to their surgeries and/or taken on more follow-up work themselves. However, during 1994–95, it made planning to move resources to primary care a hazardous process in that fundholding overspends have had to be met from DHA funds, but forecasts of the extent of overspends proved highly volatile and largely exaggerated.

The primary care strategy has supported a locality basis for service provision, but given the small size of the Island and the mainly dispersed nature of the population distribution, this is envisaged to involve a networking of existing services rather than centralising within a locality a number of primary care and community services under one roof. Similarly, given that the DGH is centrally located, at a maximum of 13–14 miles from all potential patients, there has been less emphasis than elsewhere on out-posting consultant-led services. Where opportunities for bringing services together exist they will be taken. However the overall resource position only allows for slow progress, and the competing demands of investment in premises, staffing and computers to support a growth in the effectiveness, scope and quality of primary care must continuously be balanced between each other.

A further pressure on the space capacity of primary care buildings comes from the intention to develop care management as a function of the primary care team, putting more emphasis than was possible when the care management system was first set up in 1993, on integrating health and social care assessments under one worker. Progress depends on the existing availability of sufficient accommodation or on being able to create this without great difficulty.

WHY SET UP A PREMISES REGISTER?

In a small area with relatively few practices it might once have been assumed that the personal knowledge of managers who could easily get to know all practices was sufficient in deciding how to allocate resources for premises investment. However, when in late 1992 Regional capital became available, particularly targeted at practices working from Community Trust owned property, it became clear that insufficient detailed knowledge was held by the Health Authority.

Although Regional capital was accessed for one practice for a cost rent and improvement grant to finance the purchase and development of their health centre premises, the strong GP view was that this had given unfair advantage to one practice which already had a very reasonable standard of accommodation. It was then swiftly agreed to start afresh by establishing an up to date premises register from which agreed priorities could be derived.

THE PROCESS OF SETTING UP A REGISTER

The whole process was guided by GP involvement at all stages. Having obtained agreement that the then Wessex RHA Capital and Estates Directorate would undertake a survey of all premises, a group of GPs was nominated by the LMC to work with the Authority's Primary Care Directorate to agree the terms of reference for the project, the methods to be used and the means of reporting back to practices and to officers and members.

The main stages of the project were as follows:

June

A questionnaire was sent to all practices to establish some key facts about each building for the surveyor to have in advance of the visit. A review was carried out of all information on each premises held by the Health Authority (including plans of buildings and basic profile data).

July/August

A physical inspection survey was carried out of each property (barring that of one single handed practice where the partner was due to retire within the next year). The same surveyor was used to ensure uniformity of inspection and assessment. In most cases he was accompanied by a Health Authority officer who interviewed a practice representative on plans for the development of the practice in relation to future activity, staff and service changes which would affect the need for additional/different space.

September

The survey results were presented to officers through the use of three forms for each building. The first demonstrated whether the premises met minimum Red Book standards (related to the number of GPs using the building). The second form indicated the degree of functional suitability of each building — i.e. whether it met a number of essential or desirable criteria (which were selected from the then current Health Building note for General Practices plus some additions agreed by Health Authority staff and GPs). The third form showed the physical condition of each property, identified any defects and the suitability (or not) for expansion, categorising the building overall as one of as new/good minor deterioration major improvement required unusable/unsafe. The three forms were then used to generate an overall summary form.

October

The Survey report was published for members and all practices, who all agreed that full details of their premises could be made available to colleagues.

THE RESULTS OF THE SURVEY

About 70% of premises were defined as generally acceptable in terms of their condition and suitability as GP premises but 14% were in poor condition and also not able to meet the essential functional requirements. (Of these, two were main surgeries as opposed to branches.) Over all premises there was a rough split of a third of premises requiring considerable work or development, a third considered satisfactory in terms of condition, and a third which could benefit from some investment. However, this assessment was only in relation to current services, and although a number of sites could potentially allow expansion the fact that a number of properties were rented was seen as a likely barrier to achieving this. About 50% of the main premises could not be easily expanded on their current site, which clearly indicated that proposals to enhance the capacity of primary care provision were likely to face severe challenges.

The survey defined which properties were in most urgent need of attention and highlighted such other issues as security defects, lack of access for disabled people to toilet areas, and the need for a general maintenance programme. The fact that comparable details of all properties were available to all interested parties enabled a full discussion with the LMC premises sub-group from which an investment policy was developed and then approved by the Health Authority in December. Since then the policy has been used to generate an investment programme on a yearly basis, with a review by the sub-group half way through each year to adjust decisions in the light of the actual progress achieved. With further Regional backing and in collaboration with another Health Authority who was interested in using the Isle of Wight experience to develop a similar register, a computer data base was established and the details of the survey are now entered onto this. The register can easily be updated as changes occur, and can be used to produce comparative data as an aspect of practice profiles.

ISSUES OF WORKING WITH THE INVESTMENT POLICY

The policy defines three main categories for investment and a means of prioritising within them. Category A covers small-scale improvements to existing premises, with first priority to those designed to achieve minimum standards and provide essential facilities, and second priority to improvements where basic standards are already met.

Category B covers major capital schemes addressing a wide range of deficiencies. Of top priority are existing premises where the condition and environmental limitations mean that minimum standards cannot currently be met, and there is an urgent need for major rebuilding or relocation. Of second priority are existing premises meeting minimum standards already but unable to expand activities in their current form — i.e. being seriously held back from delivering a full range of primary care activities. Of third priority are those premises already operating at a fairly extended level where further premises improvements would result in only a marginal increase in activity.

Category C covers the development of additional and new premises primarily to enhance accessibility for patients. The policy states that this category can only be considered once all outstanding needs within the first two categories have been met. Branch surgeries designed mainly to bring core services closer to patients are not a priority at the moment and hence will not receive any investment of cash limited funds.

As with all policies, implementation has been problematic in some respects. Using the categories practices were placed in one of four priority bandings (with all the top priority practices being in Category B). However, progress since this initial prioritisation in early 1994 has been patchy given the tendency for complex capital schemes to be held up by difficulties in obtaining planning permission, problems in identifying sites and funding, and changes in the costing base, as well as reconsiderations by practices. In addition, the priority order has been changed in response to other developments. For example a practice with premises defined by the survey as adequate and in good condition has developed rapidly by taking on additional patients and two more partners and by becoming a fundholder, so that an urgent need for expanded office space not foreseen 2 years ago has occurred. In another instance a practice defined as medium priority for investment has generated sufficient fundholding savings to bring forward a long planned expansion with Health Authority support in advance of other practices given a higher priority rating. Implementation of the policy has had to be flexible enough to cope with new problems and opportunities as they emerge.

While this approach has been well understood and accepted by local GPs, the slow pace of development has led to much frustration. We have been using the familiar tactics of maximising the use of improvement grants which does not involve committing recurrent funding. However, when schemes become delayed then non-recurrent money has to be brokered for the next year. A small Health Authority has a limited capacity to add to the GMS allocation, whether this be to increase the number of developments or to get round the restrictions of cost rent schemes. Although some funds of HCHS origin have been made available, pressures from the secondary care sector to enhance spending there have restricted the amount. In these circumstances the potential availability of Regional capital to boost cost rent and/or improvement grants and to allow developments over and above the cost rent limits to meet the office space needs of fundholding practices, as well as to enhance the scope for additional services, has been seen as a lifeline. However, this availability has been thrown into doubt with the changing Regional role of the NHSE Regional office and uncertainty about future NHSE capital allocations policy beyond April 1996.

In varying degrees this will be a familiar pattern, experienced all over the country. Some areas may find solutions to particular problems and clearly for an area like the Isle of Wight with very high levels of fundholding, the use of accumulated GPFH savings is one such solution. Lease backs from private developers may also have their part to play. However, moving forward in any radical way to enable General Practice across a whole district to meet the aspirations of both Health Authorities and individual practices to expand

and improve the space from which they work as providers and purchasers still feels some way off.

LESSONS FOR A PRIMARY CARE-LED NHS

In this context Health Authority managers have to put into practice a range of skills and attitudes without which a genuinely Primary Care-Led NHS will remain a statement of intent, empty of real substance.

The key principles are still being debated, but in my view must emphasise a process of decision making about the shape and pattern of health service delivery and the ways of maximising health and well being which directly and intimately involves primary care practitioners. Also to be emphasised is their involvement in taking forward a style of health care in which the skills of a range of professionals are brought together in the interests of individual patients, based on openness, team working, and clear communication between primary and secondary care for those interventions beyond the (developing) scope of primary care.

This means that primary care practitioners and Health Authority managers must work together in new ways for both to discharge their responsibilities to the population, in the realisation that the contributions of both sides of the partnership are each crucial. This partnership will be subject to nearly continual negotiation and renegotiation over time and as different issues emerge which need local solutions. The pattern of working directly with GPs to share information and reach consensus on priorities and a direction for action described here in relation to the development of a programme for investment is one small example. On the Isle of Wight we have extended this pattern to decisions about GMS and other investment in staff and computers. In each case we have worked with a subgroup nominated by the LMC firstly to establish openly the current pattern of investment and secondly to agree principles for future allocation. In each case policies are designed to find solutions to problems identified through an understanding of the cumulative effect of past decisions. Although in neither instance are all the solutions identified, and limited resources are still to some degree defined as a cause for complaining rather than imaginative action, the fact of joint working visible to all has created a different atmosphere.

In itself, this works to make possible the start of a different dialogue with practices. Practices are starting to define their own future direction and to analyse the elements of change needed to achieve it through a process of practice development planning, and Health Authorities are starting to make more explicit the expectations of managers about how these changes can be measured and the support available to make them possible. Discussing how to reach a new position and demonstrate arrival (or at least steps on the way) by acknowledging different perspectives but mutual interests is very different from requiring action and setting standards from on high.

To cope with the management of investment for developing primary care capacity while also working within a negotiated relationship. New Health Authorities need a combination of skills which span primary care development and financial planning. To achieve other than piecemeal gains they also require strong support from the NHSE at regional and central levels backed up by a detailed understanding of the different processes of capital development between hospitals and primary care. At present these processes are outdated, having been overtaken by developments generated through fundholding, the change of focus to primary care and the opportunities created by setting up contracts for services additional to core GMS with primary care teams. A Primary Care-Led NHS requires an imaginative review of capital investment across the board. This must address the linked issues of accountability for public finances made available for capital developments, the context of independent practitioner organisations where issues of ownership and potential personal gain are relevant, and the complexities of the total General Practice remuneration system. The outcomes of the current NHSE work in these areas will be the subject of considerable expectation and careful scrutiny.

Where total purchasing through fundholding is superimposed on an already complex situation, the need for the locally negotiated implementation of agreed development strategies is even more important. The initial widely promoted definition of fundholding savings as belonging to the practice for the promotion of solely practice defined goals will have to be adjusted to encompass a sense of the legitimacy of pooling resources from a variety of sources to meet local needs. New Health Authorities in 1996–97 need to grasp quickly the opportunities for such partnerships that can arise from implementing the new Fundholding Accountability Framework. The process of defining those needs as well as that of allocating investment to meet them can be assisted by building up practice profiles based on comparative data about each practice's current list, total resources and activity, backed up by 'softer' data derived from a number of sources including each practice's development plan. Using such profiles is fraught with difficulties. Primary care practitioners can be suspicious of any attempt by managers to use them to generate performance league tables based on variations from a mean (which cannot always easily be accounted for). This is especially so if investment is linked to 'high' performance, the definition of which has not been agreed. On the other hand, in a situation of limited resources, Health Authorities face difficult choices in trying to achieve a more equitable distribution of resources for patients to access in primary care settings if their policy is also to use investment as a means of encouraging progressive 'high performers' to continue to achieve. If, alternatively, they use investment to bring 'low achievers' up to speed they face creating disillusionment in the more active practices. This dilemma has clear implications for the future number and distribution of services outlets.

To develop the culture of mutual trust and cooperation referred to above these fears and tensions must be acknowledged and shared. Progress at present can only be made by building up locally agreed profiles and locally agreed standards for measuring performance in a context of openness about how these can be used to increase understanding of variations as well as inform decisions about investment. We have attempted on the Isle of Wight to link the planning of developments and investment in services to profile data, including that generated by the premises survey. This has had to be a cautious process, with methods, assumptions and conclusions being locally agreed before action is taken.

CONCLUSION

The premises survey described in this chapter has been influential locally in developing the principles of sharing information and the process of prioritising investment with primary care practitioners. As a result, the 1996 Health Authority has detailed knowledge on the standard and condition of existing practice accommodation, and practices are more able to see their individual needs in a wider context. Difficult decisions are still required and fundamental resource constraints continue, but the first steps have been taken on the route to a Primary Care-Led NHS through jointly managing investment to promote and support its development.

ACKNOWLEDGEMENT

The author is grateful for comments on this chapter received from Denise Rendell, Andrew Hollingshead, Edwin Hume and Drs Coleman and Denman-Johnson (Isle of Wight GPs).

15. Contracting for primary care

Alan Torbet

Health Authorities now have control of all the resources that can ensure the provision of effective health care for their population. They will want to invest in primary health care services which are effective, which meet individual patient needs and which also match the general health care needs of patients in each area. Whatever else, the Primary Care-Led NHS — able to provide most care, to most people, in or at their own homes — wants strategy to set some consistent directions for primary care as well as tactics to support localised provider development.

How can a new Health Authority commission services from a multiplicity of GP practices, as well as working with Trusts and other providers? How can it set strategic objectives and ensure they are met by the sum of tactical commissioning and contracting with each primary care provider? Can primary care development deliver strategic change, and how can it be measured? What is the potential for managing the market in primary care — stimulating competition or supporting providers to work together?

There are no easy answers. A hard headed 'horses for courses' approach is required. Successful primary care can only be achieved through integrated commissioning; through development contracts with Trusts; and through highly specific development plans agreed with every General Practice, which meet their requirements, and the needs of the Health Authority.

ASSESSING NEEDS AND DECIDING PRIORITIES

Pausing to get some assessment of a local area's need for primary care could be seen as a counsel for inaction. After all, does not the universality of access to primary care mean that all need — presenting as want — is met by a wide range of General Practice?

Fortunately, there is too much hard evidence to the contrary for this view to stand close scrutiny.

There is a primary health care market, but often patients are unwilling or unable to choose on the basis of quality or effectiveness. Speed and ease of access tend to be the determinants of choice. Needs go unmet or are met inefficiently or ineffectively. A service grows or withers because of a practitioner's interest (or loss of it), even if it was originally offered to meet a perceived local need.

Effective secondary to primary substitution is still some way away — even for a limited number of health treatments. The choices exercised by individual practices to extend their services do not yet add up to enough consistent capacity to allow local hospitals to make a quantum shift in their provision.

As need and consumption of primary health care are imperfectly linked, information must be gathered on both, as well as on the types of clinical behaviour and service delivery which are to be sought. Thus, a series of inter-connected indicators need to be reviewed:

- Health status
- Demography
- Consumption
- Service activity in primary and secondary care
- Effectiveness.

Primary care consumption is intensely local and parochial, but can be mapped over larger areas to take into account travelling and other social and cultural factors. The geographical spread of a GP's list can tell much about the kind of services they will be providing. Overlaying practice and community health service activity will show not only the totality of provision, but also whether one is compensating for the service weaknesses of the other, or both are having to meet hidden need, for example from homeless people or the arrival of a new and needy immigrant community.

Setting priorities and meeting needs effectively, requires all agencies to have a view of a local area which is more than the aggregation of expectations of individual GP practices. Health Authority, Trusts and Local Authority may find it relatively easy to agree a development framework for primary care in a ward, or constituency or community area, but GPs will get involved only if there is the prospect of beneficial changes for the practice and patients. Examples could include: using a local hospital Consultant as a focus for discussion on clinical practice, referral standards and guideline; the development of joint services with the Local Authority for a particularly deprived community; using Social Services area offices as a focal point for liaison and problem solving on social care practice; and local multi-agency working groups, within which service problems can be addressed, local resources deployed to solve them, and local relationships forged with the 'can do' players.

Ultimately, there is a tension between commissioning services for a population and for a practice list. This is manageable, however, if the needs which are determined by both approaches are recognised as equally valid and negotiated with practices. This will produce the tactical agreements for practice action which contribute, over time, to the achievement of Health Authority strategies.

COMMISSIONING PRIMARY CARE

Traditionally DHA purchasing of primary care services has used district and client-group need data to seek broad changes in the volume, content and quality of activity from community health service providers. FHSAs have been more able to achieve very specific changes with individual GP practices, and some shifts in activity or standards have tended to flow from the national GP contract.

Now the Health Authority has the total resources for investment in primary health care at its disposal and will need to deploy them through an integrated commissioning programme which can set general and local priorities, and contract with a range of local practice and Trust providers to deliver. Building on the experience some FHSAs and DHAs have already gained in bringing together commissioning and purchasing power, integration must achieve:

(a) Clearer strategic commissioning of primary care;
(b) Both general and local priority setting;
(c) Improved effectiveness of services purchased and better targeting;
(d) Reduced gaps and overlaps between primary and acute services, and within Primary services;
(e) Secondary to primary substitution;
(f) Primary care contracts, including primary medical care, staying within overall budgetary limits.

An integrated approach to commissioning primary health care is no less valid where most or all of the Health Authority resources for community health services are going to GP fundholders. Both eventually will have to agree a share of the GMS and CHS cake which accurately reflects the volume and content of care and the standards to which GP practice and Trust providers will work, to meet the primary health care needs of a fundholder's patients.

Integrated commissioning also make more explicit the quantum and quality of service which is being sought to be purchased for a local area, without pre-determining the share of the services which will be provided by any particular GP practice or Trust provider. Complementary contracts can then be agreed with both types of provider which ensure that effective service coverage is achieved within overall budget, and cost effectively.

Commissioning integration must ensure more effective use of the resources being deployed. For example, there is a need for flexibility between all the nursing staff at practice level, but a strategic view also needs to be taken about the level of investment in primary care nursing across each local area, and the Authority population as a whole. Increased investment in practice nursing must be balanced with the purchasing of community nursing services, and planned shifts from secondary to primary care.

Likewise, commissioning services in practice settings — for example physiotherapy and chiropody — must be managed against a clear contract between Trust provider and practices, which ensures that the patient benefits are realised.

COMMISSIONING SERVICES FROM GENERAL PRACTICE

Overall commissioning priorities for General Practice will probably include:

- Enhancing the quality;
- Extending the range of services provided in practice settings;
- Strategic substitution of services from secondary to primary care;
- Developing primary care services to meet the needs of specific user groups.

The range and standards of services commissioned should take into account general and local priorities as well as developments unique to each practice. Many will require complementary contracts to support joint working between practices and Trust staff and to ensure that the total of the national and community health care commissioned for an area meets agreed needs.

This requires a unique service agreement with each practice, within a framework which allows all of the agreements to be aggregated: to evaluate local provision, development potential, and development gaps.

PRACTICES' SERVICE DEVELOPMENT PLANS

As Birmingham FHSA demonstrated, virtually all practices can be encouraged and helped to produce structured service development plans. Each practice can be supported to implement agreed elements within them. This creates a valuable tool, and the information base, from which to achieve changes to primary care services which are both strategic and directly relevant to each practice.

Service development plans must be negotiated locally, both in style and content, but they are likely to be based on:

Clarity regarding the Health Authority's directions and priorities for primary care development

These would describe a range of needs within an area, but not how these translate into service delivery by the range of GP practices serving it.

Jointly agreed service features which can demonstrate success

These would be debated and agreed by representative samples of practitioners, or self selecting innovators. There are many service guidelines already circulating, and service features can be as simple or as complex as necessary to engage practitioner interest. Features and standards must be achievable (albeit over time) through the development resources which are likely to be available.

Some will be universal, others can be tailored to individual practice's needs — a necessary approach where the range of practitioner and practice environments varies considerably. Service features should not seek to set minimum standards applicable to all practices as these should be agreed and monitored by other means. Service development plans should be seen as developmental, not about policing.

Aspirations for service improvement for their patients, chosen and developed by each practice

Willing practice participation will be largely dependent on the culture of the new Health Authority and its relationship with practitioners. Whether practices view the invitation to respond and complete a development plan as genuinely welcome — or interfering, policing, compromising their clinical independence, bureaucratic or simply a game to be played — will affect the quality of the self-reported data and its validity and reliability. Quality of participation will also be affected by the questions asked. The manner in which practices are invited to respond has an obvious danger of alienation if the Authority aims and their own do not broadly coincide, unachievable standards are being sought, or the aims are too facile.

Service development plans will be broader than business plans and should solicit views about best practice, even if short term goals fall short of this. If the aim, as it should be, is to have all practices participate and establish a clearer picture for strategic planning, help will have to be provided to practices to facilitate the process, at least in the early stages.

Clarity regarding criteria for allocating resources and support

These would meet the competing claims from priority Health Authority developments and from practice innovation meeting very specific local needs. Different practices will need different levels of support and the main function of the development plan will change as the cycle of development evolves. Inevitably, there will be a degree of competition between achieving effective service coverage and concentrating support on the practices which are really positive about moving forward.

A cycle of development which recognises the resource needs of practices for some years to come, and tracks progress and change

Service development plans cannot be static, as needs and the resources required change. Major gains can be made in the early years of the planning cycle and the broad nature of the approach should mean that all practices will find some areas of development to agree to initially even if it becomes harder as the range of options is narrowed. Tensions can emerge about the ownership of the agenda if feelings of compulsion rather than cooperation are allowed to develop.

Business plans give practices a much freer opportunity to select their own development route. Equally, of course, the Health Authority still has to choose to support the business plans which most clearly meet its objectives.

Sensitivity in implementation, interpretation of data and acting on the results

A continuous cycle of visits to practices needs to be sustained to explain the intentions, validate the data and give practices an open opportunity to express their own agenda. Practices need to see that support and resources are genuinely available so that plans can be formulated on a reasonable expectation of success.

Plans which seek to accommodate both the practices' and Health Authority's development agenda will inevitably contain contradictions and tensions. This is manageable, with clarity about use and expectations; about the balance of resources which is felt to be fairly invested between the two agendas; about intensive support with individual practices; and retaining the capacity to evolve and develop the plans in the light of experience.

Collected, collated and analysed, practices' service development plans will give a sound indication of the potential for development of any practice in the area in comparison with its peers; the development potential of all practices in a local area and across the Health Authority; and the resources — by way of support and investment — necessary to achieve the development potential of each and all practices. Practices can compare themselves against the aggregated plans and needs for the area, or the whole district, and can get good indications of service developments which the Health Authority would be most likely to support.

Investment for change in primary care is easier to justify if the potential capacity to deliver is known in advance and can be shown to meet strategic aims. Practices' development aims can be supported if the local area needs a developed service. Other providers can be encouraged to develop necessary services where practices cannot or will not.

If primary services are to be complementary, if weak provider links are to be supported, if service gaps are to be closed and if investment in shared centres is to be encouraged, local commissioning intelligence will be required on the capacity for service development within all primary care providers, to compare against the needs of the area. Systematic and meaningful performance information will also be necessary to ensure that care, and developments commissioned and contracted, is delivered effectively and to the targeted population.

The new Health Authorities should develop a more subtle blend of commissioning and purchasing of primary care than has so far been achievable. GPs will also need help and encouragement to work together, and active performance management of primary care must support the delivery of agreed services and standards.

MONITORING PRIMARY CARE CONTRACT PERFORMANCE

To be judged effective, integrated primary health care commissioning through practices' service development plans and complementary Trust contracts will have to demonstrate changes to clinical practice, leading to health improvements. Activity changes, and better recording of them, however, are steps in the right direction.

Most community health service information systems are still barely adequate for general contract monitoring and few can have great confidence in their ability to demonstrate service success which is supportive and complementary to the performance of local practices. Commissioners will need to agree jointly with GPs and Trusts what items of information will be sought for performance monitoring, and ensure that they are collected consistently and can be readily used by everyone — including practices — to demonstrate collective as well as individual achievement.

For monitoring practice performance, the extensive knowledge which FHSAs have of individual practices and their practising environments must not now be lost, if an appropriate level and content of monitoring is to be actively negotiated and put in place in each case.

For practice developments, agreed success criteria will need to be established in advance of any investment, including the consequences of non-achievement where a minimum standard is being required. Major changes, including significant capital investment, should be subject to a service level agreement, with timescales for delivery.

The increasing amount of information which becomes available through practice plans, which allows practices to compare themselves with each other, also offers peer performance review, against criteria which practices will have had a hand in setting, and which can be developed and modified in the light of experience.

MANAGING THE PROVIDER ENVIRONMENT

Primary care provision is highly fragmented, particularly in urban areas, with a large range of overlapping practices, fundholders and multiple Trust providers. Developing individual practices with their community health services is a vital role for the new Health Authorities, but an interventionist market management, stance is also needed to influence the configuration of primary care providers.

Each practice vacancy must be viewed as an opportunity to review practice configuration, and active steps must be taken — for their benefit and for the patients' benefit — to help or manage inadequate or incompetent practitioners out.

There are a number of ways in which GPs can be supported, and encouraged to establish working relationships with each other, from which better and more comprehensive services are likely to result.

Partnerships need to be held together by effective and fair partnership agreements. The Health Authority should insist on these, with agreed standards, as a pre-condition to practice reimbursement. Partnership break-ups should not be encouraged, inadvertently, by the availability of incentives to set up elsewhere. It is a tough line to take, but GPs need to know that it is their responsibility to enter into a safe partnership agreement, failing which, if it breaks down, they are on their own.

GPs do not, however, need to be in partnership to work together. They can share surgeries and practice staff; dedicated Community Trust staff can work with groups of small practices in a local area; out of hours practice rotas and cooperatives will bring mutual support and consistency.

Single and small practices have come together to meet the minimum list size criteria for fundholding and multi funds have helped to carry a management burden which small practices could not. Fundholders are also making excellent use of the additional skills which many practitioners have — in minor surgery, for example — to cross refer patients, rather than send them into hospital.

Multifunds must also have the potential to become internal primary care development agencies but they will need help to balance their external purchasing concerns with internal reflections on the practice's own clinical performance.

Competition can be stimulated between practices, to tender for enhanced services for a local area — such as for drug abusers, minor injuries services and for homeless people. New styles of practice-based service, such as physiotherapy, chiropody and out-patient clinics, should also be subject to tender, both from local Trusts as potential providers and practices as potential hosts.

The future for primary care in inner city areas, without active management of providers looks rather bleak. With fewer trained GPs coming through, and less willing to work in difficult areas, fewer GP principals will be coping under even greater patient pressure. Patients who are more likely to benefit from extended practice-based services are less likely to get them, because many of the smaller isolated practices concentrated in these areas will be unable to respond. Large deprivation payments to GPs which could be an effective incentive to better inner city practice cannot act in this way because they are seen as a support to remuneration, nothing else. GP fundholding is probably shifting resources from poorer to more affluent areas.

In this context, the new Health Authorities may easily find themselves short on powers of intervention — and they will need to be arguing for one or two changes. They might, for example, want to contract with a local Trust to act as the primary care agency in an area, giving them the responsibility for delivering effective medical and community care. To discharge this role effectively, Trusts would need to be able to employ family doctors to fill any shortfall in quality or quantity. Trusts could also want to shift the boundaries between General Practice, community nursing and hospitals, including the use of nurse practitioners and 'walk in' primary care centres.

Health Authorities might also want to contract with groups of GPs for the management of all health care provision for a local area, providing primary care as well as purchasing hospital care. This would need a contract which went well beyond a combination of GMS contract and total fundholding. GPs taking on this responsibility would need powers and funding to employ business managers, and additional practitioners to concentrate on direct patient services.

CONCLUSIONS

Movement towards a Primary Care-Led NHS should be initiated by integrated commissioning of primary care from practice and Trust providers, and achieved through provider development and market management.

Effective commissioning of secondary and specialist services — by Health Authority and by GPs — follows on, it does not lead.

Commissioning of primary care services can ultimately be judged to be successful if:

(a) it gathers and uses information about needs and current service delivery in local areas as well as in the Health Authority area as a whole;
(b) it sets service priorities which are sensitive to local and general needs;
(c) it offers a portfolio of service requirements and changes within which individual practices and Trust providers can agree and deliver their own unique contribution;
(d) it monitors provider performance through contracts, service level agreements and development plans;
(e) it uses this information to negotiate further and future service provision.

A structured approach to GP practice development is necessary if the Health Authority's strategic objectives are to be achieved through tactical support of individual practices.

Health Authorities will need to manage the primary care provider environment at least in the deployment of GPs. More active intervention — enhanced by new powers — will be necessary in areas with acute needs which are not being met effectively by existing practice and Trust configurations.

16. Extending fundholding

Brian Maynard-Potts

Fundholding, the 1996 NHS version of managed care, is extending in two directions: the proportion of the population covered, and the scope of services included. Both of these trends are beneficial to patients, and there is much that the new Health Authorities need to do to support these processes.

MANAGED CARE IN THE NHS

'Managed care' is a term which many use but few define. Most would agree that it refers to health or social care schemes which provide a defined range of services for a defined population at a defined price (i.e. with few or no item of service payments by the user). Such schemes are funded by regular fees or capitation payments derived from subscriber or employer insurance, or from taxation. The term is particularly applied to schemes where a team of practitioners — for health care, primary care physicians — is signed up to accepting that the budget for a certain number of clients is, within a certain latitude, finite. Thus the management of health care resources is brought into the same framework as the management of patients and their care.

Decisions by such physicians are, in general, different from those by physicians who are not operating in managed care systems. The former are likely to be more careful in their use of clinical resources. This is an advantage to the patients, who should find that funds are thus available for occasional high cost procedures and new services; and to those funding the scheme who should find that the cost of providing the health care is predictable.

The well developed system of General Practice in Great Britain allows the particularly successful form of managed care we call 'fundholding' to flourish. The GP's surgery is widely understood and accepted as the gateway to health care. Our system whereby the patient registers with the GP creates the practice list of patients, a concept at the heart of fundholding. Even in these days of high social mobility, the family doctor service provides some continuity of care for the individual, and often for the family. The GP is more aware of individual patients' needs than any Health Authority manager can ever be, and is one of the first to hear when the system fails to meet them. Through fundholding, the potent combination of the professional knowledge of the primary health care team and the enterprise culture of the medical practice is applied to the purchasing of health care.

At the heart of managed care is the concept of choice. Patients choose their GPs. Practices choose whether to leave all their purchasing to the Health Authority or to be purchasers themselves. If they decide to be purchasers, they can decide the extent of this, and whether to join a consortium. Purchasers choose their providers, who in turn choose their tertiary providers.

Where managed care co-exists with other approaches in a scheme designed to achieve equity for patients (such as the NHS), it is important that secondary care facilities treat referrals from the managed and 'unmanaged' sectors differently. To fail to do so is patronising to those clinicians operating in the managed sector, and is inequitable towards their patients who, as a group, are thus forced to wait longer for treatment than those of equal need in the unmanaged sector where referrals are more lightly made.

The principle of managed care is gradually being applied further down the health care chain. Some of the more progressive Trust hospitals are giving their clinical teams their own budgets for support services, allowing them to spend any saving on developments.

An obstacle to the further development of managed care is the current central guidance on tertiary referrals. We should perhaps adopt an arrangement where secondary providers accept the risk of tertiary referrals up to a certain level, and reflect this in their tariffs; beyond that level, the patient should be referred back to the GP with a recommendation for further treatment and, for rare or novel treatments, information about the outcomes of the proposed treatment.

SUPPORTING POTENTIAL AND NEW FUNDHOLDERS

The changes that are being made to the fundholding scheme go a long way to answer the criticisms that have been made of it. The scope of the standard scheme, while being extended, is also becoming much simpler to comprehend. Almost all practices are now eligible to be fundholders by one means or another. Moves on budget setting, though necessarily slow, are in the right direction to answer the criticism that fundholding has created two tiers of service. As we have found in South and West Devon, total fundholding is potentially compatible with locality purchasing and is being introduced with due regard for evaluation.

As fundholding becomes the mainstream culture of General Practice in England it can no longer be seen as professionally divisive. The concept that clinical resources have to be managed is becoming widely accepted. Fundholder groups are often driving forward service improvements for all patients in their locality. Nationally, fundholding has achieved for primary care a centre stage position in the NHS drama that has so often been promised but never before delivered.

Health Authorities should arrange events at which fundholding GPs can share their experiences and achievements with non-fundholding colleagues. The fundholders can describe how they have been able to prioritise their waiting lists by clinical need, or offer patients the choice of travelling further in order to be treated sooner. They can explain how they have improved standards for clinical communication, developed direct access to hospital services, enhanced the range of practice-based services, or reduced unnecessary outpatient appointments.

Non-fundholders often do not appreciate the improvement in relationships that results from fundholding; that consultants actually welcome the opportunity to discuss potential developments clinician to clinician. Nor do they appreciate the extent to which the information derived from fundholding can inform clinical debate within the practice, and improve collective decision making.

Some of the new Health Authorities are using the occasion of their formation to improve their accommodation, bringing staff together on a single site. They should give equal priority to ensuring that their front line purchasers have adequate accommodation. In particular, some practices would like to be purchasers but do not have the necessary office space.

If possible, preparation for fundholding should begin before the formal preparatory year. Practices considering fundholding may be understandably nervous about the organisational development required. Issues that have been latent for years may have to be addressed. Health Authorities can help here, by providing management or pharmaceutical advice. Better still, as in the southwest, they can encourage established fundholders in the locality to be mentors to those preparing for fundholding.

ALLOCATING RESOURCES FOR TOTAL PURCHASING

Many fundholders have felt constrained by the scope of the standard scheme, and have longed to bring the benefits of fundholding to a wider range of services. As against this, the non-elective services such as emergency admissions and the high cost procedures excluded from standard fundholding have been seen as too risky for the risk to be borne at practice level. The national pilots of total purchasing by fundholders provide the opportunity to resolve this debate.

Non-elective and expensive services can be included in a managed care scheme, provided that the subscriptions or allocations are wisely set and the risks analysed and, where necessary, shared.

There are no easy answers when it comes to allocating health resources, particularly at practice level. There is a strong case for moving from historical levels of resource use to weighted capitation at a defined rate which prevents major disruption to the market. It may also be necessary to make changes in budgets to reflect changes in contracting currencies.

As the existing mechanisms for sharing risk with providers do not operate at practice level, costed practice-allocated activity can easily vary by 15% or more from year to year. Hence, more than one year's data must be used to establish the baseline.

A patient aged 85 may spend twice as long in hospital as one aged 65, and yet generate the same geriatric medicine episode charge. A practice with a high elderly population that moves rapidly to resource-related contracting could find itself under-funded. Total purchasing pilots should move forward towards a world where resource consumption at each stage of patient care can be quantified and compared with clinical benefit. Funding mechanisms should promote not smother such initiatives. Where historical episode activity is used as the baseline, adjustments may be needed.

A decision then has to be made about the formula for capitation funding. The method used for distributing hospital and community health service funds to Health Authorities in England is essentially based on the analysis of relative needs of different geographical areas undertaken by a research team at the University of York.[1] If total purchasers and districts are funded the same way, any potential charge of two-tier funding is averted. Yet there may be a better method of calculating the age-cost curve. As a significant proportion of the rate of lifetime health care accrues during the last few months of life, it may be wiser to separate deaths, and generate an age-cost curve for survivors.[2]

Whatever capitation formula is selected, the same practices are likely to be outliers on the basis of their historical activity. Moving to capitation over a defined period allows time in which the capitation formula can be refined in the light of improved knowledge about need and demand at practice level.

There is a common misconception that the adjustments for age and deprivation in weighted capitation systems are small. In fact, they are, at practice level, very significant. It is instructive to look at the ranges of adjustment we have calculated for individual practices of at least 5000 patients, in South and West Devon. For the general and acute sector of the York model, the ranges are −31% to + 38% for age weighting and −13% to +16% for deprivation. The deprivation adjustments for the psychiatric sector are typically three times as great as for the general and acute, which is particularly important in such cities as Plymouth where much publicised individual cases have highlighted the need to strengthen the community support available to mentally ill people. The separation of practice-level budgets allows one to be confident that resources are being targeted at areas of deprivation. This, potentially, can be far more beneficial in ensuring that the provision of health services fairly reflects existing inequalities of health than any number of consultative committees informing pre-April 1996 Health Authorities.

MANAGING THE RISK TO PRACTICES AND HEALTH AUTHORITIES

Practices may regularly attract a population whose health care needs are skewed relative to the age-weighted expectation for patients in that catchment area. Perhaps one day we will have sufficient up-to-date information about needs at practice level and the fair cost of programmes of care to meet those needs (according to evidence-based protocols) to allow budget adjustments for this. Such adjustments must, though, be sustainable across all practices in a district.

The very occasional patient whose care is extremely expensive poses a particular risk at practice level. A group of practices can agree to share the cost of such patients, by top-slicing their budgets to create an insurance fund. The host practice can then pay the first £20,000, say, of each patient event, the balance being taken from the insurance fund.

The annual cost of providing health care to a patient obviously varies from patient to patient in the wider population. When one takes a sample of that population, there is an inevitable variability in the mean annual cost per patient for the sample. The larger the sample, the smaller that variability of the mean becomes. Where two different sample sizes are compared (such as a practice and a district), the ratio of the variabilities of the means is equal to the square root of the inverse ratio of the sample sizes. This relationship (which is simpler than it sounds) is useful in estimating levels of risk.

Part of the fluctuation in annual costs arising from random year-to-year changes in demand can be shared with providers. The rest can be shared with the new Health Authorities through a linear budget-smoothing mechanism. Total purchasing and, perhaps, standard fund-holding practices should be permitted to roll over overspends as well as savings up to an agreed limit into, say, the four following years. Such inevitable fluctuation is different from loss of management control. The latter can more easily be monitored in a multi-practice pilot. Total expenditure across the practices can be plotted on a control chart, within confidence limits. This aids judgement as to whether any particular pattern of expenditure is likely to represent a change to a new expected level, rather than being a random fluctuation.

Many risk factors tend to be concentrated in localities. These include environmental or genetic health problems, infectious diseases and disasters, and risks associated with transient populations, as well as factors internal to the NHS such as significant local tariff changes. In South and West Devon, we are running a total purchasing pilot in which the practices are geographically separated, which should assist risk management. There are other advantages. Dealing with different providers gives them a variety of experience to share. As the practices are not competing for patients, they are not subject to some of the constraints on open collaboration sometimes experienced by neighbouring practices. If successful, this model could be widely adopted, as it does not depend on all practices in a locality being at a similar level of development.

Total purchasing practices should be expected to accept the risks of the over £6000 costs for standard fundholding services for their own patients, and for any overspend on their own standard fundholding budgets. However, it is not reasonable for new Health Authorities at this stage to expect them to accept the risk of total purchasing overspends against their standard fundholding savings.

IMPROVING THE BALANCE OF SERVICES

Total purchasing increases the credibility of fundholders as purchasers, and helps in service developments which bridge the boundaries of the standard fundholding scheme. The key challenge facing total purchasers is to turn the concept into real improvements in patient care. Many see total purchasing as an opportunity to move the balance of health care towards the community.

Many (perhaps most) people in acute hospitals either stay too long or should not be there at all. They may be waiting for an operation, recovering from one but beyond the stage where fairly intensive care is needed, or simply in hospital because the community-based services or their carers can no longer cope. Rehabilitation requires specialist skills and is best delivered in a more homely, and perhaps less expensive environment, closer to family or carers, than an acute hospital.

Given good community reablement teams, resourced to provide quite intensive therapy and patient education over a short period, not only should some patients recuperate and achieve self-dependence much sooner, but others need never be admitted. If this is true for those who one hopes will be recovering to good health, it is also true for the provision of palliative care for those who are dying and would prefer to die at home. Similar arguments apply to inappropriate A & E attendances and the over-medicalisation of maternity services.

Many previous initiatives to re-balance services in favour of the community have insufficiently addressed the issue of clinical workload. Total purchasing provides the opportunity to resolve this. In our Devon pilot we are exploring various options for the status of a community rehabilitation physician to head a community reablement team with a range of therapeutic skills, and access to equipment, transport, and support services. Such a team is a key component of the wider primary health care team of the future.

Each patient needs a care plan which takes account of their individual circumstances. The best location for that care (whether a specialist community facility, a nursing home, or their own home), will depend on the patient's wishes, and the frequency and complexity of therapy they require. Ideally, for each component in the care plan, improvement in health should be compared with cost of provision. Yet as soon as this is attempted problems of poor quality information are met.

One may find that, under existing tariffs, the cost of care for a patient spending 20 weeks in an in-patient mental health facility but going home at weekends is 20 times what it would be if the patient did not go home at weekends. How, then, can one begin to compare the clinical gain per resource consumed of alternative community-based care programmes?

We can make progress only by fundamental reform of contracting currencies, and who better to lead this than total purchasers in partnership with the 1996 Health Authorities? The fact that the process is driven by the search for better clinical outcomes answers the argument that this is just turning doctors into accountants. The days of the finished consultant episode at average speciality price are numbered!

The provider Trusts working with our Devon pilot are well advanced in allocating their fixed and variable costs to new contracting currencies which will allow prices to reflect resource consumption more closely. The rules by which providers have to calculate tariffs are generally seen as being too restrictive, but they do have advantages here. The proposed allocation of costs is openly discussed and can be challenged; if there were cross-subsidies between services, the provider would keep its calculations secret.

There are two key interfaces when rebalancing services towards the community: hospital clinicians, and local social services teams. Early discussions are essential to achieve a collaborative approach. The aim must be to achieve early discharge by consent of the consultant, not by confrontation. The key here is well-designed community services. As patients will be leaving hospital before they are stable, social services teams may have to undertake discharge assessments in a wide variety of settings. They will need to consider rebalancing or redefining the interface between their hospital and community teams.

IMPROVING RELATIONSHIPS AND ACCOUNTABILITY

In dealing with General Medical Practices, Health Authorities must avoid smothering the very qualities which make small businesses tick, a mistake which financial institutions made in taking over estate agents in the late 1980s. Having paid rather generously for the professional and local knowledge and entrepreneurial skills of these successful businesses, many of the institutions dissipated those strengths, replacing concern for the client and rapid decision making with corporate imperatives and centralist processes. Staff and clients became disaffected, and the businesses were eventually sold off for a fraction of the price paid, with great loss of corporate pride.

In recent years NHS purchasers have been measured too mechanistically. The 1995 NHS Accountability Framework for GP fundholding is a substantial step in the direction of correcting this.[3] Though covering the main issues, it omits the extensive and detailed specification of expected responses which has often characterised NHS guidance documents in the past. It sets a tone which, though right for the new NHS, sits uneasily alongside some existing requirements. Many health authorities are concerned that they will be held closely accountable for delivery of performance to which their fundholders must contribute, but for which those fundholders are only loosely accountable.

The gradual resolution of this will be very beneficial to the NHS. It should lead to quantified indicators of performance that are more meaningful, and to greater willingness to trust the qualitative judgements of performance review managers. Above all, it should give purchasers greater space to develop better patient services.

We must now increasingly focus accountability on outcome rather than process. That need not inhibit Health Authorities from challenging practices' plans, provided they do so constructively. However, purchasers will need a new sense of responsibility. It will no longer be sufficient to 'feed the beast' by producing slightly manufactured performance figures. Actual improvements in services and health must be demonstrated, especially to the public.

Health Authorities that may be wondering whether power is shifting too far towards primary care should not respond by stressing accountability to themselves. Rather they should ensure that the freedoms of primary care are counterbalanced by informed patient choice. Is there sufficient choice of primary care provision in an area where such choice can reasonably be expected? Is there sufficient information for patients to make an informed choice of practice? Do fundholders consult sufficiently about their plans, and do they report to their patients and the wider community on how they performed against those plans? One of the practices in our pilot is using total purchasing as an opportunity to explain the benefits of fundholding to the local Community Health Council, and to involve them in service planning.

The fact that total purchasing is currently free from central regulation allows a new style of working. Ideas can be explored in an atmosphere of learning together. To help this along, Health Authorities should avoid colluding with providers to reconfigure the supply side of the market and thus pre-empt innovation.

The developing sense of partnership may be put at risk as the emphasis of performance management by health authorities swings from secondary to primary care. Health Authorities may one day find themselves actively managing or regulating the primary care market, authorising applications for new partners, accrediting practices for various levels of fundholding, and publishing league tables of practice performance. Many of these developments, if they occur, will seem threatening to GPs. The challenge, then, will be to maintain the spirit of collaboration currently being developed. Supporting the vast majority of practices who wish to see clinical resource management improved will continue to be a priority.

REFERENCES

1. Carr-Hill R, Hardman G, Martin S, Peacock S, Shelton T, Smith P 1994 A formula for distributing NHS revenues based on small area use of hospital beds. University of York
2. Bevan G 1996 Personal communication. University of Bristol
3. National Health Service Executive 1995 Accountability Framework for GP Fundholding. EL (95) 54, NHSE, London

17. Reconfiguring providers

Anita Grabarz

HISTORIC TRENDS AND COST PRESSURES

The new April 1996 policy of Primary Care-Led NHS needs to be understood in the context of dramatic changes in health care over the next 10 years. Primary, community and acute services must continue not only to evolve, but come together to meet the new requirements now facing almost every aspect of health care. People are living longer and have higher expectations, and demands are outstripping resources.

The universal pressures for these changes can be summarised as follows:

- Effectiveness issues around increasing sub-specialisation and the need to achieve sufficient volumes to maintain expertise;
- Continual advances in drugs that offer new benefits, e.g. beta interferon for MS patients;
- Increasing amounts of minimally invasive surgery and day case trends;
- Technology improvement that will allow more home based care less hospital attendance and better outcomes of treatments;
- Improving patients outcomes by combining scarce expertise, equipment and skills, as a result of which not all hospitals should provide all services;
- Changing patterns of medical training;
- Changing patterns of clinical effectiveness which require more consultant delivered services;
- Decreasing availability means tasks previously undertaken by junior doctors will have to be carried out by consultants, technicians and nurses depending on safe practice;

Particularly in the major cities and their suburbs acute hospitals have adopted marketing strategies to survive by providing a whole spectrum of specialties to their local residents (and anyone else who can access them easily or wants to be referred). Trying to maintain a fully comprehensive brief across such a wide range of services is now of questionable value. As primary and community services develop, health care is being provided by other professionals; there are more opportunities for training, learning new skills, enriching existing skills, low technology developments and shared care. Patients have choices and usually prefer to use services based at their family doctor's surgery or a nearby primary care centre, than to attend the impersonal out-patient services.

In the suburbs of outer London (or instead the hinterlands of Manchester and Birmingham) there are groups of small hospitals all trying to maintain a comprehensive range of services within a few miles of each other, it is no surprise that purchasers are seeking to undertake acute service reviews. To do nothing would result in the increasing costs for advances in medical technology, hospital high dependency care, investigation and screening being multiplied by the number of hospitals within the boundaries of a District.

The new 1996 Health Authorities must undertake such reviews hand in hand with their GPs, fundholding and non-fundholding. GPs know all about their patients' individual needs and the needs of their practice population. The integrated Health Authority can bring in the broader picture of total local populations as well as the national imperatives, e.g. Health of the Nation targets. In this way effective signals can be agreed by all referrers as part of the primary-care led strategy. Purchasing intentions will then reflect need rather than historical perspectives and enable and influence acute units to address long term direction.

Small acute hospitals are facing their problems too. It becomes harder and harder to manage a 350 to 400 bedded unit as income barely matches inflation. The major source of income is via in-patient contracts but as the break away from traditional models of care gathers momentum (e.g. the introduction of more ambulatory care in the primary sector) in-patient income is reduced. And all the time their services are competing in the internal market, subject to contract changes each and every year.

OPPORTUNITIES TO ADVANCE ACUTE CARE

The NHS reforms have increased the pace and range of change. The resultant opportunities include:

Changing medical practice

Clinicians are always endeavouring to improve medical practice hence the emergence of minimally invasive surgery. This trend will continue; offering patients day case surgery rather than open surgery and inpatient stays.

Questioning clinical effectiveness

The decline of the traditional DGH is also being brought about by the need to justify clinical interventions. At last, after 40 years of the medical model, evidence of effectiveness is now being pursued on the whole range of services.

Increasingly stringent training requirements

Clinical Medical Education and Clinical Professional Development audits mean that the consultant and specialist grade posts, created to cope with the lower junior doctors' hours and provide more consultant delivered care, will have to spend more time learning. The Calman Report on medical training requirements also expects far greater teaching requirements resulting in less time with patients. For some specialties this could mean consultants with additional administrative sessions losing around one third of clinical practice time in their working week.

Increasing sub-specialisation

The need to develop and maintain expertise will hit the smaller branches of sub-specialties, particularly those within General Medicine and General Surgery. There will be requirements to obtain a critical mass to ensure: the necessary effectiveness, efficiency and economy of skills, technology and other resources to provide improved complex and high dependency care. Small 'stand alone' services run by a couple of consultants may no longer be acceptable.

Shifting ambulatory care

The 1996 policy for new Health Authorities' Primary Care-Led Purchasing is going to influence new patterns of care especially around ambulatory services. In London this has been fostered by the efforts and support of the London Implementation Group initiative, which is creating opportunities for more and more chronic disease management to be undertaken outside the district general hospital, thereby threatening traditional out-patient and ward attender services.

Shifting post-operative and palliative care

Developments in partnership with community hospitals and voluntary sector social services are now also affecting acute hospital long stay patients. Again, as alternatives take shape, the length of stay at an acute unit can be reduced as patients are offered an alternative choice of care in the primary sector.

The combination of all these factors makes planning for future health care daunting. It becomes almost impossible to do en masse. The job has to be broken down into specialty by specialty changes. Even so this can create an information overload and it is important to be clear about the methodology required to assess future demand. At New River Health Authority we use the following list of information clusters for analysis:

- Admission by condition and length of stay, broken into both emergency and elective.
- Day case activity and possibilities.
- Current volumes and activity levels.
- Referral patterns by practices to ratio of admissions (to assess what alternatives could be useful and viable, if any).
- Waiting times in terms of unmet changes in practice/skills demand and increasing low waiting time targets.
- Case mix and age analysis — standardised information for accurate comparison.
- Required consultant expertise to assess tertiary patterns now and those required longer term.
- Long term trends in demography and epidemiology.
- Best practice indicators that affect current service structures, e.g. number of required consultants and volume of experience.
- Costs per procedure/per night.

This list will vary from specialty to specialty. For Accident and Emergency one would include a lot more information on access time, skill availability by time of day, and so on. The quantitative information is only one part of the picture. We have learnt the importance of working with professionals in both the primary and secondary care sector to prepare qualitative analysis about what is currently good or bad and how this could change in the future. This needs to be stimulated by information on health care developments on a national and even international basis. A series of questionnaires, interviews, specialty conferences, focus groups, etc., can all help to educate the local stakeholders, including the purchasers and the public, on how to advance health care locally.

Having collected so much data it is then important to clarify trends for each of the services in order to build up assumptions about the future, and to be able to work on developing the process in collaboration with the primary and secondary care sectors. The London Health Economics Consortium at the London School of Hygiene and Tropical Medicine, uses a planning tool that is tremendously helpful to us in clarifying how to apply information gathered to assess trends in hospital utilisation.[1] Each new Authority requires an equivalent resource.

The lynch pin that helps draw together the quantitative analysis and quantitative analysis is the age standardised and case mix standardised admission information by condition. This should be plotted alongside length of stay (LOS) in order to examine:

1. The input stage — what alternative services save a hospital admission at the 'ambulatory stage'?
2. The LOS under 3 days — what could be offered in terms of ambulatory care? What are the commonest reasons for overnight stays?
3. The LOS between 3 days and 11 days — the management of those patients that are likely to continue to need acute hospital care.
4. The LOS over 11 days — the very ill patient, or patient requiring longer rehabilitative care or social care. What changes can be achieved by closer health and social care liaison?

Drawing together this information helps stakeholders to look at the changes needed; prioritising which conditions should receive attention first and merit piloted improvements; being careful to monitor the impact on resources.

The new 1996 Health Authorities need to remember that acute service reviews are fairly common place. Networking with neighbouring authorities is, therefore, very useful, and if these Authorities also purchase from the hospitals being reviewed, it is essential and must be part of the review process.

Not all hospital services can be addressed on a specialty basis and the interdependent nature of some services can unfortunately be too easily ignored by an individual building brick approach. It is important to take into account links between services, e.g. general surgery and oncology, in the design of different service patterns.

POLITICAL DIMENSIONS OF CHANGES TO ACUTE CARE

It will be tempting, after April 1996, for the new Health Authorities with virtually all the NHS resources at their disposal to dive into organisational solutions for solving over capacity on current sites. The best way to do this, some believe, is to take a central planning approach. First, spend a few days away visioning (preferably with a few GPs); second, put into a project format checking critical pathways; third, decide steps 1 to 12; and finally go out and sell it.

However, acute hospital Chief Executives in London and elsewhere are not tapping their fingers on the desk waiting for purchasers to produce solutions, particularly the solution that expects their exit from the market. Primary Care professionals will not consider this fair play either. Reconfiguring providers is above all about working with people, understanding the politics and the organisations.

Political support for any further hospital closures is now declining. There are fears that the changes have been too fast and that the alternatives being put in place are not yet proven. The August 1995 statement by the new Secretary of State, Stephen Dorrell, which requested greater attention be paid to local opinion on local services, can be interpreted as a directive for no more controversial actions that go against community views. Some have seen this applying particularly in the North Thames region to the 'noisy' closures of St Bartholomews Hospital and the merger of Guy's Hospital and St Thomas's.

Acute strategies are very high profile and political insensitivity can cost careers. There always needs to be communication with constituent MPs on a regular basis and not just when there is a crisis. Political acquiescence is more likely to be achieved if there is a groundswell of medical opinion for change that is being accepted by the public.

Purchasers are not yet trusted in 1996 by the population they are trying to represent. The public consider they own their local hospitals — this is particularly the case when a distinct local community is easily discernible and is highlighted by a hospital's ability to control the media through the public's basic belief in doctors. Purchasers trying to develop rational arguments for service improvements are often ignored as mere bureaucrats.

People tend to interpret change as just more cuts in health care and in this context, rational debate can cease and emotions take over. A resident population need to be informed, involved and given clear expectations about the direction of health care. Users should be encouraged and empowered towards self-advocacy and autonomy concerning their health. Purchasers and providers must remember the public now expect easier access to information on conditions covering both investigation procedures and effectiveness to enable them to demand standards on both prevention and treatment issues.

CREATING EFFECTIVE STRATEGIC VISION WITH PURCHASER AND PROVIDER SUPPORT

Using a framework of People, Politics and Organisations in Enfield and Haringay we have seen our first task as a detailed stakeholder analysis. It is worth studying each stakeholder's perspective, their amount of influence on events and the incentives that can be used to keep them on board throughout the process. The stakeholder analysis must be part of the communication strategy to support the process. Stakeholders need to be regularly communicated with about proposals and next steps, and well before any formal announcements are made.

Rules of engagement are vital to achieve a vision but are dependent on the time available and opportunistic events. For example a purchaser 'hands on' approach, with top down direction may be more necessary in cases of severe financial pressure, e.g. Liverpool had estates rationalisation issues at five of their main hospitals in 1995–96, whilst in North London the Barnet and Edgware DGHs were trying to survive supplying a population of 300 000 between them. A list of rules of engagement drawn from these could now include:

- Purchasers drawing up the boundaries, e.g. making clear the limits to what the strategy can achieve and suggest structures for leading and monitoring the process;
- All parties agreeing how medical and health professional opinion can be involved in the changes across all sectors: primary, priority, community and acute;
- All parties agreeing how medical and health professional opinion can be referenced against provider senior managers' views;

- All parties agreeing the building bricks to use to profile the current and future picture of acute hospital care;
- Purchasers and providers agreeing on methodology/calculation of:
  - Changes to specialty e.g. develop frameworks for specialty reviews that elicit advances in patterns of care and create agreed assumptions about changes in hospital utilisation;
  - Assess future demand via: population trends, epidemiological trends and changes in service patterns with implications for future investment.

It needs to be understood that invariably acute service strategies are complex with a record of coercive change management programmes. Collaboration is precious and degrees of opposition inevitable. It is important to recognise and understand the reasons for the latter and the sources of the first. We have found the following checklist helpful for these purposes:

Nurturing collaboration

- Agree common aims that stem from the quality and effectiveness of care;
- Involvement in devising and delivering a process e.g. the 'how' rather than the 'what';
- Share work, risks and rewards, e.g. joint working on key activities and attainment of milestones;
- Stress evolutionary, not revolutionary change; hospitals can feel destabilised by the very fact there is a review;
- Commitment to building long term relationships, robust partnerships;
- New language, less emphasis on the word 'change' and more emphasis on terms such as 'advances', 'health gain' and 'patient benefits'.

Barriers to collaboration

- Predetermined plan thus collaboration is perceived to be a sham;
- Real fear about the cost of change, both in organisational and personal terms;
- Win or lose stakes: nothing being offered to create win/win;
- Power confrontation: hospitals prepared to use political and media influence to expose changes to the public as negative if it affects organisational viability;

- Bad timing: good work can be lost if the sequence of consultation, communication and events was wrong;
- Too many people becoming involved to the point decision-making which becomes so long that interest wanes. There must be sufficient incentives to keep stakeholders on board.

Changes that will affect fundamental traditions, if they are to be achicvcd by consensus, need time for people to to develop trust and mutual understanding of all the different perspectives; sometimes the backtracking and attention to details will be very tedious in order to get everyone in agreement. If stakeholders cannot predict the outcome, or argue for a vision, they only have 'the how' to concentrate on. Process is all important.

PRIMARY AND COMMUNITY CARE ROLE IN ACUTE STRATEGIES

The continued shift from the secondary care sector to primary and community services is a national imperative, but there is a growing capacity problem. GPs are generally feeling that they are being overwhelmed by increasing patient expectations and demands, particularly in the London area. This has been exacerbated by problems with current GP career strutures and payments disputes around out of hours care.

This capacity problem can be relieved by the community care sector supporting GP practices who want to have more patient involvement or less acute intervention, e.g. through operating low dependency wards for a locality or consortia of practices.

Over the past 2 years the London Implementation Group's (LIG) endeavours have enabled robust improvements to be made in community and primary care initiatives and furthered the whole thrust of GP led primary care teams. In areas such as Enfield and Haringey, investment has been used to create resource centres/poly clinics or simply to extend GP premises. This has enabled GPs to offer more services from their surgery, or refer their patients to a nearby centre/clinic or even a colleague's practice, to receive care that would otherwise have been provided by the acute hospital. This has greatly improved both geographical and physical access, especially for client groups who find acute hospitals daunting, impcrsonal and unfamiliar.

Through the creation of a merged FHSA and DHA organisation there should now be a similar gain for the new Health Authorities in their primary care negotiations and planning for future services. As primary care-led services evolve beyond improvements to the lot of the individual patient and take into account population or locality needs then old referral habits can wither on the vine.

For many purchasers, there is a still general difficulty in trying to claw back money from acute hospitals as primary sector alternatives become operational. We have found that this conundrum of acute hospitals not keen on shifting any of their resources out and primary care capacity not able to take anything more on, can be improved by the emphasis being on Primary Care-Led Purchasing. Supported by needs-based assessments, PCLP can mean the delivery of care being left to those most able to provide safe, effective, efficient and more easily accessible health care. The emphasis is on primary care leading the decision making.

IMPACT ON THE DISTRICT GENERAL HOSPITAL

The DGH is better able to manage its future if it is truly aware of its competencies and stops trying to provide all services. In each District, a long term strategy is needed that plays to the Trusts strengths in the market place. Such a plan should try to reflect solutions or coping mechanisms to meet the current pressures for change. These include:

- Negotiating with the Primary Care Sector the primary care work that could continue to be offered through HCHS contracts, albeit, perhaps, at different geographical locations, e.g. dermatology being offered from community clinics or other primary care resource centres;
- Building on niche specialties to offer patients complete packages of care; demonstrating a willingness to form partnerships with community hospitals and primary care professionals for parts of the service;
- Increasing links with tertiary centres to meet demands of sub-specialisation and referral mechanisms for higher technical care;
- Creating partnerships with community hospitals to improve seamless care for patients with rehabilitation needs;
- Merging smaller specialties with another hospital (dependent on which services were most appropriate), or reaching agreements with consortia of hospitals for consultant work across two or more sites. This creates greater flexibility, makes recruitment easier and promotes the hospitals' ability to comply with new training requirements;

- Capitalising on diagnostic expertise by offering high technology investigations and one stop shops so that patients can benefit from faster diagnosis;
- Bidding for research and audit monies to demonstrate commitment, followed by timely implementation of best practice;
- Organising communication to match GP requirements and being responsive to service improvements;
- Merging hospitals to reduce management and support service costs and create sufficient flexibility to cope with health care changes in the long term.

The alternative is to carry on regardless and cope with incremental changes as they happen until the point where the market may not offer sufficient business to keep the hospital viable. This alternative is, in effect, opting for high profile crisis management.

The further development of contracting tools will only improve purchasers' manipulation of the market, through case mix disaggregation, more cost and volume contract, more market testing, etc. This will hasten the speed of change, and strengthen the imperative to reconfigure providers.

In summary, all health care professionals need now to contribute and plan for strategic change. Purchasers may 'hold the ring', but because acute services reviews touch on so many complex areas expertise across primary and secondary care divides must be pooled. Through collaboration new service patterns can be designed and achieved to offer patients and their carers: safe effective health care which is easily accessible with increased opportunities for them to exercise their autonomy.

REFERENCE

1. Edwards J 1994 Bed-for-Londoners. The Current State of London's Acute Care. London Health Economics Consortium, London School of Hygiene and Tropical Medicine.

18. Building on localities

John Kirtley

INTRODUCTION

The concept of a Locality, as a focus for service delivery or planning, has been used in the NHS for some years. More recently, the concept has been used by purchasing Authorities. There are many dimensions to the definition of a locality. This chapter describes how a locality focus was developed by the Health Commission in Portsmouth and South East Hampshire from early 1994.

BACKGROUND: PORTSMOUTH AND SOUTH EAST HAMPSHIRE

The new Portsmouth and South East Hampshire Health Authority covers a population of around 540 000. The area encompasses Portsmouth City and adjoining conurbations of Fareham and Gosport to the west and Havant to the east. To the north of Havant and the City of Portsmouth the area is more rural and extends beyond the town of Petersfield, some 20 miles inland from the coast.

For many years the delivery of community health services in the district has been based on three broadly comparable populations; Portsmouth City, with a population of around 180 000, Fareham and Gosport with a combined population of around 190 000 and Havant and East Hampshire covering around 170 000 people. In addition to focusing district general hospital services on two main hospitals within Portsmouth City, an equally important element of service development strategy in recent years was the planned provision of four community hospitals serving the population centres outside of Portsmouth city — Petersfield, Gosport, Havant and Fareham. New community hospital developments have been commissioned in Petersfield and Gosport within the last 3 years, and elements of community hospital provision are either in place or planned to serve both Havant and Fareham.

Needs assessment and service planning have also had a community focus. The third edition of a Community Health Atlas was published in 1993. This consisted of nearly 100 maps covering population and household characteristics, fertility, mortality, morbidity and lifestyle patterns. The maps were based on 23 neighbourhoods which were aggregates of electoral wards.

The establishment of the Portsmouth Health Commission in 1992 brought together management arrangements for primary and secondary care. This was the catalyst for the development of a locality focus for commissioning of health services. The strategic intention behind the development of a locality focus in Portsmouth and South East Hampshire was to ensure a Health Commission responsive to local needs for service commissioning and the development of primary care.

Locality commissioning has now been developed by many Authorities in the NHS. The structure and size of localities vary enormously, as do the defined aims for locality commissioning across the country. Some 'old' Districts of populations exceeding 200 000 have become 'localities' as authorities merged. The aims and objectives for locality commissioning in Portsmouth and South East Hampshire are set out below. This is followed by the definition of 'locality' adopted in Portsmouth and South East Hampshire.

LOCALITY COMMISSIONING OBJECTIVES

The aims of developing locality commissioning in Portsmouth and South East Hampshire were for locality commissioning managers to work with GPs and other primary care staff, voluntary organisations, statutory agencies and consumers to:

- Develop and extend primary care services;
- Establish local arrangements which ensured that the combined purchase of secondary and community care reflects needs;
- Act as the main representative of the Health Commission locally, with particular regard to health improvement strategies, quality issues and consumerism concerns;
- Ensure that local issues were reflected in the continuing development of Health Commission strategies and its own organisational development.

The overall aim of a locality focus was agreed early in 1994. Three core objectives, within the overall aims, were then agreed. These were:

- Development of primary care;
- Improved purchasing of secondary and community care;
- Locally based Health Commission representation.

In early 1994 the detailed objectives for Locality Managers within each of these three core areas were set out as follows:

Development of primary care

- Establish a database of current primary care services provided by practices and contribute to the development of a management information system;
- Develop practice plans which form a basis for additional investment;
- Develop pilot projects which extend the scope and range of services in primary care;
- Plan recurring investment in primary care to provide equitable local access to an extended range of services, following successful piloting;
- Assess and monitor resource allocation to practices within the community service provision by the local Trust;
- Liaise with Social Services to provide a commissioning input into joint planning locally.

Purchasing of hospital and community care

- Ascertain GP and public views on services being purchased and on those required;
- Provide information and advice to GPs on referral options for hospital and community care;
- Participate in contract discussions and negotiations with local providers;
- Monitor and co-ordinate views on local providers' achievements of quality requirements and promote further quality improvement and standards;
- Raise GP awareness of comparative cost effectiveness of services purchased and options available;
- Assist in the development of practice based information systems and links to Health Commission databases/systems;

- Assess the feasibility of locally held and managed budgets for agreed aspects of health care purchasing.

Locally based Commission representation

- Strengthen relationships, communications and working alliances locally and lead local discussions on health care needs;
- Act as frontline listening posts to ascertain consumer needs/expectations and satisfaction;
- Act as a facilitator for health improvement;
- Elicit local views on perceived and desired quality of services;
- Promote the development of local charters and patient participation;
- Coordinate and promote needs assessment initiatives which inform local service planning.

In 1996 the target desired outcomes which follow from these objectives remain as follows:

- Locally responsive contracts for secondary and community care;
- Extended range of primary care services;
- Patient sensitive flexibility and choice;
- Improved service monitoring intelligence;
- Local arrangements for eliciting public views;
- Improved quality requirements and standards;
- Information dissemination in terms of best practice concerning consumerism, quality, health promotion, health improvement, health gain and outcome measures.

The development of locality commissioning in Portsmouth and South East Hampshire was, from the outset, designed to be comprehensive in providing a single management focus for primary care, secondary care and the consumer. During 1994 other Authorities were focusing on a single dimension, such as consumerism. Whilst it is not claimed that the comprehensive approach in Portsmouth was unique it was, for the time, ambitious in that it was a deliberate attempt to draw together three key elements in single management posts, and it has served as a model for some Authorities now planning for the integration of DHA and FHSA functions in a Primary Care-Led NHS.

DEFINING A LOCALITY

There were several important factors taken into account in agreeing locality boundaries. The key was balancing achievable workloads, management costs, and crucially, allowing Locality Managers time to relate on a regular basis to a manageable number of GP practices.

Key 'geographical' factors also taken into account included District Council, Electoral Ward and Social Service boundaries as well as GP practice location and populations. In addition, the often quoted concept of natural communities or neighbourhoods were also an important influence. The latter are difficult to define, but easy to recognise in a local context.

Original proposals were to establish eight localities, although this was subsequently reduced to six. There was also considerable debate with GP practices about boundaries, particularly within the City of Portsmouth. The city was clearly too big as a single locality when the number of GP practices were taken into account, but options for sub-division generated considerable discussion.

Four Locality Commissioning Managers were recruited in April 1994. Following experience between July and the late autumn of 1994 a further two Locality Commissioning Managers were recruited at the end of 1994. The make up of the six localities is as follows:

1. Fareham: 10 Practices, total list size of 88 000.
2. Gosport: 11 Practices, total list size of 87 000.
3. North Portsmouth: 15 Practices, total list size of 107 000.
4. South Portsmouth: 16 Practices, total list size of 72 000.
5. Central Havant: 14 Practices, total list size of 90 000.
6. East Hampshire and North Havant: 15 Practices, total list size of 98 000.

LOCALITY MANAGERS: ASSEMBLING THE TEAM

As well as looking for individual experience and characteristics, an important criteria in recruiting to the total of six posts was the assembly of a team with a range and mix of skills. There are considerable benefits in having a range of skills available across the team of six Locality Commissioning Managers, as a resource for each other. The key requirement, however, is the ability to relate and communicate with a range of health professionals, particularly in primary care, as well as voluntary organisations and the public.

Three of the team were recruited from FHSA backgrounds. These included provision of nursing advice, team training and development, and operational management of GMS, planning and regulation. Two Locality Managers were recruited with experience and backgrounds in contracting; one from an Acute Trust perspective which included operational management, and the second from a Purchasing Authority with experience in contracting for community care services. The final member of the team provided a background in public health, which included epidemiology and also responsibility for leading health promotion projects.

A key element of working arrangements is the provision of bases both in the locality and also in the Health Commission offices. The former usually involved health centre or community hospital accommodation. Another important element of working arrangements is that the six Locality Managers are 'paired'. This provides continuity in terms of absence, but also avoids duplication in terms of participation in some Local Authority initiatives; this also reflects the tripartite organisation of community service delivery referred to earlier. The pairings are Fareham and Gosport, the two localities in Portsmouth City, and Havant and East Hampshire.

A vital part of developing the appropriate focus for locality commissioning is GP participation. Whilst it is important for links to be built up with individual practices, it was felt that there was also a role for Lead GPs for each of the six localities. Each Locality Commissioning Manager therefore has a lead GP relating to the same group of practices. The Lead GP role covers both general and locality specific responsibilities; these are summarised below under these two headings.

General: Commission wide responsibilities

- Membership of the Commission's GP Advisory Panel;
- Establishing and maintaining mechanisms for seeking views of GPs in the locality;
- Provision of, or assistance in, commissioning other professional advice;
- Discussion of policy issues with Directors.

Specific: locality issues

- Contributions to Health Commission documents, such as annual Purchasing Intentions, and to participate in local consultation on these.
- Identification of, and feedback on, service quality and access aspects of secondary care, including patient satisfaction.

- Provision of local GP views on priorities for primary and secondary care investment, including research and development. This includes issues of clinical and cost-effectiveness.
- Support the Locality Manager and help in development of this role, including evaluation of practice based projects for extending the scope and range of primary care.

Nominations for Lead GPs were sought from the District Committee of GPs (DCGP). The appointments are renewable annually. The time commitment is the equivalent of one session a week, which the Health Commission pays at the equivalent of the rate for a Clinical Assistant. Using the District Committee as a source of nominations from individual localities was the correct approach. However, almost inevitably, there were some difficulties resulting from differing elements of the role as perceived by the Commission and General Practice.

The Commission wished to ensure GP advice and input along the lines set out above in the summary of the role specification. Seeking nominations through the DCGP led to views amongst some GPs that there was a 'shop steward' representative element to the role. The key here is clarity on agreeing the mechanism for setting the agenda.

The establishment of locality commissioning arrangements, and filling Locality Managers and Lead GPs' posts was an important step in the Health Commission's own organisational development. A steering group of three Directors, covering the areas of Primary Care, Secondary Care Contracting and Quality and Consumerism has maintained oversight of the introduction and development of locality commissioning. This has included reviewing achievements against objectives, identifying support or development needs of individual Locality Commissioning Managers, and reflecting on feedback received concerning progress.

RESULTS SO FAR

Like the development of a Primary Care-Led NHS itself, the development of a locality focus for a Health Authority is long term. However, some improvements are made much more quickly.

Communications

The first improvement, though obvious with hindsight, is worth stating. Dialogue, understanding and true communication with

practices is only achievable with regular contact. These relationships take time to develop and mature. The Commission had been
making efforts to consult with practices on specific issues, such as
the annual Purchasing Intentions prior to appointment of Locality
Managers. However, the only regular point of contact for 82 practices was a single Manager, with assistance from one support post.
Locality Managers are now each responsible for relating to manageable numbers of between 10 and 16 practices, covering between
42 and 59 GPs.

Practice planning

More regular and detailed dialogue has allowed the development of
practice planning, aimed at agreeing a longer term perspective on
how individual practices can and should develop as primary care
providers. For example, in relation to cash limited GMS, this has
allowed an annual bidding system to be replaced by a more rational
planning model. This allows a greater understanding of why developments are required, how it fits into a longer term service plan,
and consequently allows better decision making on priorities.

Spreading innovation

More regular communication has also fostered a wider participation in pilot projects aimed at extending the scope and range of services to be provided in primary care. This has extended beyond
such areas as practice based physiotherapy, mental health counselling and minor surgery and into the provision of advice on
Social Security benefits and common illnesses, as well as provision
of alternative therapies and primary care for the homeless. Other
areas of innovation have also included provision of medical equipment for practices for testing and treatment in primary care, which
has demonstrably reduced referrals to hospitals.

Initially participation in pilots was limited to larger or more forward looking practices. The position has now been reached where
virtually all the Authority's 82 practices are participating and bene-
fiting from pilot funding or the roll out of successful developments, following evaluation, such as practice based physiotherapy.

More charters

Practice Charters have been developed at a swift pace. Prior to
Locality Manager appointment, less than 20% of practices were

developing Charters; within a year more than 60% had Charters completed with the remainder in development.

Towards devolved contracts

Attention has now been focused on testing arrangements to devolve current District-wide contracts to a practice and locality level. Contract areas being considered are broadly comparable to those areas covered by Community Fundholding and include District Nursing, Health Visiting, Community Midwifery, Physiotherapy, Occupational Therapy, Chiropody, Dietetics and Pathology. Community Fundholding can provide a more direct mechanism through which these can be achieved

The aim is to devolve to practice level, through Locality Managers, control of the main elements of the primary health care team. This control should allow practices to use resources flexibly to respond to increased demands, and their own views of service priorities. This is a particularly attractive development for the Portsmouth Commission, where in 1995 only 10 of the 82 practices were Fundholders.

BACK TO THE FUTURE

Regular liaison between Lead GPs and the practices within their localities has allowed a more widespread feedback to the Commission on GP views. The frequency and formality of gatherings vary, but all localities have in place some arrangements for Lead GPs and Locality Managers to seek views and test issues with all of the practices in the locality. The relationship between the Commission's Executive Team and Lead GPs as a group is also developing. However, there are areas where, at this stage, Lead GPs feel uncomfortable in giving views. For example, discussions on limitations on plastic surgery procedures for purely cosmetic reasons are characterised as a rationing debate, and not relished by Lead GPs. However, even in this area dialogue concerning definition of legitimate exceptions to blanket exclusions has benefited from useful contributions by some of the Lead GPs.

Participation of GPs in difficult areas, such as those perceived as rationing, is vital to ensure a true Primary Care-Led NHS. Primary care led should not just allow GPs the opportunity for clear expressions or views on shortcomings of secondary care provision, or priorities for additional developments, whilst allowing issues of efficiency, clinical effectiveness and value for money to be ignored.

Another key area for future development which cannot be ignored concerns the evolution of audit, quality standards and performance management in primary care itself. If the NHS is to be primary care-led then it must set an example of excellence in service provision. These will not be easy areas to address. The continuance of the Independent Contractor status within primary care is a dimension which will always figure in how these issues can be approached. For example, at the time of writing unrest and low morale amongst GPs is currently focused on the out-of-hours dispute. This makes addressing the issues of audit, quality and performance management particularly difficult. However, a locality focus provides an opportunity for genuine attempts at understanding a practice's problems and opportunities and comparing performance, however measured, both within a locality where common problems can be anticipated, and also across localities for a wider range of comparators. The aim should be clear to all concerned. It is service improvement, through investment, training and organisational development where needed. Full participation of the primary care team is essential.

Issues for consideration in introducing a locality approach include, not least, definition of management objectives to be delivered through a locality approach. The definition of localities also has many dimensions and requires a clear view on which dimensions are fundamental in achieving the agreed aims and objectives. Assembling the correct team, ensuring GP participation, and working arrangements require close attention.

Moving forward the development as a whole depends on a massive infrastructure of relationships between Locality Managers, primary health care teams, statutory agencies, the voluntary and private sector and the public. Milestones can be identified. In Portsmouth and South East Hampshire the first one was the establishment of a rational planning system for development of primary care services. The second milestone is the devolution of community care contracts to practice and locality level. Further development of a Primary Care-Led NHS, can be measured in time by success in development of a performance management system for primary care which involves the active participation of practices and their primary care teams.

The new 1996 Health Authorities have to earn the right to undertake true performance management of General Practice, with practices as full participants in the process. This requires recognising the use of appropriate peer review in clinical areas and a track record of supporting appropriate developments and initiatives for extending the range and scope of primary care provision.

It can be argued that the move to a Primary Care-Led NHS is the ultimate endorsement of a bottom-up approach. Within primary care a focus on the practice, and localities, reflects a commitment at Health Authority level to just such a bottom-up approach.

19. Planning community care

David Dungworth

The challenge of planning and integrating social and health care within the community has occupied local authorities and Health Authorities since the inception of the Community Care concept. It has been complicated by difficult legislative structures, conflicting priorities and goals, planning cycles that rarely coincide, and emergent strategies that have lead to both a sense of opportunity and confusion. The introduction of a Primary Care-Led NHS has created the possibility of a multiplicity of stakeholders challenging the very foundations of a centralised planning system. It demands an approach that is both flexible and pragmatic in dealing with very local issues from relatively small practice populations. At the same time NHS- wide issues cannot be ignored. Planning in 1996 has become the art of integrating national and local issues to form an agenda that is meaningful to all those involved.

For Community Health Services the implementation of Community Care has been neither straightforward nor consistent in its development and many political issues continue to cloud further progress. None is more difficult for both local authorities and Health Authorities (and patients and carers) than the question of charging. It has complicated joint working and planning, particularly where this has been seen to lead logically to joint purchasing. To make joint purchasing and planning meaningful the cost benefit equation must be seen to outweigh the political bureaucracy that might be introduced to ensure that patients are still receiving NHS health services free at the point of delivery. This chapter looks at the background to the new partnership that is being forged, and considers how existing priorities and planning processes can be shared to create new roles and directions for this wider set of participants. Some consideration is given to the 'extra value' that the primary care perspective can give, particularly in relation to practice based information. A number of practical, if tentative, possibilities will be considered that attempt to give meaning to those who are planning services for very large numbers of individuals against those whose main concern is doing their best for the particular individual who is seeking their help.

NHS PLANNING

NHS national Planning and Priorities Guidance has changed considerably over recent years. Gone are the planning documents that, if implemented, would lead to massive and unsustainable change in the NHS. The new reality relies on a tighter core of critical issues that can be translated into meaningful work programmes to be endorsed by the Regional Offices of the NHS Executive. Unfortunately even this can maintain a considerable tension between Health Authority purchasers and the perceptions and concerns of primary health care teams and, in particular, GPs (including GP fundholders). What steps can we take to bring GPs and their teams, with the knowledge of the populations, to the planning process? The first step must logically be their involvement in NHS planning issues as the basic building block for creating alliances with other agencies.

For many health commissions this has meant bringing GPs to the very heart of the decision and planning process. GP fundholders can be seen as being there by right because of their control of resources, but all GPs act as gate keepers for the majority of NHS resources.

In Gloucestershire, since the NHS reforms, there has been a regular pattern of visits to GP practices to consult. Often the greatest benefit has been to the Authority staff who, for too long, have concentrated on the acute sector. With the formation of Gloucestershire Health, incorporating the Gloucestershire Health Authority and Family Health Services Authority in 1993, these visiting rounds were merged into one. A countywide GP health purchasing group was formed to give regular advice and exchange of ideas. This has worked reasonably well, but it has become difficult to see how this can now provide the means of filtering local GP issues into a form that could help shape future Health Authority decisions and planning.

More recently, therefore, GP locality commissioning groups have been created in an attempt to improve understanding of, and reflect, local needs. With six localities in the county following district council boundaries, there has been room for experiment and recognition of the differing rates of development that such an opportunity creates. Since the inception of GP fundholding there has developed a supportive relationship, the continuation of which may be challenged by the growing numbers of GP fundholders and the need for a more formal monitoring process.[1] The development of locality based purchasing may provide the mechanism for maintaining a link that is based on a mutual understanding of practice-level issues. For locality commissioning groups to work effectively (and to encompass GPFHs and non-fundholders) they need to develop beyond a 'lobby' group to one that shares in the responsibility for the cash limited resources available to the NHS.

It is clear that the increased involvement of GPs in the purchasing process (whether they be GP fundholders or not) is a major challenge. We should not underestimate the gap between the aspirations and the reality of a truly Primary Care-Led NHS. Commissioning authorities were created to better understand local needs and improve the health of the population through the purchasing process and have found this role very challenging. To expect GPs to be public health physicians, to manage and prioritise resources within an overarching planning process, and to be the most significant provider of direct health care is a little over optimistic. They require management support that enables their unique knowledge to be used and facilitates continued commitment. It must be remembered, however, that others in the PHCT can make a significant contribution, as do mental health teams, learning disability teams and social workers.

To enable primary health care to have real influence those of us in the new Health Authorities must first protect it against the effects of our own enthusiasm. Not to do so will either lead to GPs drowning in a sea of involvement or, the more likely outcome, withdrawal to their direct health care role. To avoid this, their role in the planning process must be based on renewable energy. This means finding a process that is the most enabling.

If this is the backdrop to a Primary Care-Led NHS, what opportunities are presented by the existing planning processes for community care?

HEALTH AND COMMUNITY CARE PLANNING

Initial attempts, prior to the implementation of community care, to define health and social care responsibilities and activities were largely unsuccessful. They did illustrate that the grey areas of care can be used to unite social and health agencies as well as being the areas of potential strife. The introduction of annual agreements and the Community Care Plan in 1992–93 formed the major back-drops to local planning. It is still debatable to what extent the Community Care Plan is an active planning document or a public information exercise. Given that the major players operate to dif-ferent decision making and resource cycles, at best it can provide a framework for further planning. GP involvement has not been sig-nificant in the annual agreement although guidance has exhorted Health Authorities (and local authorities) to include them in the process. This must be largely due to its relative remoteness from the everyday experience of GPs.

The development of GP fundholding has, like most structural changes, consumed a good deal of time and energy. The learning curve for GPs and District Health Authorities and Trusts has been considerable. Community care planning therefore has not been perceived by these groups as the top priority. This process is now, however, well established and increasingly GPs, fundholders and non-fundholders alike, are seeking opportunities to integrate local services. In a recent article in the British Medical Journal, it was reported that 'General Practitioners said they were becoming more involved in community care; with central roles in monitoring, supporting, and caring for patients receiving community care and attending multi-disciplinary case conferences'.[2] Through this process they are being drawn into the planning arena.

Within Gloucestershire, a project based in Tewkesbury has been exploring how joint information and resources can be brought together around a group of local practices (which includes both GP fundholders and non-fundholders). This process involved the local Social Services Department, health providers, Health Authority and GPs and has not been without its moments of tension. In identify-ing local resources and needs it has enabled GPs to feel a sense of ownership of their local planning process. All parties have become better informed about the framework within which they operate and have been able to make positive contributions to targeting ser-vices to those with the greatest need. This joint purchaser/manage-ment approach appears to be breaking down the barriers between personal and health care for those who receive it. We hope this will enable us to move towards a single point of entry into the services.

THE ADVANTAGES OF INVOLVING GPs

For the purposes of planning, GPs hold significant amounts of health needs information that, as yet, is relatively under-used, particularly concerning the needs of older patients with whom they are in regular contact. The 1990 GP contract, through the annual over-75 health checks, encouraged a more formalised approach to the identifying of both social and health needs. In Gloucestershire a research project has been undertaken by a local consultant to follow a cohort of 1800 over-75s using a standardised format for recording information. It has not only highlighted that GPs hold key information on needs but provides a relatively easy means of identifying the range of resources used by them (for Health, SSD, Housing and Voluntary sector) against their levels of changing dependency. To exploit the information effectively there is a need to integrate GPs' systems with others in the Health Service, which is the major challenge addressed in Chapter Four.

These kinds of processes involving GPs and their practice based team, with their close contact with patient and carer needs, seem to be particularly successful. Local attempts at involving GPs in multi-agency locality planning teams seem less successful. The reasons for this must, in part, be as a result of the differing concerns of those involved. The meeting of national planning processes with the GPs focus on the individual can be difficult to reconcile. There is a requirement on both parties to move ground. GPs must become more strategic in their concerns while the caring agencies need to be more flexible in developing a planning process that builds up from the bottom. It is interesting to speculate how the involvement of GPs with, for instance, Social Services Committees might be accomplished without this becoming part of the existing formalised channels for GP representation.

It almost seems that the two parties are travelling in opposite directions. Social Service Departments are becoming masters at policy-making to define entitlement in response to new statutes, while GPs increasingly seek individual and pragmatic solutions. To meet with some hope of travelling together both parties require a clear set of benefits from mutual action. Distrust on both sides seems common-place. Like most stereotypes, this can be broken down only by individual contact.

A number of projects aimed at bringing care managers into the practice have been viewed as successful and desirable by GPs taking part, but the main problem seems to be the resource implications for social services and the organisational context in which they work. Other higher level approaches also seem to have been beneficial. Formal links between the Local Medical Committee and senior social services staff have fostered improved understanding on both sides. In Gloucestenshire these regular meetings to discuss community care have been chaired by the Health Authority with the aim of increasing the influence of GPs.

PLANNING FOR THE FUTURE

The dilemma for the future of Health Authority and local authority relations seems to lie in the diminishing direct influence on NHS health care services. Against this, GPs, through GP fundholding, will be directly involved or, as a result of their wider role, they will exert the key influence on Health Authority purchasing. Our existing processes are based on limiting the number of decision makers and we do not seem equipped to be able to deal with the wider range of independent contractors. If we assume that there is a practical imperative to joint action and co-operation, how can it be manifest in a Primary Care-Led NHS?

The Department of Health's answer is already set out in the monitoring arrangements for GP fundholders. This assumes that Health Authorities will be both leaders of strategy co-ordination and monitors of the performance of GP fundholders.[1] Assuming that GP fundholders will simply accept the legitimacy of the new Health Authority's role seems a little over optimistic. GPs as independent contractors have developed a culture that does not easily fit in with the structures of the NHS planning system. They often accept authority and NHS management on sufferance, only being convinced when it delivers extra resources for their patients.

It is true that GPs are only just beginning to appreciate the influence they are being offered and other parts of the NHS are even slower at realising the implications. If the new role of Health Authorities is unable to offer the appropriate leadership or direction for GPs they may well find it unacceptable and indeed they do have other issues that command their attention. In many ways an approach developed by GPs might be considered the most desirable solution by Social Services Departments confronted by a large number of seemingly irreconcilable interests. One such approach is the formation of consortium arrangements by GP Fundholders in which, due to their increased size, they are able to command the attention of key players in the wider field of community based services. Such arrangements would allow GPs to share resources, to enable time to be allocated to strategy development and negotiation with statutory agencies. The danger would be the creation of a series of mini health authorities that can be both expensive and relatively wasteful in the duplication of resources. Against this, for local authorities it would provide a group, or groups, of sufficient size to begin to simplify local planning dilemmas.

A further development of this would be an extension of fund-holding to include purchasing of social elements of Community Care. This could improve targeting of services, save duplication of service resources and solve the problem of the divide between health and social care. This approach is attractive, but requires General Practices to develop as managed care organisations with the skills to purchase social care services. With the assistance of practice-based general managers this may not prove to be a major difficulty.

Locality commissioning groups could also provide a similar approach that would need to be based on shared systems of Community Care. This would need to go beyond inter-agency cooperation and agreement to entering into discussion with local community and social care staff. The main advantage for GPs of this approach is its implicit commitment to making care more local. Such a development requires GPs and members of their practice team to consider the adequacy of the current knowledge base. The need for skills to enable a 'wider' population focus to be used points to one area of fruitful development.

These approaches provide a significant advantage for the agencies involved as they focus the debate through a structure or process that could both inform and be informed by planning and strategy. However, any approach that seeks to enhance the delivery of Community Care and health care must be based on a cultural shift within health and local government.

The key is involvement at local level rather than building hierarchical structures. Also of significant importance will be the ability of central government to construct priorities that are meaningful within a practice population and that allow for flexible local implementation. It may be shocking for some to discover that primary care is not one structured unit but rather a myriad of conflicting interests, opinions and enthusiasms. Yet, this is its strength, for it deals with the particular, and one of the major reasons for the introduction of Community Care was to ensure that packages of care meet the needs of the individual.

REFERENCES

1. National Health Service Executive 1995. An Accountability Framework for GP
   Fundholding. EL (95)54 NHSE, London
2. Kingdon D, Sumners S (1995) Community care and general practice. British
   Medical Journal 311: 823

20. Implementing strategy

Gavin McBurnie

INTRODUCTION

In Scotland all Health Boards have produced primary care strategies, the purpose of which is to develop local strategic frameworks that underpin the development of a Primary Care-Led NHS. However, no matter how articulate the strategies produced may be, they will amount to nothing if they cannot be implemented. Producing a strategy which can be implemented is, therefore, one of the key challenges facing the new 1996 Health Authorities as they move towards a Primary Care-Led NHS.

The crux of strategy development and its implementation is for the Authorities to recognise that this is a process of change management. Shifting from a position whereby 'primary care supports more specialist secondary and tertiary care to a new position in which primary care is recognised and developed as the foundation of the health service',[1] and where primary care ceases to be dominated by secondary care but instead determines secondary care provision is affecting major change. Therefore, Authorities need to consider how they will manage this process and the tactics they will adopt if they are to successfully implement their strategies.

DEVELOPING A COMMON VISION

In Fife, we have found that the key to successful implementation is a framework with which there is general agreement by the major stakeholders. Implementation therefore begins with the process of strategy development: this process is at least as important as the document produced as it provides a unique opportunity for new Health Authorities and primary care to develop new relationships and new styles of working. If Authorities do not take this opportunity to reshape their relationship with primary care then the process of strategy implementation will be much more difficult.

Strategy development is above all an opportunity to open mean-ingful dialogue with primary care about the future development of local health services. The framework produced needs to reflect both the aims and concerns of primary care professionals as well as the wider objectives and parameters within which health authori-ties operate. For this to occur the traditional health service approach to strategy development (i.e. top-down and produced in isolation from users and providers of services) will be inappropri-ate. Instead a bottom up approach is necessary. As with all frame-works, more detailed plans and actions then need to be developed. Practice health planning has the potential to act as the ideal process if the plans are developed and owned by the primary health care teams that produce them. New Authorities must resist the temptation either to produce the document for the primary care team or to prescribe too narrow parameters which affect the ability of the primary health care team to produce its own plan.

If an effective strategic framework is to be produced there needs to be a clarity of purpose within the document. This begins with a clear understanding of what is meant by primary care and a description of its defining characteristics. This is important as we found in Fife that primary care is a dynamic concept; what might have been considered to be an appropriate definition of primary care a few years ago was certainly not appropriate when consider-ing the future direction of a primary care led health service. A lack of clarity at this stage can create the situation whereby different stakeholders hold different views on the way ahead.

The strategic framework also needs to exhibit a clarity of objec-tives. The making explicit of the strategic objectives extends not only to the primary care sector which needs this clarity if it is to understand and thrive in its changing environment but also to the secondary care, voluntary and private sectors. If these sectors are to be able to manage the opportunities and threats that exist within the success of the strategy then they too need to fully understand the implications that arise from the development of a Primary Care-Led NHS.

DEVELOPING NEW RELATIONSHIPS

The process of strategy development is an ideal opportunity to build new relationships between the new Health Authorities and primary care. In Scotland, the development of primary care strategies took place against a backdrop of strained relationships between Health Boards and primary care. The principal reasons for this strained relationship were:

- Health Boards still being held accountable for the 1990 contract changes and the increased paperwork that resulted;
- Primary care practitioners experiencing a shift of work into primary care without the accompanying shift of resources; and
- Low morale in primary care, a problem about which primary care practitioners felt Health Boards were unconcerned.

Unless these relationship type problems are resolved, or at least tackled, then this also increases the difficulty of implementing the strategy. New relationships therefore need to be developed which have the following features. They are based upon:

- Openness: In Fife, during the strategy consultation process, many primary care professionals were suspicious that there was a hidden agenda behind the Board's apparently sudden interest in primary care. Primary care professionals need to be convinced that there are no hidden agendas;
- Trust: Nothing will destroy a relationship more quickly than if a health authority states it will do something, then does not. Primary care professionals must trust the word of health commissioners.
- Empowering primary care: A Primary Care-Led NHS cannot be achieved if health authorities control all the levels of power. Power needs to be devolved to primary care both in the development of the strategic framework and in their ability to determine future health service developments whether through planning or purchasing mechanisms;
- New styles of working: A Primary Care-Led NHS demands new styles of working between Health Authorities and primary care. These new styles, characterised by collaboration and partnership, need to recognise the role of each side with the consequent sharing of power and responsibility.

One of the concerns expressed by many primary care professionals is their anxieties concerning management. They fear that one of the implications arising from a Primary Care-Led NHS is that primary care will become increasingly managed by health authorities. Given that one of the attractions of a career in primary care is the relative freedom from management that exists, the belief that primary care will become increasingly managed is seen as a major threat. Primary care professionals need to be reassured that management does not by necessity have to be directive. Instead health commissioners will need to develop alternative management skills as they have often gained their management experience in secondary care. The requirement of secondary care with its emphasis on line management is not a suitable paradigm to encourage the development of primary care. Accordingly, there is a need for senior officers to develop their skills in the ability to influence, to facilitate and to support. The production of an agreed strategy with jointly agreed objectives between Health Authorities and primary care is vital. When this occurs, the importance of directive management recedes.

DEVELOPING EFFECTIVE STRATEGIC FRAMEWORKS

An ideal strategic framework will be greater than the sum of its parts as each section within the strategy reinforces and strengthens other sections. At the same time it should not be seen as prescriptive. Rather it needs to be a set of agreed principles and objectives around which dialogue with stakeholders can be held and which acts as a unifying foundation upon which flexible developments relating to specific local needs can be produced. It should give providers of services, whether in primary or secondary care, the statutory, private, or voluntary sectors a clear sense of the future direction of the development of local health services. The effective strategic framework will ensure that 'primary care ... [will become] the pervading philosophy underlying health service delivery ... i.e. 'planning from "primary care out" rather than "hospitals in".'[2] The strategic framework will need therefore to address the following issues:

- Patient Focus: Part of the rationale in developing a Primary Care-Led NHS is the proximity of primary care practitioners to patients, and the putative understanding of patient needs and requirements that this proximity gives to practitioners. The strategic framework should therefore address the methods by which services become increasingly patient-focused.
  This means balancing patient views of their health needs with professionally driven needs assessment; integrating patient views into prioritisation processes and service development proposals; to obtain patient views on the services they receive. The objective must be to ensure that the needs and views of patients are reflected accurately in all future health service developments.

- Provision of services: A Primary Care-Led NHS with its emphasis on the appropriate local provision of services raises many new challenges which will need to be addressed in the strategic framework;
- Key issues include premises development, primary care team development, management and organisational development, partnerships with other agencies, developing new models of care, developing the quality of services (both clinical and non-clinical) and the shift of services from secondary care locations to the community where clinically and cost effective;
- Planning of services: The planning of services whether they are in primary or secondary care is one of the key areas in the development of a Primary Care-Led NHS. The strategic framework should address how Health Authorities are going to bring primary care into the planning process and allows it to be the key driver in this process. As suggested earlier, practice health planning provides an opportunity to allow meaningful primary care led planning to occur if it is steered by the primary care team;
- Purchasing of services: The future is for general practice to lead the purchasing of services. This is the second key mechanism in the development of a Primary Care-Led NHS. GP led purchasing allows General Practice to make real decisions, not only about which services should be purchased, but also about resource shifts. The strategic framework needs to detail the means by which Primary Care-Led Purchasing will be supported and developed.

IMPLEMENTING AGREED STRATEGY

Producing a strategic framework which supports the development of primary care and has been agreed with primary care practitioners is an important first step, but the second is its implementation. One of the findings from Fife is that not all in primary care will agree with everything in the strategy. Primary care practitioners are far too heterogeneous a group to allow this! In Fife, the pattern has been for about 45% of General Medical Practices to consistently participate in projects aimed at developing primary care with the remaining 55% showing little initial interest although some participate later. What this indicates is that in common with any change process, the proposed change provokes different reactions from different groups — from enthusiasm through anxiety through denial to outright opposition.

New Health Authorities need to maintain their dialogue with primary care throughout the process of strategy implementation. The reason is, first to ensure the continuance of an agreed strategic vision, but secondly to ascertain the responses of different groups. They must be aware of the responses that their strategy is generating in order to take appropriate action, whether it is reviewing the strategy or performing any of the tactics now considered.

PROVIDING UNDERSTANDING AND SUPPORT

The proposed development for primary care will undoubtedly provoke a range of reactions. A particularly good example of this occurred during Fife Health Board's consultation process with General Practitioners over its primary care strategy. At one meeting, a General Practitioner stated that:

'I feel as if someone has turned over a stone and found General Practice. I wish they would turn it back over again.'

This quote is a powerful indicator of the fact that although health commissioners may believe that a Primary Care-Led NHS will be warmly embraced and accepted by primary care professionals, the reality is that many in primary care will react unfavourably. Some of the reactions (such as denial and opposition) will be due to anxiety and fear with the commonest causes for these reactions being:

- An anxiety over the perceived increase in workload that will not be accompanied by the necessary resources;
- A fear of an unknown future;
- A fear of economic loss;
- A threat to power and influence.

Health commissioners need to develop an intelligence network which keeps them informed of the different reactions that the implementation of the strategy is arousing from different groups. If the Health Authority is aware of any adverse reactions that their strategy is provoking then it will be in a position to deal with them appropriately and to provide the required support.

An example from Fife was the anxiety community nursing staff felt, and still feel, by the recent development which allows practitioners to perform community fundholding. Two principal anxieties were identified:

1. How will the nurses function and be managed in new style primary health care teams with the different power relationships that exist?
2. If nurses are contracted to the practice, do they then become employees of the practice and, if so, will they still be covered by the pay and conditions that apply to other community nurses?

Both of these examples are understandable yet neither need cause significant problems. Health commissioners working with local Community Trusts should be able to allay these fears relatively easily. The important point is that health commissioners will need to know and understand the reactions that exist if they are to successfully deal with them.

PROMOTING COMMUNICATION AND EDUCATION

It is extremely important for new Health Authorities to undertake this effectively as it is essential that primary care professionals understand why the change is both occurring and its inevitability; what change is going to occur and the nature of the benefits to be obtained. When change occurs both costs and benefits result. If it is perceived that costs exceed benefits, resistance to change will increase. I use the word perceived, as if there is an excessive focus on costs (which, for example, occurred with GP fundholding), this can create the perception that costs exceed benefits even when this is not the case (and also is the case with GP fundholding). Therefore both costs and benefits have to be clearly understood. Methods which can be used to communicate and explain the nature and reasons for change along with the benefits to be gained are:

- Regular meetings, whether with individuals, practices, localities or at authority level. It is important that senior health authority staff attend these meetings as this not only indicates the importance that the Health Authority gives to primary care, but also gives authority to the messages being given to primary care;
- Educational workshops and seminars;
- Newsletters, which are probably the least effective method. In addition, given the amount of mail now received by primary care professionals, careful thought needs to be given to the production of newsletters and whether the information can be communicated in a more appropriate way.

PROMOTING PRODUCT CHAMPIONS

Nothing encourages people to change more than to see the benefits to be gained from changing. This provides a role for both product champions and projects. The product champions are the innovative practices or health care teams which understand the benefits to be gained from changing and thus lead the change. It is with these practices that new Health Authorities can try out new projects and if they are successful the commissions can then encourage these practices to communicate this to their colleagues. Due to the history that commonly existed between the early health commissions and practitioners, some practitioners will be sceptical at the supposed benefits to be gained from changing if these benefits are advocated by health commission officers. However, if it is their primary care colleagues who are saying 'look at what we have been able to do' then this is a much more powerful statement and is much more likely to lead to change. Commissioners need to identify and work with these product champions who will lead the development of primary care.

Related to this, and of equal importance, is the role of project management. What appears to be a feature of giving power to primary care professionals is not only their willingness to work with health commissioners in testing out new models of care, but more important is for them to be the generator of the more innovative and radical changes occurring within the health service. In Scotland, the Management Executive has set up a Primary Care Development Fund, a move echoed in many health boards, the purpose of which is to test out and fund innovative developments within primary care. This type of funding is important as many of the best ideas will originate in primary care and funding will be necessary to give these ideas the kiss of life.

A word of caution is also appropriate. Simply because something is innovative, does not mean that it is necessarily a good thing. Projects have to be carefully evaluated before they become widely adopted. After all, not only are scarce resources at risk but also more importantly patient care.

EMPOWERING PRIMARY CARE

Critical to the successful development of a Primary Care-Led NHS will be the need to empower primary care professionals. Curiously we found in Fife that many primary care professionals are distinctly reluctant to be empowered. Some see it as a 'trap' which will lead them to take over the work and responsibilities of health boards while others feel simply too overwhelmed by their workload to be able to take on other tasks. In Fife it was found that there was a need to recognise these realities and to convince primary care professionals of two things: first that there is difference between being the key influence in decision making and performing all the associated work, and that second, if practices are to take on extra responsibilities and tasks then they must be properly resourced to enable them to do so, even if it is simply a case of financing time and space away from the practice to consider the issues fully.

In the earlier section 'Providing Understanding and Support' it was suggested that many primary care professionals feel anxious about their future because they feel that they lack control over it. During the process of strategy development, hopefully at least some of the professionals will begin to feel empowered and ready to take on the challenge of a Primary Care-Led NHS. However, other professionals will need to be encouraged to see the potential the future brings and to grab and shape the opportunities that they have been given. This in part depends upon the degree of trust and confidence practitioners have in their health commission to allow them to exert this power. The other part lies in new Health Authorities encouraging practitioners to use this power through mechanisms such as practice health planning and GP-led purchasing.

Pre-supposing this empowerment of primary care is the assumption that authorities will be willing to give up some of the power that they currently possess. Yet this is essential. The move towards a Primary Care-Led NHS will have significant effects upon the structure and activities. This change, leading to a strategic planning, regulatory and support function for the new Health Authorities is a challenge to which they must respond.

USING THE POWER OF THE NEW HEALTH AUTHORITY

Many people or organisations faced with proposed changes with which they do not agree or understand, will react either with denial, (that is they carry on regardless, ignoring the change that is occurring) or with outright opposition. Practices exhibiting denial need to be encouraged to understand that the change is inevitable, and supported as they come to terms with the changes and the impact that this change will have on them.

Practices or practitioners opposed to change pose different problems to health commissioners who will need to know who is resistant to change and why. Health Authorities may need to be prepared to take action, such as refusing to invest in practices to enforce essential change. Against this, is the effect enforced change may have on other elements of primary care. There is likely to be a degree of instability in attitudes within primary care and enforcing change on one group may provoke opposition from another group which, if not previously supportive, at least had accepted the change. Commissioners, therefore, need to think carefully about using force and this will include considering the wider reactions.

CONCLUSION

In the process of implementing its strategy, the key role is for a new Health Authority to *manage change*. If the NHS is to become genuinely led by primary care then primary care must be the key influence in the planning and purchasing of services. This necessitates a new relationship between Health Authorities and primary care, a relationship based upon partnership. The successful implementation of strategy depends upon the development of a strategic framework to which there is agreement by the major stakeholders and, in particular, primary care stakeholders. However, the major change that a move towards a Primary Care-Led NHS effects, will provoke a variety of reactions from enthusiasm to opposition. Health Authorities will need to be aware of these reactions and how they will manage them if they are to be able to successfully implement their strategies.

REFERENCES

1. NHSiE Management Executive/Office for Public Management. 1994
      Development Paper 1: Towards a Strategic Framework for Primary Care, p. 4
2. Ibid

21. Managing primary care

Ray Wilcox

INTRODUCTION

The significance of the words 'a Primary Care-Led NHS' cannot be overstated; neither can the words 'Managing primary care'. The whole history of the NHS and indeed its portrayal in the public mind today tells us that this statement is an aim rather than reality. Achieving a Primary Care-Led NHS is something that will take some time to achieve, even with partial success and many years to get to a state where people recognise it as reality.

DEFINING PRIMARY CARE

How might we define primary care and the management of it, for the purpose of this chapter? Everyone has their own idea of how to define primary care and that view is influenced by the individual's personal perspective, whether as a worker in it, or as a consumer of services. There is no commonly agreed definition of primary care and there is unlikely to be one for the time being as indicated in a recent review by the IHSM.[1] Some of those who contribute to the delivery and development of primary care include General Practitioners, the Primary Health Care Team (broadly or narrowly defined), Community Trusts, Social Workers, Health Authorities at a distance and a range of others. But the main pillar in the delivery of primary care is the General Practice unit, whether fundholding or not, and the thrust of this chapter is therefore concerned with the management of the arrangements in and around the General Practice setting.

WHERE HAVE WE COME FROM IN PRIMARY CARE?

It is impossible to deny history and for those looking to develop a Primary Care-Led NHS, it is essential to understand why primary care is where it is today, in terms of its current standard, practices and development. Things are slowly improving in primary care, but investment has been neglected, quality and standards are variable. Efficiency has been off the agenda and patient expectation has been tolerant. Taking a moment to reflect on this helps us to a better appreciation of the opportunities and threats inherent in moving to a Primary Care-Led NHS and managing in primary care.

Recognising that achieving a Primary Care-Led NHS is a *long* run aim is important, because 'Managing primary care', or at least the Family Health Services part of primary care, was until the beginning of this decade, almost certainly a contradiction in terms. Management in the broadest sense is seen as planning, implementing and reviewing progress; about allocating and shifting resources; it implies being in control. Yet almost all of those things have been outside the control of those who have been involved in 'overseeing' the development of doctors, dentists and their fellow independent contractors, and consequently the wider primary care arena since the beginning of the NHS. I say 'consequently' because primary care development in the wider sense flows in the main from positive and innovative relationships around general practice.

For more than 40 years General Practice had a uniquely open contract with the state which allowed it (General Practice) to be in control of its own arrangements and largely free from any state interference. During those 40 years the arrangements for controlling these services (i.e. deciding the terms under which GPs would work in the NHS) rested firmly with the Civil Service through their negotiations with the professions. The result of this arrangement and the absence of any involvement in or control by Regional Health Authorities was that GPs and Family Practitioner Committees — the forerunner of the Family Health Services Authority — were seen to be outside the mainstream of the NHS and on many occasions even referred to by managers in the service as outside the NHS altogether! For staff and professions alike, this state of affairs had both advantages and disadvantages.

For administrators working in this part of the service (they were not allowed to be called managers), there was a real sense of camaraderie and wide networks, which came from administering a national set of terms of service and a close (many said too close) bond between their organisations and the professions concerned. The disadvantages for managers were an excessively tight control on grading structures (certainly as compared with other parts of the service), and the absence of career development opportunities available in the hospital and community health services. This was inevitable because these primary care services were not seen as part of mainstream NHS and therefore not sufficiently important to include in training schemes.

For the professions, undoubtedly, the advantages were a continuing ability to keep their affairs tightly controlled through centrally negotiated terms of service including favourable arrangements for self employment. Added to that, in the sense of being in control, was the reality that in very many circumstances it was a GP who was Chairman of the FPC which had to 'oversee' the delivery of GP services locally. The disadvantage to the profession was that the arrangement meant that they practised in isolation from their colleagues in the hospital and community services and in latter years particularly, distanced themselves from the investment in management education and training opportunities that came the way of colleagues in the rest of the service. Infrastructure investment suffered too, because despite the introduction of special funding arrangements for GP surgeries in the 1970s (the cost rent scheme), investment in General Practice premises was patchy. The good premises got better and the not so good stayed that way.

PHCT development suffered too, because of this separation and the 'different' arrangements. Despite the volumes of reports and books on the subject, real primary care team working has remained an elusive dream for most. Poor premises, different organisational cultures and a lack of strong organisational structures and systems in General Practice have militated against team development.

It was not until the late 1980s — some years after it was brought into the rest of the service — that general management came into the world of the then Family Health Services and at the same time a smaller, tighter Authority — the FHSA — took over the role of the FPC. Then we began to see with these changes, and the advent of the new contract for GPs, a more strained relationship between FHSAs and GPs as 'managing' was legitimised by the Department of Health to replace the word 'administering'.

In 1989–90, at the time FPCs were abolished in favour of FHSAs, professional control was reduced as medical involvement in FPCs was severely reduced. The new contract exposed GPs to change on a scale never before experienced by them; many, even now refer to the 'imposed contract'. Not only did they experience change on a major scale, they were exposed to it without any of the expected support processes which organisations provide when such change occurs. Individual feelings and values were threatened and partners in many practices who previously had rubbed along together, largely as individuals in a shared surgery, were forced to make corporate decisions about the future nature and direction of the practice as a business. It was a muddled, frustrating and for many a demoralising experience and it ended 40 years of relative stability for UK primary care.

WHERE ARE WE NOW?

Let me bring things upto date while again reinforcing the need to appreciate some historical points about primary care, its management and development; it is important to understand history while not being hostage to it.

Against this background of under investment, of absence of training, relative isolation, low morale and the sometimes seemingly idiosyncratic terms and conditions of service of GPs which impede managed change, we are intending to build on and around existing structures, to see a Primary Care-Led NHS.

In the context of change in a changing world for organisations, Beckhard[2] argues that ' ... the dilemma for managers is to maintain stability within an organisation, while at the same time responding to outside forces, stimulating innovation and rearranging roles and relationships. ... ' Primary care in this country is built around many thousands of organisations (9000 GP practices alone), and because of this and because each has an individual view, and despite the existence of a centralised contract, creating a feeling of stability in times of significant change is no easy task. Those with a long association with this part of primary care — and perhaps those coming recently to management of this part of the service — will recognise the dilemmas referred to by Beckhard. The first attempt to institute change — but failing to maintain stability — was the introduction of the 1990 contract for GPs where the resulting tensions are regrettably all too present today with apparently record levels of stress among GPs, an upsurge in the number of partnership dissolutions and real problems of morale among many GPs.

This state of affairs must not be dismissed as a temporary blip, something that will correct itself — although it may well do that — for it was here that the first attempts to put General Practice in a more central — and consequently in a more exposed and accountable position — have shown up the weaknesses in changing a system in the face of considerable opposition, or put another way without securing sufficient ownership of the change.

One of the dilemmas for the new Health Authorities in 1996 — and it was so for FHSAs in 1990 — is to decide the fundamental relationship with the medical profession. They need to be clear whether there is a stick or carrot approach and understand what they are doing at any one time. That decision decides your stance and dictates the relationship with the profession. The functions of the old FHSA were a mixture of both (pulling and pushing) and in the years from 1989 this uncertain mixture contributed in part to the often strained relationship with the FHSA; part of that organisation fed GPs and another part asked them what value it had got from feeding them! In other words it tried to carry out an accountability role as well as a support role.

Contracting out some of the functions of the old FHSA — those involving things which have disparagingly been called 'pay and rations' (the support role?) and which have little relationship to the new role of the Health Authority — needs to be something for early consideration. But this will still leave Health Authorities with the task of forging partnerships and alliances including one with the medical profession. This will be no easy task for it also involves carrying out a performance management role on fundholding GPs within the terms of the accountability framework.[3] It will be fascinating to see how this performance management role develops, particularly the extent to which it will be made tighter than the first tentative framework and the time which elapses before it applies to all GPs.

The NHS Executive have a major role to play in setting the vision for a Primary Care-Led NHS. Health Authorities by themselves will come up against the 'central contract (for GPs) versus local need' dilemma and the Executive will give a major boost to local initiatives if some of the centralist rules and conditions can be relaxed or even better, authority for some local negotiations given. Again at a time when so much publicity is being given to local pay in the NHS (for NHS Trusts) similar development in primary care is lamentably slow.

'Pushing the boundaries of the possible' is reasonable in the short run, but if the system continues to reassert the original boundaries, those pushing the central rules and contract can feel very exposed. The 'Manchester ruling' in 1995 where the medical profession went to the High Court to challenge successfully the interpretation of the FHSA on the use locally of certain monies which came with strong central earmarking, is a case in point.

WHERE ARE WE MOVING TO?

Management

There are two organisations — the new Health Authorities and General Practice — which are central to the successful development of a Primary Care-Led NHS. Within these organisations there are three groups of people: Health Authority staff, GPs, and Practice Managers, who will be crucially involved in modifying the structures for a Primary Care-Led NHS; others may be important but these people will be crucial.

The Health Authority staff

For Health Authorities and their staff one of the challenges is to recognise the absolute importance of helping to get the General Practice unit on a sound business footing and to do this will inevitably mean the investment of resources. Here we need to tackle the vexed question of 'who invests in General Practice?' Should investment come from General Practice, the Health Authority or both; and what if GPs will not invest from their own resources — should investment come from Health Authorities alone?

One of the real advantages of integrating FHSAs and DHAs is that resources will be available (subject to priorities) through integrated funding in ways which were not possible to FHSAs or DHAs acting alone. 'Better Management = Better Health' a phrase used extensively in the NHS, is as appropriate, if not more appropriate, to General Practice than anywhere else in the NHS.

Not that every practice will recognise the need for investment or indeed allow the 'intrusion' by Health Authority staff, even where they recognise the need. The new Authorities will need to show that they understand the practice as a business unit, can demonstrate how to help to prepare it for the future and to help to train and develop key players. General Practice is no longer isolated from market forces (NHS or otherwise) and can no longer operate without the planning, objective setting and financial systems to which any business in a changing market has to conform. There is plenty of evidence to show that the successful practice is one that has grasped these issues and helping GPs come to terms with this is a challenge for the new Health Authorities.

Claire Perry articulated well the new role of the Health Authority in a recent article.[4] She referred to the fact that 'command and control styles of management are simply not appropriate in this world.' Managing in this part of primary care is more concerned with the art of encouragement, persuasion, innovation and imagination and pushing the boundaries of the possible. It is about working in partnership with the medical profession. It is to do with learning that sometimes needs will dictate that you are the dominant partner and sometimes the reverse.

Health Authorities have to start (and a few have begun to do so) to build a meaningful partnership with General Practice that takes a strategic and at the same time a pragmatic look at what is needed locally. Bringing on staff to learn the primary care business is essential and the culture and the terminology is important — how many Authority managers understand the implications of negative equity in surgery premises on primary care development, on market entry and exit and on internal movement? It is as important for the development of primary care and the new Health Authority, as understanding capital charging has been in relation to the Trust hospital.

The GPs

Secondly after Health Authority staff there are GPs themselves. With the advent of the NHS reforms including the new contract (in 1990) under which they operate, management has become what many GPs refer to as a necessary evil. In her book about Practice Management[5] June Huntington describes in great detail the dilemmas faced by GPs in facing up to the need to get organised in a more business-like way when their primary interest and training focuses them on patient care. I have referred to the morale issue already. Health Authorities and GP educators need to work together to organise management training and development opportunities for those GPs who seek them, for rather like the development of fundholding and other changes in General Practice over the years, securing ownership and legitimising change so often comes from leading edge thinking within the profession.

This will be no easy or short term task. Helping GPs to be involved in management issues, expanding career development opportunities and offering access to change management thinking, all has implications for practice management. Many GPs now really do want to be better prepared, to be involved in management issues. But unless and until substantially more do so, and the opportunities exist for them to do so, it will be difficult to develop the really well managed practice because GPs will not understand the potential of management as a discipline, nor be sufficiently aware of ways of growing the type of Practice Manager needed for the future.

The Practice Managers

Finally in this examination of the role of three groups there are Practice Managers. As I have already said, I believe General Practice is the key organisational unit around which a Primary Care-Led NHS will emerge and if it is to do so it will need to be stronger organisationally than it is now. Some Practice Managers are beginning to have an influence on the development agenda, but the vast majority are not ready or able to have the effect needed. For many practices, the role of Manager is ill-defined, many partners are not convinced of the need for a manager and there is a wide range of capability among them. As June Huntington asks in her recent book, the question is, whose business is it to ensure that we have strong Practice Management and Managers?[5]

The challenge for Health Authorities is to help practices and the medical profession locally and nationally to recognise that the development need of Practice Managers and Practice Management is of joint concern. The key words here for Health Authorities are working in partnership and resource investment. Until NHS management can seriously engage with General Practice and form an understanding about future direction and ways of working, it will be difficult to make progress with investing in the development of Practice Managers. Failure to invest and improve here will consign the General Practice organisational unit to a further period of frailty, which in turn will prevent the improvement of the structures around which primary care can flourish.

Training and career development

Much of the forgoing comment and discussion about management issues reflects a separateness that flows from history. FHSAs were separate from DHAs; GPs were separated from the FHSAs; General Practice was separated from hospital and community services. Management training schemes predominantly tracked through the hospital sector as the recognised way to the top of the management ladder in the NHS. Primary care management (if one was bold enough to use the word management), was an area which management training passed by. It is a sad fact that in the past so many of the complex issues surrounding primary care development, including particularly infrastructure investment consolidation of provision and exit policies, have not had the best minds addressing these issues. Again this was simply because these posts were never considered the necessary training and development ground for those aspiring to the most senior posts in the NHS.

However, that has begun to change and again the challenge for the NHS is to turn the training and management development system of many years on its head. We need to ensure that our programmes in the NHS reflect the primary care vision set out now and that applies both in managerial and clinical circles. The additional challenge in primary care is to cross fertilise the training opportunities and programmes at an early stage in GP and NHS Manager and Practice Manager careers (with others) and to keep that going on a continuing basis. We ought to look to the position in the near future where shifts in career direction are not just into primary care but around primary care. Some years ago in Norfolk I instituted a short term placement of senior managers into General Practice and the learning proved extremely valuable even if the time was short; I was never able to organise clinical placements in management posts, but the benefits to the parties would be considerable.

Until now such training as there has been for the three groups referred to, has been — with some notable exceptions — uni-disciplinary and outside the work setting. What is required perhaps nationally and certainly locally, is a strategy which will deliver much more *shared* training and development and of reasonable periods of duration. Each of the three groups have much to learn from the others and if they do this together there will be a much better chance of 'rooting' the move towards primary care.

Management in primary care is still in the early years of its development and much work remains to be done, but looking back only 5 years there has been so much progress on the way to a more carefully managed primary care system. Many of the changes have been authorised or decreed by the centre, some of them have been led through innovation and boundary pushing locally and some have come about through Regional initiatives particularly in the former Wessex Region.

Creating successfully a Primary Care-Led NHS depends on many factors, but it depends particularly on getting the management arrangements right and in this regard there is absolutely no room for complacency.

REFERENCES

1. Institute For Health Service Managers 1995 Management development for primary care. IHSM, London.
2. Beckhard R, Harris R 1987 Organisational transitions. Addison Wesley, New York
3. National Health Service Executive 1995 An accountability framework for fundholding. EL (95)54 NHSE, London.
4. Perry, C 1995 Galvanising primary care. IHSM Network vol 17
5. Huntington, J 1995 Managing the practice — whose business? Radcliffe Medical Press, Oxford.

22. Managing performance

Bob Ricketts

INTRODUCTION: JUMPING THE CURVE

Transforming 'a Primary Care-Led NHS' from rhetoric into reality will require more than the managerial rubric of business planning, investment programmes and target-setting. Like the diffusion of evidence-based medicine, its essence is a process of cultural change, of personal and organisational re-learning. This will be critical for the new Health Authorities. Unless they are able to jump the learning curve to new ways of joint visioning and strategy creation, and influencing performance, they are likely to achieve at best only limited incremental change through primary care. At worst, insensitive attempts to 'roll-out' traditional top-down models of performance management to practice level will risk stifling innovation and responsiveness to local needs, damaging the credibility of what the NHS policy shift is trying to achieve.

In short, Health Authorities will need to develop new strategies and tactics for influencing performance. Each Authority, together with primary care practitioners, will have to find its own solution, one which fits its culture and priorities, and is sustainable in an era of lean management costs. All will, however, need to address the following six key facets of effective performance management:

1. Developing a performance culture in the new Authorities and in primary care.
2. Focusing on the local and national issues that matter.
3. Measuring performance meaningfully.
4. Agreeing targets that are jointly owned.
5. Providing constructive feedback.
6. Creating incentives for change.

DEVELOPING A PERFORMANCE CULTURE: WINNING AS A MATTER OF STYLE

If a Health Authority is to be effective in influencing performance within primary care, as well as being clear about what it is trying to achieve, it must be credible in terms of its own performance, first, with respect to the quality of the services it provides to practitioners and the public — Service Committees, payments, GPFH administration and support, and health information. The perceived responsiveness and efficiency of these 'front-end' services will be key factors in shaping attitudes to the Authority. This implies an attention to detail by Chief Executives and a willingness to resource this key area adequately. Benchmarking such services with comparable Authorities, or preferably those that are seen as 'best-in-class', may help assure quality and value for money. The second prerequisite for credibility — the right organisational culture — is likely to be more difficult to achieve.

What do we mean by a 'performance culture'? Definitions vary, but normally include the following elements:

- Clarity of mission, values and goals;
- Ownership by all staff of what the organisation is trying to achieve and acceptance of personal responsibility for their contribution towards it;
- Strategic perspective — a clear understanding of where an organisation is going and how it aims to get there;
- Very tight controls on those areas that matter, including an attention to detail;
- Constant feedback of results;
- Curiosity about how things are done elsewhere — networking and benchmarking;
- Directed research and development;
- Values-driven priority-setting and behaviours.

Research in the United Kingdom[1] has shown that these attributes are likely to be facilitated by:

- Visible senior management;
- Flat organisational structures;
- Empowering, informing and developing staff;
- Valuing and rewarding innovation.

Having a new Health Authority culture which values performance and develops high-performing teams will not, in itself, help instill a performance culture in primary care. A critical factor is also likely to be the Authority's approach to influencing performance. Drawing on the experience of the Oxford and Anglia Regional Office's evolving relationships with DHA's and FHSA's, and our agreed implementation arrangements for the GPFH Accountability Framework, success is likely to be facilitated by a style which is:

- Jointly developed and agreed with primary care;
- Strategically driven by agreed priorities and common values;
- Focused on critical success factors and differential performance;
- Predominantly developmental — facilitating self-assessment, networking, sharing good practice, providing information on comparative performance. It is essential that the right balance is struck between supporting and monitoring practices;
- Robust and evidence-based in its assessment of performance;
- Minimal in its information requirements, relying principally on what is required for effective practice management and to ensure probity;
- Rigorous in ensuring accountability where it matters, e.g. ensuring GP fundholders contract for integrated Mental Health services;
- Adult, assuming that practices are principally responsible for their own performance and development;
- Sensitive to the independent practitioner status of General Practitioners.

The ultimate goal is to develop a performance culture within primary care. There are some encouraging signs including, for example, practices which have introduced peer review of referrals, practice quality or advocacy groups, participation in the King's Fund Organisational Audit process for primary care, or accreditation via BS 5750. Nevertheless, progress remains patchy and uncoordinated, often reliant on the energy and enthusiasm of interested individuals. It is important that Health Authorities develop a cohesive approach, making use of all the opportunities presented by the Fundholder Accountability Framework,[2] practice devlopment plans or contracts, audit, peer review, post-graduate education, benchmarking, and Practice Charters or related quality initiatives.

FOCUSING ON THE ISSUES THAT MATTER

Unless we have a clear vision and success criteria, we are unlikely to know whether or when a Primary Care-Led NHS is actually happening. NHS Executive Letter EL (94)79 set the over-arching goal of creating a system where the decisions about purchasing and providing health care are taken as close to the patient as possible by GPs working closely with patients through primary health care teams. There is, however, no single or simple definition of what this would mean in practice. To help bridge this gap and to enable progress to be measured over time, the NHS Executive South and West, Anglia and Oxford and Dearden Management have developed with practitioners and managers, a performance and development framework for national usage. As a first step, the framework assumes that what we are trying to achieve are the outcomes shown in Box 22.1.

Box 22.1 Characteristics of a Primary Care-Led NHS

- Bottom up health needs assessment
- Sensitivity to the health care of local communities
- Primary care involvement in purchasing
- A patient focus
- A strong Primary Health Care Team delivering effective services
- Open services and ready access
- Local delivery of services wherever possible
- Integrated multi-disciplinary services in the community
- Patients being managed across primary care/secondary care boundaries
- A Primary Health Care Team aware of their actions
- Primary care acceptance of responsibility and accountability
- Empowered members of the Primary Health Care Team in relation to other agencies
- Over time, different packages of care and different packages of investment
- A well informed population

Source: Primary Health Care Performance and Development indicators, NHS Executive South and West with Anglia and Oxford and Dearden Management, 1995, page 1.

The framework is still being developed and needs refining, for example, to address the outcome of a more equitable match between service provision and need. One of the key challenges we face is redressing the effects of the inverse care law in primary health care. If the development of a Primary Care-Led NHS is to be genuinely value-driven, new Health Authorities will need to demonstrate that they are serious about equity. This will mean giving priority to needs assessment and resource mapping (both in their relative infancy in primary care), and targeting investment and support where it is most needed. In some areas, this will necessitate developing creative ways of supporting, networking and empowering single-handed practices, particularly where they are serving deprived urban communities.

MEASURING PERFORMANCE MEANINGFULLY

If we were to take stock of the current primary care 'performance indicators' used by the NHS Executive and Health Authorities we would find many of the following characteristics:

- Limited relevance to Health Authorities and practitioners. For example, the percentage of practices undertaking minor surgery. Aside from telling you that this service is available, the information is of no real value. What matters is the range, quality and quantity of procedures; this is not collected.
- Little linkage to strategic or development objectives.
- Cannot be readily mapped against available resources.
- Focus narrowly on certain inputs, not outcomes. Many indices tell us little about the reality of the quality of services for patients.
- Lack of ownership by practices, leading to poor quality and inconsistent information.
- Duplication, increasing the burden of bureaucracy on General Practitioners.

Each Health Authority will need to develop with its practices a portfolio of performance and development indicators which are:

- Bottom-up: developed jointly with practices and owned by them.
- Add value: by facilitating self-audit and development planning, as well as informing discussions about performance and the allocation of resources.
- Linked to core elements of the Authority's agreed overall strate-

gic direction and strategies, e.g. for developing primary care, continuing care and mental health.

- Allowing progress to be measured over time.
- Reinforce the development of a performance and evidence-based culture in primary and secondary care.
- Minimise information requirements on practices.
- Present a balanced perspective of a practice's performance. In short, a 'balanced scorecard'.[3]

Many authorities have already gone a considerable way towards developing such an approach. For example, by the summer of 1995 nine Health Commissions in the South and West Region were already using practice profile or indicator packages. Wiltshire and Bath used their package of 20 key indicators, not just for performance review, but to assist in resource prioritisation and allocation.[4] This early work, together with parallel initiatives in Anglia and Oxford, has been refined in the Primary Health Care Performance and Development Indicators Framework now developed on behalf of the NHS Executive.[5] Extracts from the Framework are provided in Boxes 22.2 to 22.5.

The Framework is intended to be used at four levels.

1. NHS Executive Regional Office to Health Authority (Box 22.2) — a small number of key questions based on critical success criteria, intended to inform debate about performance and development planning, and contribute to Health Authority Corporate Contracts.

Box 22.2

Key questions	Strategy	Support	Monitoring
1 Is there a demonstrable framework for involving Primary Health Care organisations and professionals in strategy development and implementation?			
2. Is there demonstrable evidence that health strategy development and implementation are led by local needs assessment?			
3. Is the implementation of health strategy leading to a more appropriate and evidence based balance of care and service provision, which is demonstrated by changing patterns of investment?			

4. In enhancing the implementation of agreed local health strategies: • how have practice and locality based services been improved? • what is the level of support for service innnovation and development?			
5. How is the Health Authority identifying and meeting the personal and organisational development needs within primary health care?			
6. Does the Health Authority have a demonstrable framework for monitoring the perfomance and development of primary health care which involves primary health care organisations and professionals?			

2. Health Authority (Box 22.3) — a larger number of performance indicators and descriptions, intended to inform and facilitate self audit, development planning and organisation development.

Box 22.3

Performance indicator	Issues and comments	Data source
1. The Health Authority can show: (i) percentage of GPFH practices submitting an annual practice plan which meets the requirements of the Accountability Framework. (ii) percentage of non-fundholding practices producing an annual practice plan, or equivalent, in accordance with HA guidance. 2. The Health Authority can show the priorities and service changes in its Purchasing Plan which have been drawn directly from GP practice plans and reports. 3. The Health Authority can show which of its strategic priorities for (a) improving the health of local people and achieving the objectives of 'Health of the Nation' and (b) improving the health services available to local people, have been explicitly agreed with primary care professionals.		

3. Primary Health Care Team to Health Authority (Box 22.4)
— a small number of key issues intended to inform discussion about performance and development planning, and inform practice Annual Reports, practice plans 'corporate contracts', fundholding accountibility frameworks, and the Health Authority's strategy.

Box 22.4

Key questions	Strategy	Support	Monitoring
1. Does the practice identify and respond to the needs of patients?			
2. How does the practice seek to impact on the health of the practice?			
3. Does the practice relate effectively to other organisations for the benefit of patients and health gain?			
4. Is the practice forward looking and planning organisational and service change for the benefit of patients and health gain?			
5. Does the practice use resources effectively to purchase and provide an appropriate range of evidence based services?			
6. Does the practice effectively review organisational and service activity, and progress against plans, and take appropriate action?			

4. Primary Health Care Team (Box 22.5) — a larger number of descriptions, intended to inform self audit and development planning.

Descriptors	Issues and comments	Data source
The practice has a plan which: • includes a strategy for improving health and health services • proposes changes that can be made within available resources • identifies and prioritises training and development needs for practice staff, and the means of meeting those needs. The practice plan: • is developed and agreed with the Primary Health Care Team members • takes account of strategic objectives and priorities in the local Health Strategy • is based on local needs assessment.		

New Health Authorities and practices will find the Framework helpful when developing their own self-audit and monitoring tools. More work, however, is required to broaden the Framework to address the needs of other primary care practitioners (e.g. in community pharmacy, general dentistry, etc.) to balance the focus on General Practices and practice-based staff.

AGREEING TARGETS THAT ARE OWNED

An obvious but essential point is that any practice development or improvement targets which arise from the use of monitoring tools and implementation of joint strategies (e.g. for mental health) need to be developed jointly and owned. They need to be congruent with perceived priorities and integrated with the practice planning process, and (if fundholding) the locally agreed accountability framework. Critically, they also need to be seen as underpinning policy decisions within the practice in terms of how broader agreed strategies (e.g. integrated mental health care) will be delivered, rather than as an adjunct to a vehicle for bidding for resources.

Box 22.6

At the time of writing this report 29 of the 30 practices of Northampton Borough have been visited over a period of 5 weeks. Each meeting lasted a minimum of 2 hours with the discussions centred around priorities for the county and issues arising generally in primary health care as well as specific practice issues. This report highlights those issues which seemed to be common to most of the discussions.

It was very easy this year to make the appointments with practices and all set aside time with no question about the necessity. In the majority of practices all, or nearly all, partners were present. There was no doubt that practices appreciated the opportunity to express feelings and concerns, which most did quite volubly at the start of meetings. A pattern emerged across the range of meetings. Members of the team needed to vent their feelings about a wide range of issues before we could progress to raising awareness about care group strategies etc., completing with a review of last year's progress against plans and the practicalities of running the practice which included the need for rational business planning and discussion of resource implications for implementing plans. There seemed to be a growing appreciation of how the Authority is trying to support general practice.

Documentation is still a major problem. Many of the practices did not have the documents we forwarded, even though we had provided a folder etc. and some claimed non receipt. Time was taken going through the papers which was useful but time consuming. It was interesting to note that even the health promotion report had, more often than not, not been read and having the relevant graphs in the practice profile was useful and enlightening to most.

Although over 50% of practices submitted practice development plans this year indicating an appreciation of the process, quality varied enormously from a three stage document including all aspects of the practice, including clinical quality indicators, to a sheet of A4 which was fundamentally a wish list for funding with no outcomes defined. There is still a need to support practices in the development of approaches to planning. The implications of the FHSA monitoring the use of development funding was sometimes uncomfortable but widely accepted. The fact that we were willing to discuss the issues face to face and that we were willing to share resource assumptions and our criteria for allocations, as well as being alive to the issues of maintaining GP income levels, was seen as a real indicator of our commitment and most practices were certainly far more forthcoming than last year.

(Extracted from *Summer Report 1995 — Bridging the Gap*: Northamptonshire Family Health Services Authority)

A recent approach which has worked effectively in Northamptonshire has been to develop a Primary Health Care Planning and Development Cycle. This concept provides a vehicle within which discussions and agreements about practice, local and national priorities and subsequent practice resource allocations can take place, and has been running for two years. The approach has not been without its difficulties (see Box 22.6) and it has taken time to establish credibility and trust, but it has begun to deliver significant benefits.[6] It must be emphasised, however, that to make it work effectively puts considerable demands on any Health Authority in terms of:

- Practice profiling and analysis;
- Clarity about and linkage to strategic development goals, priorities for investment, and key success criteria;
- Collation of intelligence;
- Corporacy — practices need one key contact, rather than facing a succession of target setting visits from different managers and advisers;
- Time of locality managers or equivalents and advisers. There is no substitute for regular face-to-face contact with practices.

Ownership may be strengthened further by negotiating a 'performance protocol' between the Authority and practices covering such issues as monitoring requirements (no new types of information to be sought in-year), use and publication of information, avoidance of duplication in visits or requests for information, 'lead' contact with the Authority, etc.

PROVIDING CONSTRUCTIVE FEEDBACK

To be useful to them, practices need focused regular feedback on results. Drawing on best practice, this needs to be:

- Two-way, providing feedback to the Authority on how it has helped or hindered success, policy obstacles to implement, and encouraging constructive challenge;
- Credible, both in terms of the feedback and the person providing it;
- Consistent — it is essential that individuals/teams likely to come in contact with the practice are aware of the key messages;
- Relevant to the main issues facing the practice and agreed priorities and targets.

- Can be supported with evidence;
- Comparative, setting performance in context, hence the importance of providing ready access to comparative performance data, and preferably, encouraging benchmarking by practices themselves;
- Integrated with normal business or planning processes, e.g. the Primary Health Care, Planning and Development Cycle.

CREATING INCENTIVES FOR CHANGE

The new Health Authorities are likely to have an increasing regulatory role within primary care together with greater flexibility in the use of resources, as well as easier access to educational networks. Together with the GPFH accountability framework and practical delegation of budget-setting, use of bolt-on contracts for GMS, 'preferred provider'[7] status for other contractors or direct contracts (e.g. with optometrists for diabetic retinopathy), there are genuine opportunities for much more effective incentive structures. In keeping with a developmental approach to performance management, the focus should be on positive incentives, not sanctions. But jointly agreed systems need to be in place, which are clear, open and obvious, to address performance which falls below an acceptable level.

CONCLUSION: BRIDGING THE PERFORMANCE GAP

Ultimately, the post April 1996 Health Authorities will only be successful in having a major influence on the quality and direction of primary care if they are able to build lasting partnerships with General Practitioners, primary care teams, and other practitioners. This implies forging a common vision of the future and what constitutes 'success', and building mutual trust and confidence. In short, clarity of purpose, a focus on what is really important, and good working and personal relationships are likely to be the key to a performance culture in primary care, rather than the technology of performance management.

REFERENCES

1. Goldsmith W, Clutterbuck D 1985 The winning streak. Penguin Harmondsworth
2. National Health Service Executive 1995 EL[95]54 An Accountability Framework for GP Fundholding NHSE London
3. Kaplan RS, Norton DP 1992 The balanced scorecard — measures that drive performance. Harvard Business Review, January–February 1992: 71–79
4. NHS Executive South and West 1995 Towards a primary care-led NHS in the South and West. Internal report, p 24 (unpublished)
5. NHS Executive South and West with NHS Executive Anglia and Oxford and Dearden Management 1996 Primary health care performance and development indicators: a framework (unpublished)
6. Northamptonshire Family Health Services Authority 1995 The primary health care planning
   and development cycle: summer report: bridging the gap.
7. Sylvester N 1995 The preferred provider In: Meads G (ed) Future options for General Practice. Radcliffe Medical Press, Oxford, pp 79–92

23. Making it happen

A. J. McKeon

INTRODUCTION

The title of this chapter is misleading if applied to the Department of Health. The one thing the centre cannot do is make a Primary Care-Led NHS happen. It can set the right policy framework which will enable things to happen and give encouragement. But making them happen can only really be done by local people: Health Authorities, GPs, their staff and other members of the primary care team.

In some respects the centre has already set the policy framework. We did, after all, mint the phrase 'a Primary Care-Led NHS' and associated it with specific policy developments. This chapter tries to explain why we did that. The policy developments now need to be followed through. This chapter gives a view from the centre of how that might be done.

However, this is also a chapter about questions. A Primary Care-Led NHS is putting the spotlight on a number of issues which have lain, comparatively, in the shadows. It is also putting a new perspective on some old and familiar health service problems. We do not yet have the answer to those questions, and there is almost certainly no one right answer. But the issues are worth debating and defining the issues, namely, the questions to be addressed, is a key part of policy development. Lastly, this chapter is above all else a personal view.

'A Primary Care-Led NHS' is a phrase which many people have taken up and identified with. It is naturally attractive and appealing. Most people's experience of the NHS is related to primary care. It is the first, and usually the only, port of call. However, if it is an often used phrase, there is a great deal less certainty about its meaning. What does it mean? What are we aiming for? How will we get there? These are the kinds of questions which are usually asked of policy makers at the centre.

MAJOR POLICY DEVELOPMENTS AND A THEME

The 'Working for Patients' reforms introduced major changes to the Health Service. However, as implementation has progressed, it has also become clearer that more could be done to ensure that aspects of care are better coordinated to meet the needs of patients, and that decisions about the type of care to be provided are brought closer to patients and are made, or influenced, by those who are closest to them. They have also increased the opportunities to develop services in primary care for the benefit of patients.

The phrase 'a Primary Care-Led NHS' was originally used to encapsulate two major policy developments which were aimed at making further progress in this direction. First, the establishment of the new, unified, Health Authorities on 1 April 1996 creates new opportunities for developing and integrating health care. The centre expects them to work in new ways. They will need to work particularly closely with GPs (both fundholders and non-fundholders) in making their own purchasing decisions. They will also have important monitoring and support roles for primary care. There is much in this book about how these roles can effectively be carried out.

Second, significant changes to GP fundholding are being introduced from the same date. The introduction of community fundholding, the expansion of standard fundholding (both in terms of the reduction in qualifying list sizes and the increases in services which can be purchased), and the development of total purchasing pilots all mean that more GPs will take personal responsibility for purchasing services and that more services will come under their direct influence.

However, these two policy developments are only part of the story. A Primary Care-Led NHS clearly means much more. It is more a set of ideas and a theme than an organisational structure, or process or policy initiative. The three main elements relate to:

1. Decision making.
2. The process of delivering care.
3. Relationships.

Decision making involves a number of factors. These include, for example, access to services, the quality of services, their effectiveness, their cost, the needs of the individual patient and his or her personal circumstances and, of course, public health and other priorities. All these factors need to be taken into account. The aim is that decisions relating to health care are made at the right level and by those best placed to trade off the competing elements. More often than not, primary care is the best place to do that, or at least to have a significant influence over them.

The process of care means care or advice being provided in the most accessible way and by an individual with the necessary skills. Making services available in primary care more often than not meets both these requirements. It clearly does not mean that care or advice must be provided by a doctor. If care cannot be provided in primary care, or is required from several different sources, then the patient will need a guide. Primary care professionals can most often supply that.

It is clear that if we are to improve the process of care, ensure that decision making is effective, and take advantage of the opportunities offered by greater devolution of responsibility, then relationships between the various parties will need to be strengthened. This includes relationships between GPs and Health Authorities, between secondary and primary care, between health and social care and between and within the primary care team itself. The greater the degree of devolution and the more players in the market, the stronger the relationships have to be.

When set out in these terms, it is clear that there are three areas which need to be addressed in developing and securing a Primary Care-Led NHS:

1. Increasing the influence of primary over secondary care;
2. Strengthening primary care itself;
3. Developing and strengthening relationships between primary care and others, including social services.

The centre has a part to play in that, but it is clear that most of this can only be done locally. A Primary Care-Led NHS above all implies local solutions to local problems, not least because the essential building blocks — most usually the GP practice — are very localised in nature. The world looks very different between, for example, Southport and Hackney. But it also looks very different in an Authority — between, for example, 'inner city' Leicester and Melton Mowbray. All embracing solutions at national, regional or even Health Authority level seem intrinsically unlikely to be effective, except in delivering a few absolute bottom lines.

However, even if the centre cannot itself deliver, it can have some expectations of what Authorities might do and monitor them accordingly.

The centre must always expect Authorities to meet clear national priorities (hopefully few in numbers). It has always left room for local priorities and development. But can it rightly expect these priorities to have been properly set (are they evidenced based? do they reflect primary care views? etc) and to have some performance measures attached to them so the Authority itself can judge whether it is meeting its aims. It is even better if those performance measures can be compared with others with similar problems or priorities. These are the sort of questions which the centre might reasonably ask.

For the new Health Authorities, there also seem to be a number of essentials related to primary care and a Primary Care-Led NHS.

First, they must strengthen their partnership with all practices. Mutual respect, trust and understanding need to be established. GPs and Authorities must work together to improve the quality of primary and secondary care. GPs in particular need to be explicitly 'signed up' to local strategies for health and service improvements. That can only realistically be done in a participative way. GPs — and indeed others in primary care — need to believe that they have been 'listened' to rather then simply heard.

Second, primary care itself needs to be strengthened and developed. There needs to be positive implementation of national initiatives as well as local action. There must be a clear agenda to improve the quality of service provision, including training and infrastructure support. This entails having a detailed knowledge of the workforce and its capabilities and capacities.

Third, the GP role in purchasing needs to be strengthened. I would expect a significant increase in the numbers of GPs directly involved in purchasing, difficult though that may be.

Lastly, the acid test will be whether all this action produces real benefits for patients. I would hope that all Authorities could point to a few significant improvements in service achieved in a primary care-led way that are widely recognised by public and professionals. The process of identifying the changes to be made as well as their delivery will be important in itself.

If these are some of the key implications for Authorities, there are also some implications for the centre. The field has always rightly looked to the centre to create the necessary framework — legal, financial and moral — to deliver policy aims. The job of the centre also includes monitoring and being held accountable to Parliament and the public for the outcome. There have always been some underlying themes which the centre has tried to deliver which can most easily be summed up in the hackneyed phrase 'value for money'. However, the superstructure and some of the other aims change. We have set a framework for a Primary Care-Led NHS, but the policy is posing new challenges and in some cases throwing a fresh light on old ones.

GP INVOLVEMENT IN PURCHASING

The greater involvement of GPs in purchasing has brought new stresses and strains to the NHS as well as opportunities. There seem to be three or four particular aspects which are posing policy questions.

First, it is our established policy that all GPs (not just fundholders) should be involved in purchasing. We are also seeking a participative rather than a top-down approach based on the traditional circulation for comment of Health Authority proposals. There is a moral framework here: Authorities should seek to do this; recognising, of course, that it always takes two to tango. Whether the moral framework is effective remains to be seen. As ever, the picture is patchy, but we are making some progress.

Involving GPs in purchasing also raises questions about their capacity, particularly in terms of time, to do the job. This raises a fundamental issue: what, over the longer term, do we expect GPs to be able to do and what should be their role? This clearly raises questions about the shape and size of the future workforce (see below) and its training. This issue, by the way, clearly needs to embrace professions other than doctors. There are likely to be several different views which will need to be reconciled: the profession itself, the Government, NHS managers and, of course, patients and the public who individually and collectively will have a view of the service they expect.

A Primary Care-Led NHS also raises new questions about budget setting. A lot of progress had been made in ensuring that Health Authorities received funds according to an equitable formula. However, it has always been more orientated towards the acute sector — the data are better. Also, introducing many more smaller budget holders raises new questions on resource distribution and equity.

This is not solely an issue of fundholding. It applies whenever Authority budgets are broken down into smaller units for purchasing purposes. The 'Holy Grail' is a weighted capitation budget but applied to much smaller localities, perhaps even individuals. But, like the real Holy Grail, whether it will ever be reached is another matter. Again it is an area where we are making progress. The centre can give a lead, but it is requiring new approaches to policy making. The real experts are in the field; they actually have to set the budgets, we do not. Also, diversity is increasing. Where the acid test is a 'felt fair' one, the approaches adopted could be different in different localities. This is not wrong; it could mean a more locally fine tuned approach. It is an area which the centre needs to monitor carefully and seek an increasingly sophisticated framework to ensure that policy aims remain intact. Clearly, new approaches to accountability need to be introduced to match the devolution of budgetary responsibility.

The greater involvement of GPs in purchasing, the spread of fundholding and the introduction of total purchasing are all bringing benefits. However, there are some dangers of which we need to be wary. Transaction costs are an obvious example. High transaction costs need to be (and are being) tackled although we need to bear in mind that transaction costs are related not only to the number of purchasers, but perhaps more importantly, to the linking of contracts to individual patients and the opportunity for more detailed (and more personalised) specification that goes with it. More accurate costing, more detailed analysis of caseload and better targeted resource allocations in secondary care are to some extent being driven by primary care requirements: 'just what care is being provided for my patient?'

We also need to be careful that the greater involvement of GPs is not seen as a substitute for the greater involvement of patients. GPs are clearly not the same as patients; we need to develop ways in which patients' views, and those of their representatives, can be properly heard when there are many players in the game. Representative groups (again not the same as patients or the public) had familiar and well worn routes into Health Authorities. The world is now beginning to look different, especially as primary care involvement begins to spread more generally beyond the acute care and elective surgery. A framework is being established, but it undoubtedly needs to be further tested and developed.

Finally, in this context, the greater freedom that increasing budgetary devolution brings as well as the greater sense of experimentation and diversity, place greater emphasis on ensuring that the financial incentives within the system as well as its regulatory framework are correct and effective. Probity is not really the issue, although of course it is always there. Efficient use of resources and 'value for money' are. Something which seems to be a good deal at local level may actually turn out to be an inefficient use of resources or may lead to a bad deal for the taxpayer. Some quite sophisticated systems have been developed over many years to secure value for money for the taxpayer. Interest in disease management packages for example has involved new challenges to those arrangements. The centre may have to learn how to adjust its arrangements or to regulate activity more closely in the light of new developments in the field.

THE IMPACT OF A PRIMARY CARE-LED NHS ON PRIMARY CARE

I now want to move on from policy questions relating to GP involvement in purchasing, to the impact of a Primary Care-Led NHS on primary care itself and the challenges it seems to face.

The last few years have seen major changes in primary care and the range of services now offered. Many of these have been gradual developments, but they have often been hastened by GP involvement in purchasing and particularly by fundholding. A Primary Care-Led NHS does not imply or require a shift of services from secondary to primary care, but in practice, it is turning out that way.

Several consequences seem to follow from this. First, it could become increasingly unclear what a GP should be expected to provide and what a patient might expect. There has never been a clear definition of General Medical Services; they are simply what a GP provides as a GP. Patients might once have had reasonably clear expectations of what might be expected from an average GP, but that seems increasingly unlikely to be the case.

The same point arises in respect of emergency services. My cosy, rose tinted and probably narrow view of the world is that once, if one had an emergency, one either went to the GP or he (nearly always a he) came to you, or one went to an A&E department ('Casualty'). Now, there are trauma centres, A&E departments, minor injuries units, primary care centres, GPs doing their own night calls, co-ops and deputising services. One might well be seen by a nurse, or a paramedic, or simply have one's phone call screened and advice given.

This raises questions about the services required, how they work together, and the skills needed. They also come back to the fundamental question of how do we see primary care developing. The centre doesn't have the answer to this — it may have a view — but not the answer. A clear direction needs to be set for the service before organisational underpinning for the future can be considered.

My second point concerns diversity again. Primary care is already diverse; it always has been. However, diversity is likely to increase as different localities take different routes. This makes it harder to look at processes (see below on monitoring) and even more important to look at outcomes. It also implies that single national blueprints look increasingly archaic.

Third, the development of the service raises serious questions about resourcing both in terms of money and people. Leaving aside questions of funding, the centre has a significant task in ensuring that the right financial structures are in place. It is well known in the service that, although there are well known paths for capital investment in general medical services, the way is relatively uncharted for investing in non-general medical services in primary care. As well as raising questions about the relationship (and distinction) between the two and the implication of one for the other, this kind of investment clearly has implications for Trusts and achieving a level playing field between the players.

However, there are also clearly implications for the workforce, and the roles of the individual professions and their training. The workforce itself is changing. Increasing numbers of GPs (and particularly trainees) are women. There are also more part-timers. Different attitudes to General Practice and its traditions seem to be emerging. These facts together with the increased opportunities for services to be delivered in primary care, all mean that different styles and approaches are likely to be required to provide primary care. The centre must adjust the framework to enable that to happen. There are already straws in the wind, for example, the introduction of nurse prescribing, and the development of nurse practitioners.

As well as focusing on primary care service development, a Primary Care-Led NHS has also highlighted some relatively hidden aspects of primary care itself. Questions are now being asked about the distribution of primary care resources, whether this is equitable and how, if it is not, greater equity can be achieved. This is most usually expressed in terms of revenue and manpower. The same point also applies to premises and capital.

Finally, a Primary Care-Led NHS raises new challenges for the centre (and indeed Authorities) in terms of monitoring and of justifying the expenditure. Again, it is a challenge of diversity. We inevitably monitor what we can count, even though it has always been important to look at outcomes. We have looked at inputs (money and people), processes and outputs (FCEs, visits). The 'Efficiency Index' was a major step forward nationally in monitoring outputs, but it is well known that it does not recognise sufficiently the diversity of provision now emerging. Capturing outputs in primary care is going to be much more difficult, and may not help with monitoring or comparative analysis, because of the different local approaches adopted to service provision. This puts a greater emphasis on looking for consistent measures and linking them to intermediate outputs (e.g. avoidable hospital admissions) or accepted quality indicators. Some tentative progress is being made here, but there is a long way to go. The greater focus on audit and quality may also help to answer the now frequently asked question 'What is good primary care?'

I make no apology for ending this book with a series of questions rather than clear statements and answers. A vision has been sketched out; we are at the start of a Primary Care-Led NHS; an initial framework is in place. As a result, the world is changing, and we can see some of the way ahead. There are exciting opportunities as well as some apparent problems. The centre, like the service, will have to adjust in order to make sure we achieve all the benefits possible.

INDEX